3

Desegregated Schools

Appraisals of an American Experiment

Desegregated Schools

Appraisals of an American Experiment

Edited by
RAY C. RIST
New York State College of Human Ecology
Cornell University
Ithaca, New York

ACADEMIC PRESS   New York   San Francisco   London
A Subsidiary of Harcourt Brace Jovanovich, Publishers

ACADEMIC PRESS, INC.
111 Fifth Avenue, New York, New York 10003

United Kingdom Edition published by
ACADEMIC PRESS, INC. (LONDON) LTD.
24/28 Oval Road, London NW1 7DX

Library of Congress Cataloging in Publication Data
Main entry under title:

Desegregated schools.

Includes indexes.
1. School integration––United States
––Addresses, essays, lectures. I. Rist, Ray C.
LC214.2.D46   370.19'342   79–6958
ISBN 0–12–588980–1

Contents

Contents

Chapter 2
Patience and Prudence in a Southern High School:
Managing the Political Economy of
Desegregated Education   65
GEORGE W. NOBLIT

Chapter 3
From Courtrooms to Classrooms: Managing School
Desegregation in a Deep South High School   89
THOMAS W. COLLINS

Part 2
THE NORTHERN EXPERIENCE

Chapter 4
Color, Class, and Social Control in an
Urban Desegregated School   117
JACQUELINE SCHERER AND EDWARD J. SLAWSKI

Chapter 5
The Social Context of Learning in an
Interracial School   **155**

JANET WARD SCHOFIELD AND H. ANDREW SAGAR

Chapter 6
Contacts among Cultures: School Desegregation in a
Polyethnic New York City High School   **201**

MERCER L. SULLIVAN

Numbers in parentheses indicate the pages on which the authors' contributions begin.

DOROTHY C. CLEMENT (15), Department of Anthropology, University of North Carolina, Chapel Hill, North Carolina 27514

THOMAS W. COLLINS (89), Department of Anthropology, Memphis State University, Memphis, Tennessee 38152

MARGARET EISENHART (15), Department of Anthropology, University of North Carolina, Chapel Hill, North Carolina 27514

JOE R. HARDING* (15), Department of Anthropology, University of North Carolina, Chapel Hill, North Carolina 27514

GEORGE W. NOBLIT† (65), Department of Sociology, Memphis State University, Memphis, Tennessee 38152

RAY C. RIST (1), New York State College of Human Ecology, Cornell University, Ithaca, New York 14853

H. ANDREW SAGAR (155), Department of Psychology, University of Pittsburgh, Pittsburgh, Pennsylvania 15260

* *Present Address:* Distribution of Mental Health Professionals, Southern Regional Education Board, 130 6th Street, N.W., Atlanta, Georgia 30313
† *Present Address:* Desegregation Studies Team, National Institute of Education, 1200 19th Street, NW, Washington, D.C. 20205

JACQUELINE SCHERER (117), Department of Sociology, Oakland University, Rochester, Michigan 48063

JANET WARD SCHOFIELD (155), Department of Psychology, University of Pittsburgh, Pittsburgh, Pennsylvania 15260

EDWARD J. SLAWSKI (117), Rochester, Michigan 48063

MERCER L. SULLIVAN (201) Horace Mann–Lincoln Institute, Teachers College, Columbia University, New York, New York 10028

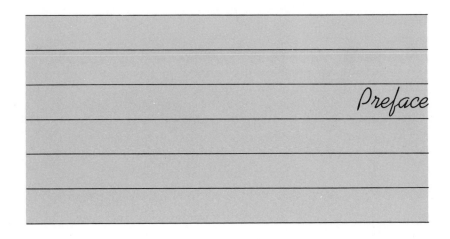

Preface

It is right and proper that this book should appear at the time of the twenty-fifth anniversary of the monumental U.S. Supreme Court decision, *Brown* v. *Board of Education*. With the unanimous vote cast by the justices to declare illegal the principle of "separate but equal" in education, the nation was set on a new course—one uncharted and traveled by no other country in modern times. The United States has sought, under the mantle of *Brown* and subsequent laws, to redress systematically the inequities and injustices perpetrated upon its own minority group citizens.

School desegregation has been one of the most visible and widely undertaken efforts in this direction. But perhaps to speak of a "direction" suggests that there is a clear consensus of where we have been and where we are headed. This is hardly the case. What *Brown* and other school desegregation cases have accomplished is to make explicit that where we were as a nation with regard to the segregation of the races was unacceptable; where we are to go is to be worked out. Thus I write of school desegregation as an "experiment." It is an experiment, for we must learn as we go. The guideposts are few and no other examples exist that might guide our actions. The impetus provided by *Brown* was one of morality rather than method.

Yet it would be foolish to assume, in the absence of clear goals, that we simply devote our energies to the development of a methodology. Sophisticated methods lead nowhere. That we are not certain of what form and content we wish our race relations to take has had its impact on the efforts to achieve school desegregation. Indeed, black–white relations are an enduring American dilemma and there is no reason to believe schools should have sorted this out more readily than any other sector of the society.

We are stymied: a quarter-century after *Brown* and it is difficult to tally up the cost–benefit sheet and learn where we are. The laws mandating school desegregation equivocate; the political will to do more in the struggle to achieve desegregation seems spent; and the research that is available does not give definitive answers to the macro questions of pupil achievement, the utility of busing, or the attitudinal outcomes of having experienced a multiracial school environment.

In the midst of the millions of words that have been written and the countless research reports that have been published, there stands a curious omission. We are hard pressed to find accounts of what is "really going on," of what the day-to-day realities of school desegregation are for teachers, students, parents, and administrators. Little is available to inform us on the subtleties of interrelationships between students and teachers, between whites and blacks, or between administrators and parents.

This set of papers addresses that omission. Their substantive focus is on the processes of school desegregation as such desegregation is experienced and lived out in countless classrooms across the nation. The sites reported on here vary from New York to Memphis, and from the industrial Northeast to the Midwest to the Deep South. They also vary by organization (elementary, middle, and high school), by the black–white ratio in students and faculty, by patterns of administrative leadership, and by levels of community support and/or resistance.

That the papers reflect such a diversity of school desegregation settings and programs is what makes them so vitally important. For if we are to avoid the reification of our understandings of school desegregation to some few statistics on white flight or arguments over the utility of busing, we need to have the complexities and nuances brought to our attention.

This volume should encourage those who believe that federally supported social science research can inform us on the basic issues in our society. The findings reported here are from a 3-year project sponsored by the Desegregation Studies Staff at the National Institute of Education and entitled "Field Studies in Urban Desegregated Schools." Awards were made to the authors of this volume to undertake an intensive, longitudinal examination of a desegregated school setting. The emphasis was to be on the processes involved, how the participants viewed and involved themselves in the desegregation effort, how the school as a social system responded to change, and how the values toward integration influenced the subsequent program.

That the results are mixed, even discouraging to those who have labored long and hard for school desegregation, should not come as a surprise. Schools do not exist in a social and cultural vacuum. They do not respond to our efforts at social engineering with the speed or deftness we might wish. Furthermore, the decentralization of educational decision making, the mixed messages from Washington, the unwillingness of the white majority to support viable *means* of achieving school desegregation, the political web of schools, banks, real estate, and city politicians, plus the tenacity of racism within American education have all mediated against any "quick fix" of a difficult and complex problem.

What we have accomplished as a nation in these past 25 years can be viewed optimistically against the pages of history, or pessimistically against the expectations of those who still wait to have their constitutional rights fulfilled.

Introduction

RAY C. RIST

There are many in America who see the matter of racial equality in general and school desegregation in particular as *passé*. The political will to implement the *Brown* decision and thus strike down segregated education is spent. We find ourselves on a plateau.

While a number of school desegregation cases are still in litigation, particularly in the northern and western states, it is apparent that the legal gains made in the 1960s and into the early 1970s will have to suffice for the immediate future. If one is optimistic about the long range development of desegregation efforts, the term is cautious advancement; if one is cynical, the term is retrenchment. Regardless of perspective, judges, lawyers, politicians, community leaders, and civil rights advocates tend now to couch their comments in carefully guarded terminology, stressing the "enormous difficulties and complexities," the tenacity of "second generation" desegregation problems, and ambiguity of *de jure* versus *de facto* desegregation, and the present backlash in white America against any further efforts at changing the status quo in race relations. Regardless of the rhetoric, the message is the same: Where we are is as far as we are likely to go for the indefinite future.

The current malaise stands in sharp contrast to the recognizable

1

DESEGREGATED SCHOOLS
Appraisals of an American Experiment

gains made in recent years in the area of school desegregation. (Some might argue that the malaise is a logical consequence to a period of rapid and systemic social change.) Indeed, in a slightly larger perspective, much the same can be stated for several key aspects of black–white relations in general. Ten years before the *Brown* decision, a Swedish social scientist, Gunnar Myrdal, published his assessment of race relations in America. His classic, *An American Dilemma: The Negro Problem and American Democracy*, stands as one of the benchmarks against which we can assess change within our society. What makes Myrdal's book of continuing interest and central to any discussion of American race relations is that he brought into full relief the gap between the creed of equality and the fact of racial inequality. He laid bare the schism between words and deeds.

Myrdal contended that this contradiction was so indefensible that it constituted an inherent flaw in the fabric of American democracy. Its presence, he posited, would become evermore intolerable to white America and thus lead inevitably to improvement for black people. So long as the American creed retained its legitimacy, the driving wheel of change would be the moral conscience of white people.

While Myrdal's analysis was prophetic in many respects, it did have its Achilles' heel. The good will of white America has not been infinite, especially when vested self-interests are at stake. Under such circumstances, white Americans have seemed eminently capable of living with contradictions between their words and deeds. Perhaps the current resistance to further change suggests that many have reached the limit in how far they are willing to move to close the schism.

It is, in hindsight, open to debate as to whether it was white guilt or black protest that provided the main catalyst for changes in American race relations. Regardless of which causal factor one chooses to emphasize, the fact is that the nation has made dramatic gains in the direction of an egalitarian society. In comparing Myrdal's time with our own, the most striking difference is that the entire, elaborate panoply of legalized discrimination has been swept away. Be it in the areas of voting rights or equal access to public accommodations, housing, employment, and education, there are now constitutional protections in place to enhance the free and unfettered right of black Americans to participate in society as they wish. At the very core of this legal transformation is to be found the *Brown* decision.

School Desegregation: Shadow and Substance

The particular strength of this present volume is that it provides in-depth understandings of a number of desegregated school sites across the nation. Yet it is well to briefly sketch the broader context in which these studies have occurred. To trace out some of the macro-level changes with regard to school desegregation can assist our understanding of how we have come to have what we find reported here. School desegregation is neither ahistorical nor apolitical—thus the necessity to elucidate both history and policy as backdrops to school situations as they now exist.

In a seldom quoted passage from the 1954 *Brown* decision, the justices wrote:

> Today, it [education] is a principal instrument in awaking the child to cultural values, in preparing him for later professional training, and in helping him to adjust normally to his environment. In these days, it is doubtful that any child may reasonably be expected to succeed in life if he is denied the opportunity of an education. Such an opportunity, where the state has undertaken to provide it, is a right which must be made available to all on equal terms.

The fact that education was not being provided "to all on equal terms" is what brought the *Brown* decision into being.

In examining the material offered in support of the plaintiffs, it is apparent that much of the basic social science data relevant to the case had to be generated by the plaintiffs. There simply were few, if any, good studies of the impact of segregated education upon children and into this void stepped several scholars, offering what material they could. That the final text of the *Brown* decision did make reference to social science evidence should not be the basis to infer that evidence was either extensive or overwhelming. Indeed, the citations tally up to several on doll play, others on small scale attitudinal surveys, and still others on the opinions of social scientists. (Parenthetically, here is but another instance of confirming that constitutional principles must be moral and political in their foundation and not based on any collection of research data.)

The *Brown* data are cited, not to disparage those who collected and used it, but to suggest just how fragile and partial has been the available evidence on matters of school segregation–desegregation. Indeed, it is difficult to even ascertain what impact *Brown* had for the first 12 to

15 years that it was law due to the near total absence of even the most simple tabular data.

Prior to 1964, no systematic data on the implementation of *Brown* were collected, tabulated, or analyzed. The general consensus among those who have studied this period is that fewer than 1% of all black children in the 11 southern states attended desegregated schools. For a full decade, it was as if *Brown* had not occurred. (Cynically, one might suggest that for this reason there were no data to collect.)

In 1964, the Congress passed the Civil Rights Act forbidding discrimination in education and authorized the withholding of public funds from segregated school systems. During this same academic year (1964–1965), the first private efforts at collecting data on the 11 southern states began. Findings suggested that 2.2% of all black students in these states were attending schools where white students also attended. In the fall of 1965, the federal government began to collect data. These data for 1965–1966 indicate that 6.6% of students in the deep South were in desegregated schools.

The pace of desegregation in the South quickened. By 1968–1969, the number of black students in desegregated schools had reached 32%. This figure then more than doubled in the next 2 years; 1970–1971 found 77% of the South's black pupils in desegregated schools. A year later it was 84%, and in 1974–1975, the figure stood at 86%.

The first national statistics on school desegregation became available with the 1968–1969 academic year. In that year, 23.4% of all black students were in majority white schools, as opposed to 18.4% in the South alone. Within 2 years the shift was dramatic as the South had 40.5% of all black students in majority white schools and the national average stood at 33.1%. In 1974–1975, the figures for the South and the nation were 44% and 33% respectively.

In addition to reporting on the number of black students in majority white schools, it is important to provide data on the numbers of black students who remained in schools where the black population was 90% or greater. The data for the 5 years (1970–1975) are in Table I.1.

As is evident in the previous discussion, school desegregation efforts in the United States have been relatively recent and intense. These same efforts have now waned. Succinctly, most of the school desegregation that has been achieved in this nation has been achieved in a matter of 3 to 5 years—or in a slightly different time frame, 36 to 60 months. From the standpoint of changing patterns of behavior, institutional

TABLE I.1

Percentage of Black Students in Schools with 90% or Greater Black Enrollment, 1970–1975

YEAR	NATIONAL	SOUTH	MIDWEST	WEST	NORTHEAST
1970/1971	46.44	34.20	64.38	50.52	52.48
1971/1972	42.60	26.62	63.69	48.44	53.54
1972/1973	42.00	25.72	63.93	46.88	54.63
1973/1974	40.84	23.54	62.73	46.15	56.36
1974/1975	40.53	23.37	63.19	45.05	57.80

SOURCE: Center for National Policy Review, *Trends in Black School Segregation.* (Washington, D.C.: School of Law, Catholic University, 1977).

arrangements, and normative standards, it is an incredibly short time in which to address any national goal. That the United States has succeeded as it has needs to be recognized. That there is yet so much segregation (cf. Table I.1) which will not be confronted must also give us pause.

There is an interesting collection of data which bears on this issue and highlights the volatility of efforts to bring about school desegregation. In a sample of 615 school districts which had undergone some form of desegregation, the United States Commission on Civil Rights sought to learn of the catalyst for that change. Table I.2 reports these findings.

Immediately apparent is the impact of different actors at different times. Until 1967, state and local educational authorities were responsible for the majority of instances in which school districts did desegregate. For 3 years, 1968–1971, both the courts and the Department of Health, Education, and Welfare were extremely active; they accounted for 263 of the 343 school districts undergoing desegregation. But just as quickly as this engagement began, so it ended. By 1972, the courts and HEW accounted for 17 of the 55 instances of desegregation. The figures of 1974 were much the same, that is, 22 of 53 cases.

While data such as these give stark evidence of the variations in effort and involvement of different agencies and organizations, they do not give us an understanding of why such variations exist. They simply tabulate that which did occur. As but one example of trying to place these data in context, consider the Department of Health, Education, and Welfare. HEW was mandated by law to continually review the compliance of northern school districts with respect to school desegrega-

5

TABLE I.2

School Districts That Desegregated, by Source of Intervention, and by Year of Greatest Desegregation

TIME PERIOD	COURTS		HEW		STATE–LOCAL		TOTAL	
	NO.	%	NO.	%	NO.	%	NO.	%
1901–1953	—[a]	—	—	—	7	3	7	1
1954–1965	13	6	18	12	53	21	84	13
1966–1967	8	4	19	12	46	18	73	12
1968–1969	53	26	42	28	34	13	129	21
1970–1971	107	51	61	40	46	18	214	35
1972–1973	12	6	5	3	38	15	55	9
1974–1975	15	7	7	5	31	12	53	9
Totals	208	100	152	100	255	100	615	100

[a] None in sample.

Source: United States Commission on Civil Rights, *Fulfilling the Letter and Spirit of the Law.* (Washington, D.C.: U.S. Government Printing Office, 1976, p. 135.)

tion. Whereas HEW undertook 28 new reviews in 1968, the number declined to 15 in 1970 and to 1 in 1973. The message to school districts from the Nixon administration was clear—Washington was not going to observe, let alone interfere, with the manner in which they implemented their desegregation plan. That HEW backed off so dramatically from their legal responsibility resulted in the agency being ordered three times by federal judges to perform their duties. It is information such as this that helps us to understand how we have come to where we are.

School Desegregation: Research versus Realities

The mosaic of school desegregation in the United States confounds efforts at grand generalization. School desegregation has brought forth some of the most severe and strident aspects of our race relations; it has also been the source of countless instances of cross-racial cooperation and tolerance. Thus it is not possible to respond to questions like "What good is busing?" or "Isn't the neighborhood school worth preserving?" without an understanding of the particular context in which students, teachers, administrators, and parents find themselves. The elaboration of the differing contexts in which school desegregation is undertaken and implemented is a major focus of this book.

While the chapters elaborate on the situation in five different school settings, they are not meant to infer that they represent the range of possible programs. They do vary and the programs they analyze differ fundamentally among themselves. Yet in the absence of a literature on the internal order and logic of desegregated settings, we have no way of knowing just how representative these present sites in fact are. What we do know is that they collectively represent one of the most intensive and indepth efforts ever undertaken within the United States to study the day-to-day realities of a number of desegregated school settings. The degree to which they vary will only become apparent as further studies are conducted. To paraphrase an adage, "Each school is like all other schools, like some other schools, and like no other school." This holds true for the sites analyzed here.

A crucial dimension in understanding the dynamics of school desegregation is to learn of the ways in which the schools in this study are or are not like "some other schools." It seems profitable not to concern ourselves with the manner in which each school is like all other schools—for then we are propounding universals and a grand theory of schooling. Likewise, to focus on how each school is like "no other school" leaves us fixated on nuances and idiosyncratic minutiae.

The "middle range" view, as it were, is important. Despite the pressing need to learn more of the political and social dynamics of school desegregation, of the interactions within multi-racial student populations, and of how schools learn to cope with new discipline and community relations matters, the research has been extremely limited. The very large majority of studies have not been grounded in the analysis of the day-to-day working out of school desegregation.

One explanation for this gap in our understanding is that the majority of studies in the area of school desegregation have dealt with interracial attitudes in contrast to interracial interaction. We have probed and prodded thousands of students, teachers, and parents to share with us their perceptions, values, and aspirations related to school desegregation. Seldom have we taken time to observe their actions, particularly in a natural context. It is a strength of these present studies that the direct observation of behavior in desegregated settings was the primary methodological focus. (Just how unique this approach is can be inferred by reference to a search of the desegregation research literature in 1975 by St. John. Of the 19 research reports she located on desegregation and intergroup behavior, only one involved actual observation.) While several studies have appeared in the few years since St. John reported her findings, the point remains—we know preciously little about how it is that the persons involved resist, adapt, support, or ignore the realities of school desegregation.

The longitudinal dimension to this research (2 to 3 years on site) provides a unique window through which to view various aspects of school desegregation. The authors are able to analyze the desegregation process as precisely that—a process occurring and unfolding over time. Most of the available research is focused on the first year of a desegregation effort. Thus the early adaptations are not studied for a sufficient period to observe how they evolve. Seldom have we located data that allow us to learn how schools have moved from the press of the first months and weeks of the program to a more steady state, be that organized or chaotic. Several of the chapters report on programs just beginning, others analyze efforts now underway for nearly a decade.

School Desegregation: A Comparative Perspective

In developing a cross-site perspective, there are a number of strands of analysis that could be developed. What are offered here are several that are thought to be important in furthering our understandings of the day-to-day realities of school desegregation. Of concern is the focus on how the presence of school desegregation either creates, compounds, or alleviates conditions in schools. This focus is critical for schools have troubles, regardless of whether or not they undertake to desegregate. Thus the conceptual need is to differentiate between problems common to all schools and those specific to desegregation efforts.

A first issue apparent in these studies is the manner of individual and group adaptations to the desegregated experience. As one might anticipate, given the salience of race to desegregation, the most important characteristic was to define a student's experience within the school setting. The racial cleavage reported time and again in these studies suggests that while the student populations may have been desegregated, they were not integrated. Indeed, not a single site among the five could be said to represent an "integrated school."

Given the racial definition of the school experience, there were two other characteristics that were evident—gender and social class. Each of these tended to confound and complicate the situations *within* racial categories. Thus one found situations of considerably different relations to the school between, for example, middle-class black males and lower-class black males. But as noted above, data from none of the sites would suggest that class or gender was more critical to the social organization of the school than was race. Racial or ethnic origins were constant: Other attributes had varying influence and within different contexts.

The presence of varying adaptations within the desegregated school setting should give pause to those who ask "Does desegregation work?" An honest answer, based on these chapters, is that it depends first on which group one is interested in and second, on how one defines whether a program is or is not working. The present material suggests that an appropriate adaptation for one group would be inappropriate for another. It is naive to assume a commonality of adaptations among lower-class black males—whom the schools have generally served least well—and white male students from middle- and upper-class backgrounds. In a complex organization such as the school, intersected by considerations of class, color, age, social status, and power, it is only to be anticipated that one is likely to find diversity and heterogeneity in how the institution is both valued and used by persons associated with it.

Alluded to above is the matter of ascertaining when a program is or is not working. Overwhelmingly, the data available here imply that a program was thought to be working if the level of violence and interracial conflict was kept to an absolute minimum. Teachers and principals both thought they were "ahead of the game" if they could "keep the lid on" and minimize disruptions. Few and far between are those indications that success was based on pedagogical or instructional criteria for teachers and on academic performance for the students. For most participants, school desegregation spelled trouble, and to keep it at an arm's length was thought to be success enough. That this view was so prevalent suggests that interracial interaction was thought to be tenuous and fragile, capable of breaking apart at any moment. The anticipation was not that things would go smoothly or that both groups could work out differences. Violence was thought to be just below the surface of daily behavior. A "good day" was a day without confrontation.

To have such a baseline for measuring efforts at school desegregation can be characterized in several ways: (*a*) a realistic approach, given the current state of American race relations; (*b*) a cynical view and one unwarranted by the experiences in countless schools across the nation; (*c*) a self-destructive view in that it creates the conditions of a

9

self-fulfilling prophecy; (*d*) an unfair view, one emphasizing a phenomenon that is a common unsolved problem of the society and for which the schools can no more be held accountable than can any other public institution; or (*e*) an irrelevant view, one focusing on nonacademic criteria. Each perspective profoundly influences the kind of assessment that would be made about a desegregation program. That so many differing views are not only possible, but widely held and acted on by persons both in and out of the school system suggests something of the difficulty in assuming any consensus is possible on what we have heretofore accomplished. It is ironic that as this book is published, 25 years after *Brown*, we are so easily led by what we do not like but nearly void of serious reflection on where we might go.

As a second cross-site perspective, the papers suggest that fundamental aspects of social organization are critical to any understanding of the dynamics of school desegregation. While it may appear simplistic to note, school desegregation does involve changing patterns of social organization, be they at the level of the school system, the individual school, classrooms, or within the informal groups of different participants. Thus, characteristics of social class, social status, and power all manifested themselves.

As noted earlier, the criterion by which students grouped themselves was that of racial or ethnic origin. Such grouping also evolved a status hierarchy within the school. As is reflected in other sectors of our society, the racial attribute of being "white" carried high status, while that of being a member of a racial minority carried low status. Given that so many members of the minority groups were also economically poor meant that status characteristics were reinforced with class characteristics.

It is this particular combination of class and color that makes the desegregated situation a potentially difficult one. For schools to deal either with matters of social class differences or racial differences is, in and of itself, a complex and challenging task. To confound them simply heightens the difficulty. It is also worth noting that there are few other institutions in our society where such a mix is encountered. The schools find themselves embarked on an effort for which there are few guidelines and even less experience.

The reality of power and power politics is evident in all of the schools analyzed here. Whether the situation be one within the school involving different groups of students vying for power among themselves or vis-à-vis teachers and administrators, the fact is that power

relations have an influence upon the life of the school. In several instances, there was a fragile "balance of power" among the contending
groups. Even a mild upset to this relation could send the informal as
well as formal organization of the school into a crisis. Students, grouped
by racial categories, periodically tested the limits of power held by
others. The power systems might have been fragile; they were also
thought to be fluid and open to realignment.

That an internal power structure existed in the schools should not
come as a surprise. It is a dynamic that we are fully aware exists in
myriad other institutional settings. What gives it special potency in
the present instance, however, is that the factor of race is introduced.
Race provokes anxiety on the part of participants and thus what is a
normal aspect of organizational life takes on threatening and ominous
overtones. If one couples the racial dimension of the power system to
that of the continual anticipation of violence, the outcome is one where,
frequently, standard procedures no longer apply and prior practice is
rendered null. That the factor of race generated such free floating tension and anxiety at several of the schools can only reinforce an earlier
contention: Desegregation should be but a first step, not the last. To
have it otherwise is to continue to have to confront situations that can
at any time get worse, but not better.

If power arrangements exist inside the schools, they exist external
to them as well. School desegregation is anything but an apolitical
event. The very fact that school desegregation is profoundly political is
what gives it varying approaches and programs in different communities. The political realities, the necessary compromises, the manner of
external intervention by the courts or other agencies of government,
and the vested interests of different groups all impinge upon the desegregation effort. Politics constitutes the art of deciding who gets what
when, and at whose expense. Transposing this to the matter of desegregation suggests that costs as well as benefits are necessary outcomes.

In the past, whites paid when they had to and blacks gained when
they could. In the present, whites say the bills are paid and blacks claim
they are long overdue. In the future, the decision as to what happens
with school desegregation will more than ever be made by black people.
The options are several: hold fast to what now is, lay back and take
over the cities, or continue to demand payment. Whichever is chosen,
the fact remains that the decision will be made by blacks, not whites.
That of itself says something about the impact of *Brown*. It also por-
tends the future of race relations in the United States.

11

Part 1

The Southern Experience

Chapter 1

The Veneer of Harmony: Social-Race Relations in a Southern Desegregated School[1]

DOROTHY C. CLEMENT
MARGARET EISENHART
JOE R. HARDING

The reorganization of American social-race [2] relations that has accompanied school desegregation is crucial to an understanding of the relevance of desegregation to equal educational outcomes for black and white students. Anthropologist Elizabeth Eddy's (1975) analysis of the process of desegregation in a rural Florida district makes this point well. She describes how black administrators and teachers were eased into a subordinate role, losing the small amount of control they had held prior to desegregation, while whites gained an even firmer (albeit more subtle) control of schooling. Although the schools were no longer segregated by social race, the equalization of black–white positions, and

---

[1] The research upon which this paper is based was conducted under contract (No. 400–76–0008) from the National Institute of Education. Sylvia Polgar, Joan True, and Norris Johnson provided helpful comments on an earlier version of the paper. Reactions and comments from teachers and the principal at the study school were also useful.

[2] *Social race* or *color* is used in place of *race* in order to distinguish between race as a biological concept pertaining to populations and race as a pseudobiological folk concept used primarily in reference to individuals. *Social race* is used to refer to the latter meaning (see Harris, 1975, for further elaboration).

DESEGREGATED SCHOOLS
Appraisals of an American Experiment

Copyright © 1979 by Academic Press, Inc.
All rights of reproduction in any form reserved.
ISBN 0-12-588980-1

Dorothy C. Clement   Margaret Eisenhart   Joe R. Harding

therefore educational opportunity, foreseen by the early proponents of desegregation was no closer than before.[3]

The social-race relations that have developed in an urban desegregated school in North Carolina described in this chapter are less clear-cut and more dynamic than the situation described by Eddy. The black community has gained rather than lost decision-making authority in the district, and district policies have deemphasized academic differences among students.

Social-Race Identity and School Organization

In the past, cultural and biological traits were the primary variants by which ethnic and racial identities were categorized. However, recent contributions of Naroll (1964), Barth (1969), LeVine and Campbell (1972), and others have drawn attention to the social identities that ethnic and racial categories confer upon individuals. In other words, the focus has changed from actual differences among groups to the manner in which individuals so categorized are expected and constrained to behave when interacting with members of other groups.

Similarly, in the anthropological study of schools, the focus has shifted from subcultural differences as an explanation of minority students' problems (see Fuchs, 1969; Gallimore, 1974; Valentine, 1971; Wax and Wax, 1971) to the social significance of the categories of sex, social race, class, and ethnicity. A case study by Rist (1973), for example, provides insight into the subtle structuring of student roles in an urban school according to social class. In the "general cultural theory of education" developed by Gearing and associates (n.d.) and built upon the findings of Rist and others, social identities (whether ethnic, racial, sex, social-class, or otherwise) are a central feature associated with societal barriers to the flow of information and therefore of learning. Ogbu (1978) similarly stresses the importance of structural constraints on the education provided to and exploited by minority groups.

These developments suggest that the organization of interaction

[3] These results are reminiscent of the outcomes feared by activist proponents of black equalization in the late 1960s. At that time, some began to place more emphasis on gaining decision-making authority than on desegregation. For a description of attitudes toward desegregation as represented in the literature, see Clement, Eisenhart, and Wood (1976).

among people classified by socially significant characteristics such as race reflects the structural position of these groups in society and, in turn, constrains the education they receive. Here we are concerned with the organization of black–white relations in a southern desegregated school and, specifically, with the manner in which social race is interwoven into the fabric of school life and the factors that seem to promote this organization of social-race relations. We have searched for situations in which social race may or may not be stressed and for conditions such as the political and economic, which have elaborated and maintained social-race identity over the long term. (See, in addition to the references above, Fennell, 1977; Foster, 1974; Jones, 1976; Manning, 1974; and Nagata, 1974.)

The following section of the chapter describes the general nature of black–white relations in the district and specific district policies that bear some connection to black–white relations in the school.

Community Politics and Education in Bradford: A Brief Sketch [4]

In Bradford's dual community system, as in many southern cities, patterns of racial segregation in housing and in education were only two of many aspects of the traditional division between black and white communities. Business and social services were also distinct for each group; for example, white funeral homes were not (and are not) patronized by black clients, and vice versa. In Bradford, a particularly bifurcated community organization developed, with Bradford blacks supporting their own university, schools, small businesses, churches, social structure, and network of leaders.

---

[4] Bradford and Grandin (the study school) are pseudonyms, as are all the names of individuals. A more comprehensive discussion of community politics and education is given in Clement, Eisenhart, and Harding (1977). The primary method used for this aspect of the study was regular attendance at meetings of the school board, an informal group of community leaders, citizen's steering committees, and the school PTA. In addition, some 30 interviews were conducted with district administrators, other principals, school board members, and community leaders. In addition to informal interviews with parents, 17 parents were interviewed using a standard set of questions on desegregation.

Dorothy C. Clement   Margaret Eisenhart   Joe R. Harding

The existence of these separate systems has been important in the development of the character of Bradford politics as interest-group interactions. In the city's history, one can see the increasing definition of the black community as an interest group that has become progressively more involved in the political arena.

When compared to black groups in other cities, black business in Bradford enjoyed an unusual degree of economic viability, giving the group a certain degree of independence from the local white economy. Although leaders of both sectors have a common interest in maintaining conditions conducive to better business, basic dependencies have been limited to such areas as the need for black labor in manufacturing industries (and, conversely, a need among blacks for employment). The success of black business also promoted the emergence of black "upper" and "middle" classes that provided a growing core of black leadership. After 1940, this leadership increasingly involved the black community in city affairs as a political interest group. A formally organized group, in fact, representing black business and political interests since the 1930s, has pursued the objective of access to and influence in the formal political structure of local and state politics. Thus, blacks have consistently sought representation on the city council and later the county commission. They have used their control of the black vote to influence other city councilmen and to seek local and, more recently, state elective positions. Additionally, black interests have focused on efforts to improve black schools and, since 1954, to achieve desegregation of the local school system both in the city and the surrounding county.

Today, the bases of the dual system remain in many respects. There is still a residence pattern that concentrates population by socioeconomic status and social race, though the lines between middle-class blacks and whites are becoming somewhat blurred in the suburban neighborhoods in the county. The political power base of the blacks lies within the city, and their political voice carries more weight there than in the county, particularly with regard to education. In comparison, the traditionally powerful white interests, the economic "power elite," find their political support among the county voters. It is possible to see the current development in city–county demography and relations as only a shift in the relative location of the segments of the dual system. Blacks have increased their influence and population in the city, whereas white groups have moved themselves and their power base into suburbia and, as far as the schools are concerned, into the county district.

DESEGREGATION, COMMUNITY RESPONSE,
AND BLACK REPRESENTATION IN
DISTRICT AFFAIRS

The first desegregation of Bradford schools was brought about by a 1970 court order. Fearing violence and civil disorders in the desegregation process, the city struggled to keep political struggles backstage and nonviolent. At a basic level, parents feared for the safety of their children in the schools. Bradford's civic leaders, both black and white, saw a threat to local business and other interests (e.g., political) should the school changes provoke the riots and confrontations that had occurred in other southern cities. Bradford succeeded in avoiding violent confrontations, even though resistance to desegregation could be found in groups from low-income to upper-class status.

In the spring of 1975, black plaintiffs won an additional decision and the federal court required a new step in the desegregation process. The school system was directed to achieve a racial balance in each school that reflected the black–white ratios of the system as a whole. This change was not accompanied by fears of violence and the extensive preparation to avoid it characteristic of the 1970 order.

The increasing power of the black community became more apparent at this time. At about the same time as the desegregation plan was in preparation, the city council moved to have the school board elected rather than appointed as it had been previously, ostensibly to make the selection process less sensitive to political pressure, much of which at this time was coming from the formally organized group representing the black community. The new procedure removed the city from formal responsibility in the troublesome problems of Bradford education, an action consistent with the pattern of withdrawal from the internal affairs of the city schools by the white political interests after desegregation. Thus, the black leadership has accomplished desegregation, succeeded in at least formally dominating the school board, and placed several blacks in the school administration, some in key positions. By court order, the faculty has been desegregated (each school to reflect the systemwide 1970 ratio), and the black influence in administration and on the school board should affect future staff hiring. Although black leaders stress the many goals yet to be accomplished, their influence on city school affairs has increased substantially in the past 20 years.

Dorothy C. Clement   *Margaret Eisenhart*   *Joe R. Harding*

CHANGES IN DISTRICT POLICY

Avoidance of conflict might also be associated with district policies evident during the period of desegregation, particularly before the election of the majority black school board in 1975. These policies, such as changes in the grading system for the elementary school, probably defused possible sources of race-related conflict.

During the last decade, there have been some indications of a reorganization of district policies away from the traditional reward structure of the schools, with its clear designations of successful and unsuccessful students, toward a system in which the standards and rewards for success and failure are muted. In place of the traditional system, an emphasis has been placed on alternative modes of instruction described as remedial programs. Efforts are made to bring students who fall behind, as measured by standardized tests, up to standard through programs based on individual instruction. During this period, quality remedial programs for math and reading have been emphasized, although they are not yet available to all who are eligible for them.[5]

It is important to note that the new system may have distinct educational advantages since it avoids some of the negative labeling of the traditional system and allows for learning that might not otherwise occur. As it affects social-race relations, we emphasize that the new system, besides its possible educational advantages, might also have spared the district considerable conflict in that it (*a*) deemphasizes enforcement of evaluative and attendance policies; (*b*) downplays overt markers of a student's ability or progress relative to other students; (*c*) places less emphasis on contact between teachers and parents; and (*d*) attempts to make evaluation and disciplinary procedures more objective. The policies developed or maintained by the central office during this period do not all necessarily have their origin in desegregation, of course, yet they have accompanied this period and have a bearing upon the conflicts that might have been expected in the wake of school desegregation.

After the 1975 court decision, Bradford schools were directed by central office officials to avoid the establishment of any racially identifiable class (that is, a class nonrepresentative of the student body, which

[5] According to the SRA tests administered in the fifth grade, 73.3% of the study schools' fifth-graders were reading below grade level. Although all of those below reading level were not necessarily eligible for the remedial program because of funding constraints, only 27% of the fifth graders were in the remedial reading program.

20

at the study school, for example, was approximately 65% black) lasting more than 1¼ hours. At the same time, the central office espoused the principle of *mainstreaming*, in which all students except those with severe physical or educational handicaps are kept together for most instruction. Students in remedial math or reading, in classes for the exceptionally talented, or in classes for the "educable mentally retarded" are separated from their classmates for one or two class periods only. In addition, fairly lengthy procedures were established to determine the eligibility of students for the special resources classes, including those for the exceptionally talented. Instituted in the 1975–1976 school year, these procedures include a teacher recommendation for the class, parental permission to test the student, administration of an IQ test, and review of the student's case by a screening committee comprised of the principal, resource teachers, the school psychologist, and the resource supervisor. Finally, parental permission must be obtained to transfer the student to the special class.

The principle of mainstreaming, the demand for racially balanced classes, and the procedures required for admission to special classes have made charges of unequal treatment on the basis of social race more difficult to sustain. Officially, the students are treated as equals entitled to remedial or special education only under special circumstances, including permission of the parents.

Changes in student evaluation procedures in elementary school and the acceptance of "social promotions" have also served to reduce conflict.[6] The new report card forms, introduced after the first significant desegregation of the schools in 1971, do not have a category of "failing." Rather, the student is marked by a system of three numbers: 1 indicating "very good," 2 for "satisfactory," and 3 for "having difficulty." Although students dread 3s, the evaluations are not quite so clear-cut as they were under the grading system used in the past. Not until junior high does the student face the possibility of an F. Social promotion in junior high is reportedly less common. Teachers are freer with Fs and willing to fail students. In other words, at the elementary level students can proceed through the grades at the same pace and with relatively little official differentiation. At the same time, remedial programs are provided for as many of those who need them as possible. For those students who do not receive remedial assistance or for some other

[6] "Social promotion" refers to an undeserved promotion in the eyes of the teacher as assessed by student performance and mastery of materials. Whether the practice substantially increased after desegregation is unknown.

reason do not catch up, institutional failure is delayed to later years. At that time, it is harder to sustain a charge of discriminatory grading because the school can demonstrate the student's lack of skills or failure to master course content.

An additional point concerns the lack of sanctions for poor attendance. Extremely poor attendance is a sufficient cause for retention. At the study school, the one fifth-grade student who failed during the 1975–1976 school year did so because of poor attendance. In general, however, the district has maintained a fairly lax attendance policy and has had relatively ineffectual enforcement methods; the matter is left up to the parents and the personal efforts of the teacher and the principal. Some teachers bring to this task a great deal of skill and interest. Others bring little.[7]

These grading, attendance, and promotion policies in effect delay institutional differentiation among students according to success and failure until later and perhaps save the school from the wrath of parents irate at the evaluations of their children's performance in grade school. Thus, potential sources of conflict are decreased.

Regulations have also been established to reduce the possibility of conflict over the administration of corporal punishment. A teacher must warn the student of the offense and the proposed punishment, and spanking must be witnessed by another teacher. These procedures tend to ensure that the teacher's purpose is a legitimate one and not susceptible to racial interpretation.

In brief, then, since desegregation and especially in the last 2 years, there has been an increase in the representation of blacks in the decision-making bodies of the school district. Although there is a current counter trend, during the 7 years that the schools have been desegregated, the district has adopted or maintained policies decreasing the differentiation of students by achievement in the elementary grades and increasing the use of explicit procedures in assigning students to groups and in meting out punishments and rewards to students. The district discouraged the use of social-race categories in the formal or semiformal[8] systems of the school (except for the purpose of achieving

[7] A policy revision has been implemented since the end of the study in June, 1977, in which each absent student is to be contacted to ascertain the reason for the absence.

[8] See Gordon (1957) for an explanation of the formal, semiformal, and informal level of school organization. These distinctions relate to the source of legitimization of the rules, regulations, and roles that are followed. Formal and semiformal

racial balance in the schools and in the regular classrooms) and otherwise has attempted to eliminate the potential for discriminatory charges by making procedures more explicit.

Aspects of Social-Race Relations in the School

At Grandin, the study school, we find a complex and somewhat tenuous organization of social-race relations. At the formal and semiformal levels of school organization, the category of social race is used only as permitted by the district. At the informal level, however, we find that social race is still an important category in how people interact with one another. The relevance of social race is evidenced by the linguistic terms that people know and sometimes use, in the interpretation that people sometimes give to their experiences, in the norms that people attempt to encourage one another to follow, and in the friendship patterns that tend to form. An examination of these four areas allows for an analysis of the nature and importance of social-race relations and the factors that support their maintenance and development. Examination of social-race terminology, for example, allows access to the cultural knowledge that people use to describe, address, and refer to one another. These terms also provide information as to how social-race relations are socially structured. In the past, blacks in the South were constrained to enact socially inferior roles, many of which were signaled in terms of address and reference. Today, although knowledge of such terms is still maintained, social rules prohibit their use in many public contexts.

The second and third types of information that will be examined are symbolic encounters and unusual characters. The analysis of symbolic encounters—or racial incidents, as they are sometimes called in the newspapers—and the study of how they are reacted to in public reveal

---

rules are ones that are dictated and backed up by recognized groups that control certain resources and continue to exist despite a turnover in personnel. Semiformal groups differ from formal groups in that they are recognized only by a portion of those who recognize the formal groups; and they are vulnerable to policy made by the formal groups but not the reverse. Informal groups are those which are not officially recognized, which control resources indirectly if at all, which back up their rules by social pressure, and which are susceptible to rapid change owing to turnover in personnel. The concepts as they are used in this study are further explicated in Clement *et al.*, 1977.

difficulties that beset black–white interaction and the means that people have for resolving them. Analysis of individuals who are singled out by school participants as being unusual or deviant with respect to how they interact with members of another social-race category allows the inference of norms for social-race interaction. Finally, we examine the actual friendship patterns between blacks and whites in order to assess how social-race identity constitutes a barrier to the formation of significant relationships in the school.

The information on these four aspects of social-race relations was gathered in the course of a 2-year ethnographic study at Grandin Elementary School that focused on fifth-grade students in 1975–1976. They were followed through the fifth and sixth grades. Methods utilized in the study included participant observation, standardized observations of a judgmental sample of 25 focal students, elicitation or ethnosemantic interviews, sociometric interviews of all students at the end of each year, standard-schedule interviews with teachers and a small sample of 17 parents, and a period of weekly open-ended ("talking diary") interviews with 10 of the focal students. The many hours (over 1,000) of informal observation in the school constitute important complementary data to the various types of interviews, especially since the topic of the study, social-race relations, is a sensitive one in the district and in the school. (For more details on methodologies, see Clement *et al.*, 1977.) These data have been reviewed for relevant information on the four categories to be described.

SEPARATING WORDS—SOCIAL-RACE TERMS

In studying social-race terminology used at the school, we follow a commonplace approach that anthropologists and sociolinguists employ to gain information about important social categories and distinctions: studying the existence in a group's lexicon of many different terms that finely discriminate categories of a single phenomenon. Additionally, investigation of the selective use or nonuse of available words in various contexts can reveal information about the relationships considered socially appropriate for those contexts. In this section we are concerned with linguistic labels referring to social-race identities that are available to and used by school participants. Through an examination of the meaning of these terms and their use contexts, insight is gained into the means by which social-race identities enter explicitly into social interaction and into aspects of social-race identities that are significant at Grandin.

The Legacy of Social-Race Terminology

In the United States, there are a variety of terms that refer to the social-race identity of a person. The number and distribution of these terms attest to their importance in American society. Barth (1969) argues that when groups of differing cultural backgrounds come into contact, features that distinguish the groups will be seized upon as socially significant. Often the cleavage between groups is reflected in and perpetuated by linguistic labels that refer to these socially significant features.

K. Johnson (1972) argues that cross-race terminology historically served as a marker of the highly constrained roles allowed blacks in cross-color interaction. Words that reflected social-status differences between blacks and whites, such as *my boy* or *my nigger*, were used by whites as terms of patronage; *bossman, captain,* and *master* were used as terms of deference by blacks.

As often happens when a group is a minority, blacks also developed special linguistic conventions to which most whites did not have access. Black terms of self-reference included distinctions of physical characteristics as well as labels such as *Uncle Tom* and *Oreo,* which referred to attitudes of blacks toward whites. Such terms were primarily understood and used by blacks.

Whereas blacks had many terms to characterize themselves, whites as a group had few, if any, labels of self-reference. Whites lacked a variety of terms for themselves, Johnson believes, because the boundaries of racial identification were never central to their self-definition relative to other whites. Instead, in their self-definition they focused on class, regional, occupational, or other features as more significant than racial identification.

In the past, then, social-race terminology reflected a pattern of social-race relations in which social race conferred upon individuals social identities of utmost importance in interaction. Terms of reference and address used in black–white interaction signaled the relevance of these identities and the nature of black–white relations. At Grandin, we find both continuity and discontinuity with the past.

Social Race Terms Used in the School

The data reveal two important dimensions of meaning coded in the social-race terms used in the school: (*a*) group identity and (*b*) physical typing. Phenotypic characteristics are attributes of all social-race terms by definition; however, most social-race terms, at least for some segment of the population, also imply social characteristics. Here, terms that emphasize physical characteristics are referred to as *physical typing*. Terms that are used when the social attributes are more salient are referred to as *group identity* terms. As we shall see, there are also a number of terms that are known but not used in public.

Publicly Used Group-identity Labels. *Black* and *white* are by far the most frequently used social-race terms. More than just physical distinctions, they are also group labels. One teacher, during a social studies class, clearly expressed the idea that there is more to the terms *black* and *white* than skin color alone. In response to a student's question about what to call a person whose racial traits are mixed, this teacher replied,

> *I don't know, I guess it depends on what culture you go with. If a Negro and white marry and the children stay with the black culture, then they'd be black. If Chinese and white, then they'd probably go by white unless they went to China.*

Additionally, blacks have a variety of group labels that are used in talking about other blacks, including *nigger, slave, colored, New Jersey African, tar baby,* and *knottyhead*. Whites do not have a variety of group labels for their own group. Rarely do they use even the label *white,* that category being more often implied by use of the pronoun *we* (or *us*).

Publicly Used Physical-typing Labels. Physical-typing labels, regardless of their context or manipulative function, were found to be used almost exclusively by black students, and that terminology is relatively elaborate. *Yellow* (as in *yellow muther, yellow boy, yellow Indian*), *red, light-skinned, dark-skinned, dark complexion,* and *chocolate* are examples of terms used by blacks to differentiate among other blacks according to phenotypic features.

White students do not seem to have developed any comparable terminology based on skin color for intragroup physical-type reference and do not use the blacks' self-reference terminology. To our knowledge, blacks and whites only occasionally use terms such as *blond* that distinguish whites from one another according to physical type.

Infrequently Used Labels

Our observations in the school and the reports we have obtained from school adults show that the use of social-race terms is infrequent, especially in comparison with the use of other social-identity terms such as *boy, girl, teacher,* and *child.* Elicitation interviews with a number of school participants produced a set of terms that were heard even more infrequently in public. *White cracker, soda cracker, honky,* and *white honky* are negative terms said to be used by blacks in referring to whites; and such negative terms as *nigger, black tar,* and *ace of spades* were reported used by whites to refer to blacks.

The findings based on public usage suggest that social-race identity is more important to black students than to white. At least in the domain of self-reference terms, blacks have a fairly elaborated set of words to distinguish one another. Whites appear to have few words available by which they may designate members of their own or the opposite social-race group. The additional data provided by the elicitation interviews suggest that a large number of cross-race terms are known and available to both blacks and whites, yet such terms are apparently not considered appropriate for public usage at school. These terms all have negative connotations; no terms that signal positive cross-color relationships were heard in public usage or discovered through interviews. The significance of these findings is evidenced by further examination of the context of use of social-race terms.

Context of Use for Social-Race Terms

Theoretically, terms that signal social-race identity could be used in any context involving descriptions, explanations, or forms of address of individuals or groups. We find, however, as indicated above, that their public use at Grandin is quite restricted and that fewer contexts are available to white students than to black.

To some extent, the restricted use of social-race terms is guided by teachers. Students' linguistic behavior, like other aspects of their behavior, is partially constrained by what teachers do and allow.

Teacher Usage. In general, teachers rarely refer to social race. District policy mandates that specific attention be devoted to social-race groups in the curriculum at one time only—during black history month. The social studies texts used made some references to social race. For example, the anthropology section of one of the texts stresses the "races of man." For the most part, however, teachers are left on their own to decide how much stress to place on instructing students about social race or social-race relations. Given the sensitive nature of the topic in the district and the lack of a clear mandate, teachers vary in the emphases they place, with some making no direct reference at all.

Although they varied among themselves, the fifth- and sixth-grade teachers at the school appeared to follow different norms for the use of social-race terminology. The fifth-grade teachers rarely mentioned any social-race terms with children present. One of the few times they were mentioned was during black history month. Here, the terms were used mostly to explain the condition of blacks in the past and to refer to blacks in American history.

In contrast, the sixth-grade teachers more often made reference to social race, particularly with regard to social studies curriculum content. Topics that provoked discussion involving explanations in terms of social-race identities, such as what a presidential candidate will do for blacks, were more often raised in the sixth-grade hall. Discussions comparing conditions of minority groups in other countries with those of blacks in the United States were also more common in sixth-grade classes. One day, for example, a sixth-grade teacher was discussing the caste system in India. The teacher asked the class to compare the effects of the caste system with segregation patterns in the United States. In the discussion that followed, both black and white students, as well as the teacher, mentioned a number of restrictions that had been placed on blacks in the past. These restrictions included the fact that blacks could not go to school with whites, could not drink the same water or eat the same food, and had to do much of the whites' dirty work. At times, sixth-grade teachers also exhorted students to behavior on the basis of social race, as when one chided black students in the class for knowing less than whites about black history.

These teachers also occasionally recounted personal experiences that cast black–white relations in a favorable light. One sixth-grade teacher, for example, told the following story about the community where the teacher had grown up.

> *The teacher talked about how kind the blacks were in the community. The teacher told the class that blacks had just built a new school when the white school burned. The blacks let the whites use their new school while the white school was being rebuilt.*

The occasions when social-race terms were used by teachers to reveal information about positive social-race relations were rare relative to the use of the terms in descriptive and explanatory contexts in reference to the past. As a result, use of the terms often reflected negatively on whites, who were portrayed as the perpetrators of injustices to blacks, while at the same time raising the specter of social inferiority of blacks.

Student Usage. As fifth-graders, the students appeared to follow their teachers with regard to social-race usage in formal situations. Only after the introduction of a subject with a clear focus on race, such as slavery or racial stocks, by the teacher (or, in one case, by a particularly precocious white child) did students use social-race terms. Even then, they were always used in an explanatory fashion, usually relating to the past. When researchers asked some of the fifth-graders to describe other children in the class, social-race terms were almost never used.

Like their teachers, the sixth-graders appeared to use social-race terms in class more than when they were in the fifth grade, especially in giving explanations during social studies periods. In a few cases, children also used social-race identity as a way to explain the present-day behavior of social-race groups. For example, one black child explained in class that the reason black children have a hard time in school is that they have a hard life outside school.

In the formal classroom setting, children use the group labels *black* and *white* primarily in explanatory contexts. Other group labels, and the physical-typing terms that are heard from students in a variety of other school settings, are not employed in the classroom either by teachers or by students in exchanges with teachers.

Outside the constraints of the formal classroom situation, students expand the range of social-race terminology that they use. In informal situations, group-identity labels and physical-typing terms are more commonly used to describe or address others, to explain actions, and to encourage behavior based on social-race identity. Informal use of the terms in these contexts is more frequent among blacks than whites.

In informal contexts, terms may be used in a neutral fashion to ask about or designate a person from among others or to describe someone not present at the time. Black students, particularly, were often heard using social-race terms in a descriptive fashion such as, *Who's that black lady?*

Black students also frequently use social-race terms to tease or taunt each other. One light-skinned girl, in particular, was the object of considerable teasing. For example, one day this girl, Helga, and two other black girls were sitting together at lunch when an ant crawled across the table.

> *Jan accuses Helga of bringing the ant in her lunchbox. Helga denies the allegation. Then Jan, pretending to speak for the ant, says, "Let me go to a white girl's lunch—so it picked Helga." Helga does not respond. Gwen, the other girl, picks up the tease, "Then the ant said, 'No, I want a black girl's lunch to eat—so it went to Helga.'" Gwen and Jan laugh. Helga makes no comment. She looks straight ahead and ignores their laughter.*

Another common form of in-group teasing used by black students is name-calling that incorporates social-race terminology, as in the following exchange.

> *One black boy was trying to attract another's attention. The boy yelled out, "Hey, red man." The target of the address (a boy frequently called this name because of the reddish color of his hair) immediately turned around, smiling, and yelled back, "Go on, you black tar nigger."*

Appellations such as *black gargoyle, blackie, black biscuit,* and *nappy head* are other examples.

These words as well as others, especially the word *nigger*, are often used informally as address forms by black students. When used by blacks as a form of address, as in *come here, nigger*, these terms may have positive connotations, being nearly equivalent to *friend* or *brother*. Although use of *nigger* in this way is common among blacks, in only one or two cases were white students allowed to use these words when addressing black students.

We observed few instances of whites singling out others on the basis of group identity or physical typing except in an explanatory context where they might use the group label *white*. We have no examples of whites exhorting each other or addressing each other using social-race terminology.

In spontaneous cross-race references, *black* and *white* are sometimes used negatively. For example, Frank (black) and Edward (white) were pushing each other in the hall when Edward finally yelled at Frank, who would not stop, "I've got enough of black germs already." On another occasion, the same white boy called several black boys *black niggers* when they systematically kept him from scoring in an improvised game they were playing. The few instances of whites and blacks' insulting each other through the use of social-race terms seemed to be cases of lashing out in frustration or anger rather than attempts to taunt or provoke.

One such instance shows clearly how potentially threatening and powerful the structuring of a cross-race confrontation and social-race identity can be for some white students.

> *Martha, a white girl, and her white friend, Chris, are sitting on the seesaw. Two black girls, Mandy and Joanne, come and try to take over the seesaw. Martha shouts to the two black girls, "You can't get on here!" Mandy replies, "Just 'cause you white. . . . You ain't even white, you red." Martha says, "I'm white . . . God made me that way and I like it." Mandy screams, "If you were white, you'd be the color of your shirt." Martha: "I don't see any of you. . . . I don't hear you either." After this statement, Martha and Chris vacate the seesaw.*

In this argument, Martha could not cope with the racial interpretation of this incident and refused verbally to accept its validity. However, she did relinquish the seesaw to Mandy.

We have no examples of whites and blacks successfully teasing one another on the basis of social-race identity. The only time researchers heard words playing on social-race identity used and accepted in jest occurred during a mixed and public activity at Grandin.

> *The class is staging a talent show. Two black boys have chosen to provide the commercials for the show. One boy stands in front of the class, holding a paper cutout of the bottom of a shoe. The other boy pretends to be filming the first. The boy with the cutout begins, "Black sole . . . guaranteed to make the run to Africa!" The whole class laughs hard. The boy puts down the cutout and picks up a jar. He continues, "Knotty Sheen . . . guaranteed to make your hair un-nice, full of dandruff, and you won't have to worry about ugly girls." The class and their teacher break up in laughter again.*

Interestingly, this example comes from one of the few occasions where students were given a free hand to structure their own performances.

In short, we see that Grandin students, particularly blacks, have the terminology available to emphasize social-race distinctiveness at the school. These linguistic labels differentiate blacks and whites and place negative valuations on out-group members. Although there are labels that can be used to express in-group solidarity, no such terms exist to

31

express cross-race friendships. Instead, the terms that students know for use in cross-race situations are ones that tend to enhance the social distinctiveness of the two groups rather than bring them together. On the other hand, there is no evidence for negative (or positive) labels that describe an individual's posture toward members of the other social race. Among the children, there are no terms such as *Oreo, Uncle Tom,* and *nigger-lover* that traditionally labeled blacks and whites who, from the point of view of same-group members, overstepped the limits of their respective social-race identities. Nor are there special terms applied to cross-color relationships that are not applied to same-color relationships. Thus, the terminology that students know is similar to that of the past in that it distinguishes black from white, is more elaborated among blacks, and carries negative loadings for cross-race reference; it is unlike the past in that terms marking superordinate and subordinate positions in interaction are not found, nor, for this age group, are terms found that describe an individual's posture toward or relationship with members of the other group.

A second significant point is that social-race terms are not used very often in mixed situations. The roughly 1000 hours of observation in the school yielded only 100 examples of the spontaneous use of social-race terms. Most of these did not occur in cross-race situations. In addition, the cross-race situations in which the terms were used generally involved conflict or competition. Students, if overheard by teachers when using these terms for derogatory effect, were reprimanded. Thus, although teachers introduce and allow the use of social-race terms to describe history or in reference to current events on a national level, they do not usually use such terms, nor do they allow students to make social-race identities explicit in negative interaction with one another.

The deemphasis on explicit invocation of social-race identities raises the question of indirect reference. Could it be that social-race identities are referred to in a camouflaged manner? Labels such as *good at sports, non-reader, EMR (educable mentally retarded) student,* and *bus rider,* for example, may be hidden references to black students who are overrepresented in these categories. It is possible that both teachers and students manipulate these relational terms in lieu of social-race terms in some cross-race interactions. The public use of words marking social-race identity has clear implications and is susceptible to emotionally charged interpretations. For this reason, students and teachers at Grandin may not wish to use them, preferring other labels that more ambiguously refer to the social-race identity of others. In any event, it is clear that explicit reference to social race is very much constrained, especially in cross-race interaction. Students have knowledge of terms that could be, but are not, used. In public contexts, negative terms are explicitly disallowed. These findings suggest that a norm against provoking conflicts based on social race exists at Grandin.

SYMBOLIC ENCOUNTERS AND THE AMBIGUITY OF INTERPRETATION

In the ethnographic data collected for this study, as well as in other anthropological literature on schools such as Fuchs (1969), there are numerous accounts of incidents that arouse the emotions of those involved. For example, during a talking diary interview, one of the students recounted the following incident that occurred with a substitute teacher:

> *We were at the lunch table about ready to leave and [the teacher] took this tray and shoved it to me and then the tray hit me. Then she said, "Hey, boy, take my tray." I said, "I don't want to take your tray." She said, "You take my tray or go to the office." I said, "I'd rather go to the office 'cause I ain't going to take your tray"; like that, so I went to the office.*

Incidents such as these, which evoke a strong reaction, are referred to in this section as *symbolic encounters.*

Symbolic encounters are actions that are deviant in that they convey unexpected positive or unexpected negative information about a social relationship. All encounters that involve exchange between humans convey social information about the relationship between the participants and are thus symbolic. The term *symbolic encounter*, however, is used here to draw attention to those encounters which are distinctive by their impact. A symbolic encounter causes an emotional response because it implies a redefinition of at least one participant's view of the relationship, the "self," or the "other." In the case described above, the student was outraged at the teacher's evident disregard for his dignity. He chose to go to the office rather than perform the simple, but loaded, act of carrying the tray to the counter. Positive symbolic encounters could also be noted. Various students, for example, reported incidents concerning classroom exchanges with teachers that were both surprising and pleasant.

Symbolic encounters having to do with social race stand out be-

33

cause they deviate from what an individual expects or will accept from another having a given social-race identity. The encounters that are vulnerable to interpretation in terms of social race, the feelings that these encounters produce, the means available for settling them, and their frequency reveal important information about the organization of social-race relations at Grandin. Although these symbolic encounters could conceivably be positive, as will be seen, they rarely are. In symbolic encounters that are interpreted as having to do with social-race identities, the tone is generally negative.

Frequency

The number of race-related symbolic encounters that became topics of discussion at Grandin, were described to us, or were observed by us over the 2-year research period is small. Between 15 and 20 such encounters came to our attention. Although these were almost all negative symbolic encounters, they certainly were not daily occurrences, as might be imagined by someone familiar with southern patterns of race relations as recently as 10 or 15 years ago. (The reasons for their relative infrequency, including norms that serve to suppress such interpretations, are discussed in the third section.)

The relative infrequency of these symbolic encounters does not, however, mean that they are insignificant for individuals and for relations in the school. As will be apparent, these incidents are upsetting and are particularly hard to resolve because they are so much a matter of interpretation. The following examples are given to show the types of incidents that occurred and the difficulties such incidents pose because of the impossibility of definitively determining what occurred and why it occurred.

One of the more striking examples of a social-race incident was related by a student in the talking diary interviews. The interviewer was asking Martha, a white girl, what had gone on the past week in school. Martha, after talking for a while about a problem with another teacher, began the following:

> . . . *we was talking about races in social studies. And everybody said, "What do you call black people?" And they said you call 'em . . . Nigeroid. And then they said, "What's the correct name for white people?" And these black people hollered out "honky" and [the teacher] laughed with them. [The teacher] did! And everybody, all the white kids looked at [the teacher] 'cause if we just said that then she woulda got us . . . prejudiced—I been noticing it but I never told [the*

teacher] nothing about it because, well [the teacher] started laughing . . . laughing, you know . . . and I never noticed that before 'cause I just thought [the teacher] was so nice and sometimes . . . now that [the teacher] said that, I been paying attention and like on baseball teams, all the blacks are picked first and then the whites are picked last and then never get to hit. I never noticed that until [the teacher] laughed. And then they said "white cracker" and then they kept on raising their hands to say different names and it hurt. . . . I used to didn't notice that—until yesterday.

In the four prior interviews, Martha had always talked fondly of this teacher. In the following interviews, when asked about the teacher, she always referred to the previous incident:

Remember that time I told you how the teacher was? I told you . . . she prejudiced. . . .

Furthermore, after that point, she frequently included reference in her discussion to the social race of students, something she had *not* done before. She also talked for some time after this interview of wanting to go to a private school.

Martha was unpopular and was aware of negative feeling directed at her. Provoked by the teacher's apparent condoning of anti-white sentiment in the classroom, she began to attribute her negative treatment to racism.

Martha did not discuss this incident with others at the school. When the interviewer asked if she did, she said:

[The other white students] just looked funny and most of them put down their heads. . . . there's eight white people in our class and then they just felt sort of funny; they didn't say nothing cause if they did then they would've got it.

Thus this incident, which was a very significant episode in Martha's developing understanding of social-race relations, was not communicated to others. No one knew that she had interpreted the encounter as she did or that it was so pivotal to her. It did not become an incident that was talked about in the school.

Only two or three race-related incidents actually did attract widespread public attention during the 2 years of the study.[9] A recurrent difficulty with these incidents and the one reported above is that they tend to be ambiguous; a number of plausible interpretations can be

[9] The possibility that such events were hidden from us is discussed below.

given for each. Thus, the significance of these encounters and their interpretations are disputed by school participants. One encounter concerned the class assignment of a student; the other concerned a teacher who allegedly put liquid soap on a student.[10]

In the first case, there was a disagreement among some of the fifth- and sixth-grade teachers as to whether a particular student, a black girl, should be retained in the fifth grade or whether she would be better off in the sixth grade. The reasons put forward for the student's difficulties and the assessments of her needs caused some disagreement. The settling of the argument by the procedural point that the girl and her parents already had been notified of her failure did not really clear the air. The disagreement was interpreted privately by some as having to do with social race. Others denied that this was a meaningful interpretation. All, however, agreed that an upsetting encounter had occurred.

In the second case, the teacher denied that an upsetting encounter had even occurred. The teacher in this encounter had become, during the year, a target of student hostility and experienced increasing difficulty in managing the class. Near the end of the year, the normally polite relationships among the teachers were disrupted by an alleged misuse of some liquid soap by this teacher. This incident was described by a student in one of the talking diary interviews:

> *Well, Virgil, he got some musk and he kind of put too much on and then he went in the room and it started smelling and [the teacher] didn't like the smell of it and she sent somebody down . . . to get some stuff to clean him 'cause of not liking the smell of what he had on. [The teacher] cleaned around him and then wiped his pants. [The teacher] wiped it on his pants and then started walking around the room, cleaning other things.*

The white teacher involved in this incident denied that the act was purposeful and argued that the students reporting the incident were known to fabricate stories. One of the consequences of the encounter was a confrontation of sorts between this teacher and a black teacher in the school. The ill feelings associated with this event were escalated rather than resolved.

[10] The details of these incidents have been altered somewhat in an effort to deemphasize the question of culpability. None of us was present at either event. Even if we had been, we would not have had access to everyone's innermost motivation, and thus we cannot in good conscience judge those involved. Furthermore, the point is not to pass judgment on these incidents, but to examine instead what they indicate about the structuring of social-race relations at Grandin.

This encounter, the disagreement over student assignment, and the case in which the black teacher seemed to be condoning anti-white sentiment have much to offer in illuminating the nature of race-related symbolic encounters and their consequences.

Ambiguity

Three perhaps not unrelated features of these race-related symbolic encounters are that they are usually negative, very upsetting, and often ambiguous. This ambiguity stems from two sources. First, what is considered demeaning, discriminatory, inappropriate, or unfair behavior if perpetrated by a white against a black, or vice versa, is culturally determined. Second, the encounter usually can be interpreted from at least one framework other than that of a social race.

Cultural Differences. It is well known that what is considered demeaning behavior in one society may not be so considered in another. Or, for that matter, what is considered demeaning by one individual may not be so considered by another. The incident of the tray described in the initial paragraph of this section might not have been upsetting to another student. The talking diary interviews produced another example:

> You do **not** come in my face, you do not hit me in the face, you is a fool. I don't care if you a teacher or a principal or who, 'cause ain't no teacher never smacked me. One threatened to smack me. And you know what I told her: "Here go my face; you smack me." Now I was in the fourth grade . . . and the teacher said, "You—if you fight or pass a lick, I'll smack you." Me and this girl was playing, but [the teacher] thought we was hitting and then I hit the girl but she wouldn't hit me back because, see, she wanted to see me get in trouble. And [the teacher] tole me: "I told you that you better not hit that girl and if you did I would smack you" but see [the teacher] a fool; don't nobody smack me . . . my mama don't even smack me.

The significance this student attached to having her face hit is not unique. Many of the black students, in elicitation interviews, indicated that smacking someone on the face is very serious. Yet, the teacher described may very well have been unaware of the severity of the act to the student.

The point is that people learn what is considered demeaning or inappropriate. In a period where the status of a group of people is changing, or in a situation where there are cultural or subcultural differences, members of one group may not be aware of what the others consider demeaning. Without access to this knowledge, they may continually offend without recognizing that they are doing so, unbelievable as it may seem to those whom they are offending.

Because of the culturally determined nature of race-related symbolic encounters, individuals may not recognize the overtones of their actions or may dispute the attribution of racism to their act. In one situation, for example, one of the white teachers wanted to take advantage of an opportunity for the classes to view the movie *Gone With the Wind*. When she talked with the other teachers about the possibility, she was informed by a black teacher that the movie was inappropriate for black students because of the manner in which black people were depicted. The white teacher was shocked. To her, the times presented in the film were long past with little significance for the present. She lacked the information that would have rendered the negative view of the film intelligible and so attributed it to oversensitivity on the part of the black teacher. Nonetheless, the white teacher acquired, albeit in a somewhat painful manner, some information about what black people (at least some) consider unacceptable.

Multiple Interpretations. The second source of ambiguity in symbolic encounters involving social race is the potential for most of these encounters to be interpreted according to some other framework. This point can be made by examining a number of examples.

When asked how she felt about Grandin, one of the parents related how a teacher at the school had punished her son for fighting. The two boys involved in the fight were treated differently by the teacher. The black boy was not punished by the black teacher, whereas her son, a white youngster, was. The mother suspected, according to her son's report, that the differential treatment could be explained by the social race of the parties involved. She was angered by this possible discrimination, yet did nothing. One reason for her inaction was that she was unsure of her son's interpretation of the incident. She thought perhaps her son had misinterpreted the incident and thus might be mistaken in trying to explain it in terms of social race.

One of the white principals in the Bradford district related his difficulty with a black teacher.[11] The teacher, by various indicators, seemed to the principal to be a poor teacher, yet he felt constrained in

[11] A number of principals in Bradford were interviewed in addition to the principal at Grandin.

his efforts to remove her from the school since the subjective element of teacher evaluation opened such an action to a possible charge of discriminatory criticism. Eventually, the principal made a negative assessment of the teacher. The failure of the black district official to agree with the assessment was in its turn interpreted by the principal as resulting from the social race of the people involved rather than from any assessment of the teacher's quality. It is clear, however, that either or both the district official and the principal may well have been sincere in their respective assessments of the teacher.

One of the researchers learned that an outside teacher had, during a brief visit to Grandin, gathered a distinctive impression of the school as racist. A white teacher, said the visitor, had advised her to go to certain black teachers for information on one black student, since they had a better understanding of the boy. The way the teacher said this was interpreted by the visitor as indicative of racism. The secondhand nature of the story makes it difficult to analyze, yet we note that the Grandin teacher might not necessarily have held the racist sentiment inferred by the visitor. The teacher, in fact, may have believed that the particular teachers she named happened to know the student better than she did. One black teacher in the school, for example, is regarded as an unofficial counselor who knows many of the students quite well.

The point here is not to present a case for the actual existence of racism in any of these cases. Instead, the objective is to indicate why there may be differences in the interpretations of encounters. The point that these encounters are inherently ambiguous can perhaps be made more clearly by the inclusion of an edited section of field notes taken from the second year.

> *I was standing in the hall talking to one of the white teachers who was away from her classroom. We happened to be near the kindergarten class. As we began to talk, I heard the sound of sobbing from the health room across the hall from the kindergarten. Soon a black kindergarten student, a girl, stuck her head out. It distressed me to see her crying, but I didn't do anything, as the teacher ignored her. Our conversation continued while the little girl continued to sob, now lying on the floor. The girl moved partially out into the hall where she was visible to us. She said she didn't like the school and wasn't coming back. The teacher interrupted our conversation to tell her to be quiet: "OK, we've seen your face, now stop making that noise; we've seen you, now be quiet." Later, she said she would stay out. The teacher said, "Go ahead." This happened a few times until finally the little girl was quiet, falling asleep curled up half in and half out of the health room.*

As we continued with our conversation, I considered the incident. It was the first act that I had seen at Grandin that so clearly fit my stereotype of outright discrimination. To me, the little girl was distressed and needed to be comforted, yet the teacher not only ignored her but castigated her as well. It was so apparent to me that the thing to do was comfort the child that I could only surmise that the teacher did not do so because the child was black.

The apparent meaning of the encounter was so clear that I scarcely managed to recall that the act was not compatible with the view of the teacher that I had formed over the last 2 years. She had made some statements about blacks as a group and some adults in particular that were derogatory. On the other hand, in talking about students particularly, the teacher interpreted behavior as psychologically motivated and seemed to view all the students she discussed as using a variety of similar strategies regardless of their color.

Thinking of the discrepancy between my view and what I had just witnessed, I asked the teacher if she knew the kindergarten student. The teacher then related a long description of the student and her methods of avoiding work and avoiding the rules that other students had to follow. She explained what she thought was the best way to socialize the student and, thus, what had motivated her treatment of the student. The teacher's analysis and ideas about how to treat the student were similar to those she had previously discussed in reference to other students both white and black that she considered behavior problems.

When the hall incident is evaluated, its ambiguous nature is clear. It could be portrayed as a clear-cut case of simple, direct racism. But it could also be portrayed as a case of discipline and socialization. If the social race of the characters is stressed, the encounter acquires one meaning. If the school roles of the characters are stressed, the encounter becomes one in which a teacher or socializer attempts to modify a student's behavior to fit certain standards.[12]

This encounter and those described earlier are all interpretable from at least one other framework besides racism. Not everyone involved agreed that the encounters should be interpreted as having to do with social race. Similarly, the response of the teacher who seemed to

[12] Obviously there are other frames that could be applied as well. The influence of the kindergartener's social race could have affected what happened to her in the hall in more subtle ways. A student who behaved similarly but was smaller or fairer-skinned, for example, might have been interpreted as having different motives. Perhaps the student's behavior, because of her appearance, was misinterpreted by the white teacher as conveying an adult-like manipulative quality.

condone anti-white sentiment may well have been misinterpreted by the student.

The meaning of race-related symbolic encounters is almost always ambiguous. In all these cases, then, people are responding not necessarily to the reality of the situation but rather to its appearance. Perhaps because of the increased power of blacks to affect both political and school affairs in Bradford, whites are especially sensitive to racist interpretations of their actions. It is also difficult, by the same token, for someone to prove racial discrimination. The inherent ambiguity of many of these incidents, in other words, means that it is difficult both to take action against and to defend oneself against charges of racism. Thus, as is further discussed in the following section, conflicts interpreted from a framework of race are likely to fester unresolved.

Resulting Difficulties

When schools were segregated, symbolic encounters were more likely to be attributed to collectivities. Two black teachers, for example, who had gone to school in Bradford themselves, related how black students were given textbooks previously used by people they had never met. The books used in the black schools were discarded from the white schools. This unequal treatment was attributable to whites as a group. In desegregated schools, in contrast, the encounters are more clearly associated with individuals who are often one's colleagues or classmates, potential friends, fellow committee members or teammates, and so forth. It is in this context that the possible impact of ambiguity of symbolic encounters must be calculated.

Conflicts tinged with suspected racism are very difficult to resolve. A charge or implied charge of racist behavior is a serious one that may sever ties among individuals who have to cooperate in many ways, and it is almost sure to be denied. To solve the matter in a direct fashion is almost impossible, and even when the issue can be handled directly, as in the case of *Gone With the Wind,* the problem is complex. If lack of information or lack of awareness prevented recognition of the racial overtones of an act in the first place, it is unlikely that merely being advised of the overtones will provide the framework needed to make sense of why such acts are distressing. The other party, meanwhile, sees the racist nature of the event so clearly that apparent failure to recognize it seems incredible and, therefore, suggestive of possible hidden prejudice.

Social race can be a divisive issue among groups as well as among

41

individuals, as in the case of the student assignment and liquid soap episodes described above. Because troublesome disagreements associated in part with social race are so difficult to confront on an individual basis, individuals may involve their friends in the problem. In some cases at Grandin, struggles got to the point where there was a mobilization of sentiment and sometimes action taken against another teacher or student. If the target of negative action has simultaneously mobilized sentiment and action, factionalism can occur. Racism is a potent issue that can divide groups.

At Grandin, such factionalism has not developed to any great extent. However, there is some tension associated with the possibility of race-related symbolic encounters. This tension creates an additional problem: the reinforcement of barriers to the establishment of cross-race relationships in which information about student styles and sensitivities can be exchanged. Interpretation of behavior can be affected by the misreading of simple subcultural differences in behavior or sensitivities. Teachers cut off from open exchange with colleagues who understand these differences are forced to make repeated needless errors that limit their effectiveness.

Salience of Social-Race Identities in Interpreting Interactions

We have argued above that the ambiguity inherent in race-related symbolic encounters renders them difficult to resolve and therefore potentially disruptive to friendships, to groups, to the school as a whole, and to the transfer of information about subcultural differences. As has been indicated, the occurrence of such encounters at Grandin is relatively rare. The factors that seem to decrease the frequency of such occurrences are (*a*) the apparent low saliency of social-race identities as an explanatory framework for most of the students and teachers, and (*b*) norms against the revelation of social race as a source of conflict.

There is little tendency at Grandin to dwell upon possible racial interpretations of encounters in general. This is true for both teachers and students. Both tend to restrict such interpretations to conflict situations and, even then, to a very limited number of conflict situations, as reported above.

Some incidents are interpreted or explained by students as having to do with social-race identities. A clear example was described earlier in which a black girl accused a white one of trying to use her whiteness to prevent the black girl from playing on a seesaw. Other such examples include a white girl's refusal to speak with a black boy who was beckoning to her in the cafeteria. Her white girlfriend teased her, saying that Gordon probably wanted to go with her. She retorted that that was silly because blacks and whites do not go together. These examples, however, are some of the few that occurred. Despite explicitness on the part of students about the racial overtones of some incidents or actions, many encounters that could conceivably have been interpreted as having such overtones were not so interpreted.

Students' lack of reliance on social-race identities as an explanatory framework was also revealed in the following case. A class discussion led by a white teacher inadvertently approached the subject of racism. The session was held near the end of the school term. Its purpose was to give students a chance to air their gripes about school that had been smoldering for years. The students, however, were more anxious to talk about things that had happened that year. They wanted to discuss teachers who had upset them. The teacher allowed them to do so, guiding their conversation so as to look at the situation from the teacher's point of view as well. As the students began to catalogue their grievances against two teachers in particular, it began to sound more and more as if they suspected the two of being racist. They described one example after another of the teachers' treating white children better than black children. Finally, in an effort perhaps to bring the subject out in the open, the leader asked the students if they thought the two teachers were prejudiced. Only a small number of the students thought so, even though the leader had suggested what were the obvious racial overtones of what was being said. The teacher, who seemed to be ready to help students think about this interpretation, appeared a bit surprised that most of the students disagreed that the teachers were prejudiced. She then assured the students that from what she knew, none of the teachers at Grandin were prejudiced, and went on to another topic.

Adults at Grandin are even less inclined than students to interpret encounters overtly as resulting from the social-race identities of the participants. Nonetheless, teachers clearly differ in their views of the importance of social race or racism as a perspective from which to interpret things that happen at Grandin. As one of the black teachers told a researcher: "To me, a cracker is the saltine variety that comes in a box; a nigger is a person who doesn't conform, who behaves inappropriately." Others say that in their role as teacher, they lose awareness of the students as having social-race identities. Another black teacher spent many weeks in deliberation before she finally decided that a white student's refusal to come to class must be because she could not accept having a black teacher. These positions, which downplay the importance of social race, contrast with those of other teachers who attribute the problems of most of their students to white teachers who lack the background to understand and handle black students coming from neighborhoods like those of the Grandin students. And there are other teachers who never mention social race at all. Because of the differences among all teachers, black and white, there is no clear demarcation of attitude along social-race lines. In the disagreement concerning the assignment of the fifth-grader, which to some constituted a type of racial incident, the sides were *not* homogeneous, with blacks arrayed against whites.

In fact, should an attempt be made to mobilize one set of faculty against the other on the issue of social race, it probably would fail. Not only is there a lack of consensus among faculty as to how important social race is, but also, at present, an effort to forego interpretations of racism and avoid conflicts rooted in social-race issues seems to be the norm.

This norm, which is discussed in detail in the following section, suggests the possibility that we as observers were shielded from some race-related symbolic encounters. It is also true that many such encounters, like the case described at the beginning of this section, were not discussed with people in school at all. In the weekly open-ended interviews that were conducted with 10 students, at least 3 described upsetting encounters that we had not heard about from them or from others while at the school.

In sum, examination of the frequency of race-related symbolic encounters at Grandin has revealed that such encounters are relatively rare. School encounters usually are interpreted at Grandin in terms of social identities other than race, a pattern that can be attributed partially to norms against the airing of race-related issues in public.

Although such encounters are rare, as indicated by our data, they have a powerful impact. Potentially, they can disrupt relationships among teachers, among students, and between students and teachers, spilling over into larger groups and contributing to an atmosphere in which social race constitutes a barrier to cross-color friendship and to the exchange of information. At Grandin, polarization among school participants along social-race lines does not seem imminent on a large scale because of the variance among teachers and students regarding the relevance of social-race interpretation of interactions at Grandin. Rather, suspected episodes of racism are generally kept private.

The aspects of Grandin life so far described clearly point to the existence of norms associated with cross-race interactions and exchanges at Grandin. These norms can be further highlighted by an examination of a third source of information about the organization of social-race interaction: *unusual characters.*

UNUSUAL CHARACTERS

Unusual characters are individuals who attract attention because they chronically violate expectations. They are like symbolic encounters in that they are deviant cases, attracting attention as a result of their extraordinary nature. They achieve notoriety or fame because they markedly exceed or fall short of expectations. Here, interest focuses upon those individuals considered unusual by their fellows in that they violate anticipations or expectations about how white school participants act toward and relate to black school participants, and vice versa.

Among school participants, there would probably be little agreement about and awareness of the individuals to be discussed. This is not surprising since, as discussed above, there is little consensus on the importance and relevance of social race in school affairs and little public discussion of such matters. Barriers to the flow of information prevent the development of a school-wide consensus about what the norms regarding social race are and who has violated them. The following discussion centers upon people who were pointed out by one or more students, teachers, or the principal as being unusual and who were treated differentially by others.

Unusual Students

Student rejection of a teacher on the basis of social race is very unusual. Although students may comment in private on social-race-related characteristics of a disliked teacher, social-race identities do not normally prevent individuals from accepting one another as teachers or as students. (See Strauss, 1959:71, for a discussion of interfering identities.) One student drew the attention of others because she began to be absent with what were considered flimsy excuses. Giving the teacher's size as the reason for her fear of him, the student studied at home with books from school. Eventually, she transferred to another school. Her unusual behavior was finally attributed by the teacher, after much deliberation, to an inability to adjust to having a black teacher.

Rejection of peers on the basis of social race is more common and does not occasion comment unless it goes beyond a certain point. Perhaps because they are in the minority, white students who have difficulty interacting with their black peers stand out more than black students who have difficulty with white peers. Some of the white students confine almost all their interactions to white friends and fellow students. They seem to avoid their black schoolmates studiously. In general, these students are not considered remarkable or strange by the people at Grandin. One of the teachers, for example, felt that such patterns could be expected because the white students, especially the girls, fear the challenging behavior of some of the black students. The teachers, in general, talk about this avoidance pattern among the students without surprise. Some parents indicated in the parent interviews that because of differences in backgrounds and interests, they did not expect their white daughters or sons to become too friendly with their black classmates.

Although students who associate exclusively with others of their own social race are not considered deviant, there are some cases in which white students are so unfriendly or exclusive that they provoke teacher or student reaction. One of these girls, Jill, had difficulty on the Powderpuff [13] patrol apparently because of her aloofness and air of superiority. She and a close friend were considered, according to one of the directors of the patrol, to have inappropriate attitudes. Jill was also observed to be the object of somewhat unusual student treatment.

> *Jill was on her post as patrol outside the door to the cafeteria. A group of five black girls standing near her were openly violating a rule that she was supposed to be enforcing. When she finally said something to them, they gathered close around her and began to taunt her. They informed her that they were powderpuffs too. She was obviously uncomfortable and at loss as to what to do. They finally moved away when another situation attracted their attention.*

[13] The Powderpuff patrol was organized by one of the sixth-grade teachers and is composed of approximately 30 sixth-grade girls. Patrol members are stationed at various places in the halls and cafeteria in the morning before class begins. Their job is to monitor the behavior of other students as they arrive for school and eat breakfast. Although time "on post" is restricted to less than a half hour each morning, a Powderpuff patrol is considered to be on duty all the time. Thus, one's authority as a Powderpuff might be evoked at any time when a rule infraction occurs. According to students, Powderpuffs are supposed to maintain exemplary behavior as well.

In an interview where a black girl not involved in the incident was asked to describe Jill, she said, "She's prejudiced; she only likes white people; she treats people bad she don't know."

Martha is another white student considered to have unusual difficulty in getting along with black students. In one class, she was the subject of group discussion and private discussion with the teacher, who explained to her the aspects of her behavior that caused problems. The teacher originally had thought that Martha had trouble getting along with black students but eventually decided after observation that she lacked white friends as well. Martha's tendency to see a challenge in any student action directed toward her, along with her "tattling" tendencies in the sixth grade, was perhaps the cause of her difficulties.

A few other white students were considered unusual because of the opposite extreme. One of these was pointed out to us early in the study; more accurately, his relationship with Lamont, a black student, was considered worthy of mention. These two students were quite close friends—a rare cross-color relationship at Grandin. In fact, Andre was one of the few white students accepted almost on equal terms among the black students. His incorporation was so complete that he was able to use social-race terms with his black friends in a solidarity-promoting fashion. Although the situation of Andre and other white students who achieved such acceptance was not emphasized a great deal, close cross-color friendships such as that of Andre and Lamont were occasionally mentioned as an exception to the usual pattern.

Unusual Teachers

Teachers at Grandin were not quick to make direct statements, particularly negative statements, about one another. However, some teachers are seen by one or more of their fellow teachers, principal, or students as unusual with regard to their behavior toward students and colleagues of the other social race.

In independent discussions with some of the white teachers, the lack of teacher "flexibility," or adaptability, was discussed as an attribute of an unusual teacher. One teacher was mentioned as an example of someone who clung to the old standards of dress and deportment and attempted to force the students to uphold them. This teacher tried to prevent the students from using certain kinds of language or wearing hats and unbuttoned shirts, and expected students to accept the teacher as an unquestioned authority. This teacher and a few other white teachers were singled out by another teacher as lacking the understanding and knowledge to teach Grandin's present students effectively. Along with the new teachers being turned out by the local university, these teachers, it was argued, had not mastered the styles in interaction and discipline that succeed with Grandin's students.

Another case involved a black teacher faulted by a white teacher for her tendency to see racism where it did not exist. Oversensitivity was also pointed out as a characteristic of another black teacher in the case of the film described earlier.

As described in more detail below, 2, or at most 3, of the 22 teachers were disliked by students primarily because of what could be interpreted as unacceptable treatment of black students. The classes of these two teachers came the closest to exhibiting what Gallimore *et al.* (1974) have termed a *culture of conflict.* (In a situation ruled by a culture of conflict, students and teachers develop patterns of mutual hostility, behaving in ways they normally do not. A *schismogenesis,* to borrow Bateson's [1972] term, arises in which the disruptive action of the class produces more disliked actions on the part of the teacher, which elicits more disruption on the part of the students, and so on.) In these two classes, moments of mutual acceptance seemed rare, and the students and teachers, at least to the observer, appeared to treat one another in a manipulative manner uncharacteristic of other classrooms. The students seemed to delight in provoking the ire of the teacher. They appeared to act in ways that would counter the teacher's purposes, not because they were caught up in some student-organized activity, but simply to spite the teacher. A student who sided with one of these teachers complained to us that the students treated the teacher like another student.

Before drawing conclusions based upon these unusual characters, one additional point must be made. In the preceding section, several cases were discussed in which white students felt that one of their black teachers had discriminated against them because of social race. Martha was hurt and confused by her teacher's apparent support of anti-white attitudes among the black students. Edward felt his teacher had unfairly punished him but not a black boy who, in Edward's eyes, was equally at fault. In two additional incidents, black teachers also came under charges of discrimination. One black teacher disparaged a student whose parents were politically active in a black nationalist group. Eventually, the distressed parents moved the student to another school. Another teacher was the target of charges of religious discrimination by a student. This student, who wore clothes unlike those of the other girls and whose religion reportedly proscribed the wearing of pants for females, felt that she was discriminated against and made fun of by one of the black teachers for this reason. Thus, although white students do encounter what they interpret to be discrimination from some of the black teachers, there is no consensus about which teachers are discriminatory or about the reason for discrimination. Of the five cases alluded to above, none involved the same teacher. None of the black teachers has acquired a reputation among the students for treating whites unfairly. In some part, this may be because the white students who are sufficiently upset to share an experience they consider discriminatory are unpopular or, for some other reason, are unable to mobilize support. The student who thought she was being discriminated against on the basis of religion, for example, lacked a wide circle of friends and thus could not circulate her complaint or mobilize support. One of her main confidants was Martha, the "unusual character" described above.

In sum, the various bits of evidence suggest that as far as social relations go, the teachers who appear remarkable to others are those who represent inflexibility and/or a limited ability (for whatever reason) to establish working relations with the black students at Grandin. Among students, none of the black teachers has yet acquired a reputation as behaving in an unacceptable manner relative to social race. A couple of black teachers, however, are thought by one or two whites to be oversensitive, interpreting cases of race discrimination where none have occurred.

Norms for Social-Race Relations

The individuals described above are considered unusual because their cross-color relationships exhibit patterns that are outside the normal range, providing a source of data from which the norms for social-race relations at Grandin can be inferred. This source is augmented by a consideration of the reaction to symbolic encounters and attempts to control certain uses of race terminology.

First, it is apparent that the norms apply to overt behavior. Public practices and statements that are interpretable as exhibiting racism are to be avoided. This is true for teachers and students. Students are punished if in a conflict they try to insult another student by derogatory reference to social race.

Dorothy C. Clement   Margaret Eisenhart   Joe R. Harding

Nonpublic sentiments about social race receive less focus. Actual feelings and opinions, those expressed in private, sometimes are subject to speculation but do not seem to be of much public concern. No one "beats the bushes" to uncover concealed prejudices or derogatory beliefs. Additionally, there is some pressure against interpreting encounters as having to do with social-race identities. A teacher who does so may be accused of being oversensitive.

Teacher–student relations are governed by norms promoting the primacy of the teacher's responsibility to the student and vice versa. Teachers are expected to be able to manage their classes effectively regardless of the type of students who make up the class. Thus, teachers must not allow any negative feelings about people of a given social race to interfere with or be manifest in relations with a student, no matter what the student's social-race identity. Neither is it expected that students will be unable to accept an individual as a teacher because of the person's social race.

The informal expectation is that at a minimum, standards of politeness will be maintained in black–white interactions. This set of norms might be thought of as "polite cooperation." In teacher–teacher interactions or in student–student interactions, there is an expectation of courteous and polite treatment commensurate with what might be expected among acquaintances of equal status. Consistent violators of these requirements of at least a minimum level of sociability, such as Jill and Martha, are pressured to conform. Those like Andre who are able to go beyond superficial sociability are considered exceptional.

As revealed by the fact that Andre is considered unusual in having a close friend who is black, the politeness demanded in cross-color interactions does not necessarily entail close friendship. One of the white teachers called attention to the superficiality of the sociability among black and white teachers by suggesting that such relationships would probably not extend to informal social exchanges outside school. A black teacher pointed out that although everyone is polite, the friendliness goes only so far. When the teachers get into cars to go to a mutual destination, whites ride with whites and blacks with blacks. To her, the superficial sociability is a poor substitute for the warm relations she experienced in the past with colleagues in all-black schools.

Notwithstanding later revelations of a degree of shallowness in the sociability, this sociability among blacks and whites was a factor of Grandin life that a number of people wanted us to see. An argument by

one student, Tricia, that the students altered their behavior to give us
the impression that blacks and whites got along is pertinent in this regard. One day at lunch, Tricia suggested to one of the researchers that
all the students were modifying their cross-race behavior just because
they knew we were studying black–white relations. Normally, she argued, the blacks would not sit near or interact with the whites (as they
were doing at that moment) but rather would look at them in hostile
ways, which she demonstrated on the white girl sitting next to her. Her
description, which she went on to explain was accurate only for the
period when the students were not used to us, was interesting because
it suggested that if students wanted to mislead us, it was in the direction of seeing rosier black–white relations than really existed.

In this last talking diary interview, Joseph was asked what he
would see at Grandin if he were to come as an anthropologist. He first
answered:

> *Well, I'd try to find black and white friends, being friendly to each*
> *other, playing games with each other.*

When the interviewer asked if he would really find that, he answered:

> *Not really, I don't think that would be real.*

Although he confessed not to believe it, he apparently was interested in
suggesting harmony and friendship.

There also was some indication that some adults edited their comments in order to underplay the possibility of racial conflict. One
teacher said that little had been said to us about the disagreement over
the retention of the fifth-grade student because it *appeared* to be a
racial problem.

These incidents support the likelihood that some teachers and
students wanted us to get a happier picture of black–white relations
than they were convinced really existed. In spite of norms that promote harmonious relations, perhaps the problems associated with potential racial incidents and the availability of negative social-race
terminology undermine the certainty that good feelings are solidly
founded. As we have seen, it also bothers some that there tend to be
few close cross-race friendships. Although amicable cross-race behavior
is not uncommon, at the level of close friendship, patterns of informal
segregation are observed. Thus, the process of exchange of information
that might facilitate cross-race understanding is proceeding very slowly,

and the personal bonds that could serve to reinforce the harmonious relations now engendered by social mechanisms tend to be absent. These patterns of informal segregation are described in the next section.

Informal Segregation at Grandin

For the most part, all teachers interact with one another regarding school procedures and activities. On matters of scheduling, testing, and supervising of students, conversations among teachers occur freely. Such conversations are usually short, to-the-point, and infrequent because of the uniformity of procedures from year to year. Teachers also make requests of other teachers such as to allow students to run errands, help out on special projects, or participate in preparation for special programs. Disagreements over these activities do not seem to occur along social-race lines, as a general rule.

Teachers also interact about ways to facilitate their jobs as teachers. They may, for example, decide to group students by ability for reading in order to improve the teaching situation or agree to supervise another's students at PE one day in exchange for a reciprocal action later on. They also mobilize their classes to accomplish certain tasks in cooperation with other teachers, such as preparing for field day, the school banquet, or some other school event. Teachers in these informal groups, which in some but not all cases include cross-color membership, come together repeatedly over similar school concerns, such as what to do about a student who has problems at home or who is not working up to his or her potential. These teachers often speak favorably of one another and may frequently interact, exchanging ideas about disciplining, course material, or strategies for dealing with special or unusual students.

Although participation in these groups constitutes some important cross-race relationships, most of these relationships do not go beyond work-related contexts and rarely seem to encompass an exchange of information about more than school-related matters. Groups of teachers who are frequently found talking about their families, friends, or non-school activities to one another in the hall, in the teacher's lounge, or in one another's rooms after school are almost always segregated by social race. Teachers at faculty meetings, at PTA meetings, and at staff gatherings that take place outside the school almost always sit together by social race, although there are some regular exceptions to this pattern. The reason for these patterns is found, say some, in differences in styles and preferences—in what people have in common. A white teacher explained why it would be unlikely for cross-race social interaction among teachers to occur outside school.

> . . . I don't want to be black. I don't want to know things only blacks are interested in. Where I used to teach, I had a good friend who was black. I'd invite her to do things outside school and she'd invite me, but we never really had anything in common socially.

Thus, it appears that teachers interact openly with one another over general procedural matters related to schooling. In informal school activities black and white teachers tend not to interact. Where interaction concerns personal information, gossip, or just talk, teachers generally have friends of their own social race. The student pattern is similar.

By law, Grandin students are grouped into their regular classes based on the ratio of black to white students in the school. Therefore, all grade-level classes contain approximately two-thirds black students and one-third white students. For these class groups, there are times the students have some freedom in deciding with whom they will sit, talk, or play. With few exceptions, students, when free to do so, sit with others of the same social-race group. This pattern of informal segregation is apparent in classes or during special activities where students can choose their own seats, during free time when students congregate to play games, and at breakfast and lunch tables.

Where student participation in special activities is voluntary, the activities are frequently dominated by one social-race group. For example, it is mainly the black students who participated in the Friday afternoon dancing period organized by one teacher, whereas many of the white students joined the student chorus, which practices at the same time.

Student friendship groups are similarly segregated by social race. Although there are a few students who consistently interact with cross-race peers, they are clearly in the minority. Those who try to establish such relationships often have difficulty becoming accepted by members of the opposite group. Systematic observations done in the regular and special classrooms, at meals, and on the playground revealed that students ordinarily choose to interact with members of their own social-race group. Other observations in the halls while students were changing classes, on field trips, and during assemblies and meetings confirmed this tendency. "Friendship" interviews, where students were asked to name people in their class and then describe them, provided additional evidence. Although cross-color classmates might be characterized as "nice" or "always smiling," the category "friend" was usually reserved for members of the same social-race group.

In brief, in spite of official concern over percentages of blacks and whites in schools and classrooms and the subsequent effects on the formal system, evidence of separation of groups by social race is found at the informal level. As has been seen in the previous section, there are no norms against close cross-race relationships except as revealed by some white girls regarding "going with" black boys. Nonetheless, there are many fewer close cross-relationships than would be expected by chance. This pattern occurs because of such things as residential segregation, the fact that black students must ride the bus, and some subcultural differences. (See Clement *et al.*, 1977, and Clement, 1977, for further discussion of the problem.)

IN SUPPORT OF HARMONY

As pointed out previously, despite the divisive potential of social-race terminology and the interpretive framework of racism, and despite the relative lack of close friendship bonds, a degree of harmony is maintained. During the 2 years of the study, this calm was disrupted only twice by incidents that were thought, at least by some, to have racial overtones. This harmony is achieved and supported by a number of aspects of the organization of social-race relations, the social organization of the school in general, and district policy. Unlike those of other desegregated schools that have resorted to more overt means of conflict control,[14] the mechanisms at Grandin are relatively unobtrusive.

"POLITE COOPERATION"

The "polite cooperation" norms governing social-race relations at Grandin tend, on a short-term basis at least, to suppress and avoid conflict. The disallowance of overt racism, the emphasis on politeness, and the emphasis on the teacher's duty as teacher and student's duty as student—regardless of the social-race identities of the individuals involved—

---

[14] In the high school described by Slawski and Scherer (1977), for example, lunch was abolished out of fear that such a large congregation of students would lead to violence.

could be seen as tending toward a situation in which conflicts are de-emphasized and less likely to be given public expression.

The normative system works to the extent that everyone chooses to honor it. There are few effective means to sanction violators of these norms. Teachers' methods of applying pressure to one another, which were observed at Grandin, are limited to approaching the colleague directly, mobilizing the sympathy and support of friends, or bringing the problem to the attention of the principal or offending teacher's supervisor. Confronting such issues is very risky, given the emotions involved. Going to a supervisor or a principal entails some risk. Although Grandin's principal does serve as a willing mediator of disagreements, the complainer takes a chance of acquiring a poor reputation if a number of episodes occur. Reliance upon friends is an indirect method that is unlikely to affect the behavior of anyone not in one's informal group and may stimulate the development of opposing antagonistic groups.

In controlling the behavior of fellow students, students have options similar to those that a teacher has in trying to affect the behavior of a colleague. One alternative is to try to bring about adult intervention, although the method may backfire. Students who are considered deviant, perhaps because they lack friends, are often said to complain for inappropriate reasons and to ask for help when they in fact should be able to handle the situation. Students also voice criticism of unacceptable behavior to their friends. Unlike teachers, students are more likely to confront one another concerning the offensive behavior, especially if the number of friends one can muster is greater than the number the other person can muster. Again, the potential for the creation of antagonistic groups is present.

The norms for social-race relations at Grandin, in sum, at the minimum promote an outward show of courteous cooperation and a suppression of potentially divisive symbolic encounters. As a force, however, they depend upon individual acceptance. Violations of these norms are difficult to suppress. Since the norms constitute informal rules, involving an authority is difficult, bringing them up to an offender is a serious challenge, and group action is likely to be met by antagonism. If these norms were all that prevented the eruption of conflict, it is not likely that they would succeed. As it happens, they are complemented by the district policies discussed earlier and by other norms that allow diversity.

The district-level policies of lax standards of attendance, social promotion, deemphasis on overt markers of students' relative ability or progress, some deemphasis on parent–teacher contact, and an effort to

55

ensure objectivity in disciplinary and student placement procedures have probably all contributed to the low level of conflict at Grandin. Judging from the disagreement that arose among the teachers over the retention of a student and the problems some students have with certain teachers, retentions and student assignments seem to be areas about which emotionally charged conflicts can arise. A student's problems, if attributed to a teacher's rather than to the student's difficulties, can engender unpleasant discussions. The district's policies reduced the potential for these conflicts by allowing a relaxation of the sorting system that had operated previously. Should the district move in a reverse direction, toward the traditional reward system of emphasizing relative failure and success rather than depending on remedial programs to bring students up to standard, the source of conflict might be increased.

RULE PLURALISM

Two other mechanisms that have reduced the potential for conflict seem to have arisen spontaneously in the school. One is rule pluralism. As has been described previously, teachers have differing behavioral standards that the students must follow in class. In the resource classes organized for individual instruction, students must learn to operate using a very different set of rules from those used in more traditional classrooms. It is expected that students will be able to manage these two sets of rules and others as well. In some classes, for example, wearing hats or chewing gum is considered improper, whereas in others it is not. The acceptance of heterogeneity by the teachers, with the expectation that students will follow the rules of the teacher whose class they are in, is obviously an adaptation to the existence of different standards of behavior among the faculty. The adaptation devised is one that logically could be thought of as avoiding conflict.

EMPHASIS ON SOCIAL CLASS

A second mechanism that may serve to limit the amount of conflict among teachers at Grandin is the attribution of student problems to their class background rather than to their social race. Student difficulties are attributed to problems that the students encounter at home— the poor conditions for doing homework, the disruptive environment, the necessity of dealing with a tough neighborhood. Roughly 80% of Grandin students are from lower-income families, as indicated by the receipt of government-provided free lunches.[15] Unlike social race, class or income level does not have the potential of dividing the faculty. Though it is acceptable to blame poor performance on factors related to social class, it is not acceptable to attribute it to social race. To the extent that there is a consensus that the poor achievement scores of some Grandin students can be attributed to social class, conflict among the teachers is spared.

WITHDRAWAL

A final mechanism that serves to control conflict is an individual one: withdrawal. Teachers and administrators who are unhappy with the direction in which the system is going drop out. The previous principal of Grandin reportedly retired early because he could not adjust to the changes that occurred in the school after desegregation. In the past, the school had had an outstanding reputation. After desegregation, among other things, the test scores fell and nothing the principal tried seemed to make a difference. Former teachers in the district can also be found who quit because of their lack of interest in or dedication to the new system. Students drop out or are taken out by their parents and sent to private schools, to other schools, or to districts more compatible with their desires. The winnowing process is undoubtedly aided by the pressure exerted upon those who seem unable to adapt. Teachers, for example, as described above, may find themselves a target of student hostility. A classroom in which an escalating hostility between teacher and students is developing is not a very pleasant place to be.

Aside from leaving the school altogether, students also have means of temporary withdrawal. They prepare excuses and get involved in other activities in order to miss classes they dislike, or once in the class they misbehave so as to be dismissed, as observed in the following notes:

> When the teacher announced that it was time to go to [the special class], Quintin said he couldn't go because he had an earache. The teacher told him: "I'm sorry but you'll have to go anyway." Next, Ashley told the teacher that his head hurt, that he didn't want to go. He and some others hung around in the regular classroom for a long

---

[15] The requirements for free meals and milk are that the family income be below a stated minimum for size of family (e.g., below $6,250 for a family of four) or, if above the minimum, that the family have unusually high medical bills, shelter expenses, special educational expenses resulting from the mental or physical condition of a child, or disaster or casualty losses.

time. Finally, the teacher sent them on. A few minutes later, Jackson came back into the room and it became apparent that he had been kicked out of [the special class]. Then Quintin came back, complaining about what the special teacher had made them do. Several more students returned to the room. Russell started predicting who would be next to be kicked out. He was pretty close. Then Russell warned the others to go hide in the bathroom so that the regular teacher wouldn't find them upon returning to the classroom.

Students also withdraw by staying home or playing hooky. The average number of absences for the students we were observing was 11.8 days and 11 days for their fifth- and sixth-grade years, respectively. Some students had more than 50 absences. Staying away, as stated by students, is one way of avoiding teachers that are disliked or problems with fellow students.

Other clear cases of withdrawal are exhibited by students who participate only minimally in class. Perhaps the most extreme case observed was a student named Jake. During his time at Grandin, he was never observed to initiate an interaction with anyone. He did as he was told but remained completely passive despite the teacher's efforts to engage him. The teacher later told one of the researchers that she had seen Jake on the street one day with his brother and that she could scarcely believe his animation and activity. By drawing little attention and minimizing responses when called upon, a student can withdraw from the class. One fifth-grade student, Chris, a teacher remarked, had been so passive that no one had noticed she could barely read.

The most bizarre case of withdrawal was that of Samuel. Samuel managed to defy all efforts to bring him into conformity. He went so far as resorting to having bowel movements at his desk and threatening suicide if he were made to acquire certain skills such as cursive writing. By eliminating demands made upon him, he was thus able to spend his time reading whatever he chose despite the protests of the other students, who wanted to know why he did not have to do the work everyone else did. Although Samuel's method of withdrawal was too flamboyant to avoid conflict, most withdrawal methods used at Grandin do serve to eliminate conflict in that one of the antagonistic forces drops out for all effective purposes.

Temporary methods of withdrawal are also available to teachers, but on a restricted basis. A teacher is not as free to miss class as are students. Medical leaves are possible for termination in the middle of the year, but again this is an extreme measure. Another method is to have only minimal involvement in the class, filling up the time with various devices such as television programs, seat work, and films. These learning experiences, of course, can have educational value if they are integrated into the lessons. On the other hand, they can be used simply as time-fillers. Generally, withdrawal of this sort is possible because there is difficulty in assessing the feedback that teachers get about the effectiveness of their teaching and because there is no way for someone who is not present in the classroom to know whether the material is being integrated or not.

Summary and Conclusions

In the school described in this paper, social-race identities are seldom explicitly referred to in public. This is particularly the case when both black and white people are present. Although black students make reference to one another's social-race identity to indicate solidarity, to tease, or to taunt, social-race identities are generally brought to the fore in mixed groups only in restricted situations of conflict or competition when anger has been aroused. No obvious vestiges were found of the older etiquette of southern race relations. Blacks are not constrained to enact inferior positions in interactions with whites and, in fact, have and use as many negative terms for insulting whites on the basis of race as whites have for blacks.

A primary situation in which social race does become an explicit identifying factor in reference to a mixed group is one in which prejudice or discrimination is suspected. These highly emotional situations, which are difficult to resolve because of the ambiguity involved, occur less frequently at Grandin and in the school district in general than might have been anticipated from knowledge of traditional Southern race relations. It is important to note that although there are relatively few incidents, the possibility of their occurrence creates anxiety, especially among whites. Although both whites and blacks cite incidents of suspected discrimination, whites believe they are more vulnerable to charges of racism than are blacks. In private, whites—both students and teachers—ruefully describe situations in which they argue that a charge of racism would have been brought had the perpetrator been white and not black. Charges of blacks' discriminating against whites simply lack the symbolic force that the history of race relations in this country and years of black struggle in Bradford lend to charges leveled against whites. Thus, whites must worry more about avoiding racist-appearing acts than must blacks.

This framework of racism, along with the negative social-race terminology and the history of race relations in this country, makes difficult the development of positive relations in the school and contributes to the expression of hostility and schism. In the face of this potential for cleavage, however, we find that relative harmony is maintained in the school.

Support for this harmony derives from three sources. First, the normative structure tends to deemphasize the importance of social race and acts against public proclamations of suspected racism. Norms also prohibit overt racism, favoritism, and explicit reference to social race except in very restricted contexts. Norms of polite cooperation favor, at the least, an air of sociability and mutual acceptance.

A second area of support for harmony at Grandin derives from a shared perspective among teachers concerning the origin of the educational problems of many of Grandin's students. School adults agree that lower-income children are often faced with poor home conditions that cause them problems in school. Thus, problems that in the past might have been attributed by whites to social race, are now attributed to social class. Teachers, students, and administrators who do not share in this consensus, who violate norms against favoritism and sociability, or who for other reasons have not been able to adjust to the changes accompanying desegregation, have tended to withdraw. A third basis for harmony lies in district policies that have decreased potential sources of black–white conflict and competition. At the elementary school level, district policy has tended to mute the traditional reward structure of the school and replace it with dependence on alternative programs for those who fall behind. The muting of the traditional reward structure through a lax attendance policy, social promotions, more explicit procedures for distributing rewards and punishments, the practice of mainstreaming, and the switch in elementary school to a less specific grading system have all tended to decrease emphasis on differential school performance and therefore conflict. There is less for teachers to disagree about among themselves in the rewarding of students; there are fewer clear indications of the success of black students relative to whites and fewer decisions for parents to dispute. Deemphasis on the school's differentiation among students may have promoted student harmony as well. Unlike schools described by Lacey (1970) and McDermott (1974), wherein students were markedly differentiated by the school, no anti-school group has developed among Grandin's students.

The harmony achieved at Grandin is only so deep. Few close friendships have developed, and the exchange of information about differences in styles and preferences is proceeding very slowly. Harmony is achieved by social mechanisms rather than by personal ties. As have been described, patterns of informal segregation, especially among students, tend to be the rule.

In a second sense, the somewhat superficial nature of the harmony is indicated by privately revealed cross-race problems. Although there are few incidents that are described in public as having racial overtones, both teachers and students have experiences that trouble them because they sense an element of prejudice. These experiences affect both blacks and whites. Although the teachers and principal sometimes catch wind of student feelings of this type, there seem to be a number of situations in which they go undetected. Teachers are left virtually on their own to decide to what extent and how to instruct students about social race or understanding of cross-race problems. Students are encouraged to behave appropriately relative to the norms of polite cooperation that are fostered in the school, yet they have little rationale or ideology to motivate this behavior or to explain incidents that violate the norm.

Despite these problems with the emerging organization of social-race relations found at Grandin, it must be pointed out that the situation could be much worse. Although the harmony that has been achieved is tenuous and in some respects superficial, many more negative possibilities have been avoided. The legacy of social-race relations in the South and in the country in general provides few positive models of black–white relations, yet polarization and demeaning behavior are held in check in the school. Obvious patterns of discrimination are absent. The credit for this outcome must go to school participants and to the situation in Bradford. The black community has been politically organized for some 30 years and has managed to support relatively strong black upper and middle classes. The years of organized political struggle for black interests have perhaps assured blacks more equal status in interaction with whites and drawn energy for conflict away from interpersonal relations and into the political arena. In the school district, the dual system has been eliminated and blacks have begun to achieve representation in the new system—in the administration, on the faculty, and on the school board—that is commensurate with student ratios.

These factors have undoubtedly affected the tone of social-race relations in the school.

One of the more interesting questions about the future of social-race relations in the Bradford schools concerns the shift away from the traditional reward structure. The use of remedial programs could be viewed as simply a diversification of modes of instruction for those who for whatever reason do not profit sufficiently from the regular approach. Pressures to return to a more traditional approach in which, for example, students are suspended for missing too much school and report cards are made more clearly evaluative, have been exerted in the district.[16] Were there to be a return to such a system rather than an attempt to develop a new system—perhaps one with less punitive methods of handling students' school problems and more focus on alternative modes of instruction geared to the strengths, weaknesses, and orientations of the particular students—then we may guess that lower-income children would continue to show relatively poor results and, thus, that black children, who are overrepresented in this group, would continue to experience lower educational achievement.

References

Barth, F.
  1969   "Introduction." Pp. 9–38 in F. Barth (ed.), *Ethnic Groups and Boundaries*. Boston: Little, Brown.
Bateson, G.
  1972   "A theory of play and fantasy." Pp. 177–193 in G. Bateson (ed.), *Step to an Ecology of Mind*. New York: Ballantine Books.
Clement, D. C.
  1977   *Interethnic Peer Socialization in a Southern School*. Paper presented at the meeting of the Southern Anthropological Society, Miami.
Clement, D. C., M. Eisenhart, and J. R. Harding
  1977   *The Emerging Order: An Ethnography of a Southern Desegregated School*. Final Report, "Field Study of an Urban Desegregated School." Washington, D.C.: National Institute of Education.
Clement, D. C., M. Eisenhart, and J. R. Wood
  1976   "School desegregation and educational inequality: Trends in the litera-

---

[16] Thus far, such pressures have been resisted. A policy has just been instituted, for example, to contact each absent student each day rather than to suspend the student for too many absences.

ture, 1960–1975." In *The Desegregation Literature: A Critical Appraisal.* (National Institute of Education, U.S. Department of Health, Education, and Welfare.) Washington, D.C.: U.S. Government Printing Office.

Eddy, E.
1975   "Educational innovation and desegregation: A case study of symbolic realignment." *Human Organization* **34**(2):163–172.

Fennell, V.
1977   *International Atlanta and Ethnic Group Relations.* Paper presented at the meeting of the Southern Anthropological Society, Miami.

Foster, B. L.
1974   "Ethnicity and commerce." *American Ethnologist* **1**(3):437–449.

Fuchs, E.
1969   *Teacher's Talk: Views From Inside City Schools.* New York: Doubleday.

Gallimore, R., J. Whitehorn, and C. Jordan
1974   *Culture, Behavior and Education, A Study of Hawaiian-Americans.* Beverly Hills: Sage Publications.

Gearing, F. O. *et al.*
(n.d.)   *A General Cultural Theory of Education* (Working Paper #6). Buffalo, N.Y.: Program in Cultural Studies of Education, S.U.N.Y. at Buffalo.

Gordon, C. W.
1957   *The Social System of the High School, A Study in the Sociology of Adolescence.* Glencoe, Ill.: Free Press.

Johnson, K.
1972   "The vocabulary of race." Pp. 140–151 in T. Kochman (ed.), *Rappin' and Stylin' Out.* Urbana, Ill.: University of Chicago Press.

Jones, Y.
1976   *Language and Politics: The Use of Inclusionary Symbols in the Acquisition of Power.* Paper presented at the annual meeting of the American Anthropological Association, Washington, D.C.

Lacey, C.
1970   *Hightown Grammar: The School as a Social System.* Manchester, England: The University Press.

Levine, R. A., and D. T. Campbell
1972   *Ethnocentrism: Theories of Conflict, Ethnic Attitudes, and Group Behavior.* New York: John Wiley.

Manning, F. E.
1974   "Entertainment and black identity in Bermuda." Pp. 39–51 in Thomas K. Fitzgerald (ed.), *Social and Cultural Identity.* Athens: University of Georgia Press.

McDermott, R. R.
1974   "Achieving school failure: An anthropological approach to illiteracy and social stratification." Pp. 82–118 in George A. Spindler (ed.), *Education and Cultural Process: Toward an Anthropology of Education.* New York: Holt, Rinehart and Winston.

Nagata, J. A.
    1974   "What is a Malay? Situational selection of ethnic identity in a plural society." *American Ethnologist* 1(2):331–351.

Naroll, R.
    1964   "Ethnic unit classification." *Current Anthropology* 5:283–312.

Ogbu, J. U.
    (1978)   *Racial Stratification and Education: The Case of Stockton, California.* Prepared for Institute for Urban and Minority Education, Teachers College, Columbia University.

Rist, R. C.
    1973   *The Urban School: A Factory for Failure.* Cambridge, Mass.: MIT Press.

Slawski, E. J., and J. Scherer
    1977   *The Rhetoric of Concern—Trust and Control in an Urban Desegregated School.* Paper presented at the meeting of the American Anthropological Association, Houston.

Strauss, A.
    1959   *Mirrors and Masks: The Search for Identity.* Glencoe, Ill.: Free Press.

Valentine, C. A.
    1971   "Deficit, difference, and bicultural models of Afro-American behavior." *Harvard Educational Review* 41(2):137–157.

Wax, M. L., and R. H. Wax
    1971   "Cultural deprivation as an educational ideology." Pp. 127–139. In Eleanor Leacock (ed.), *The Culture of Poverty: A Critique.* New York: Simon and Schuster.

Chapter 2

Patience and Prudence in a Southern High School: Managing the Political Economy of Desegregated Education

GEORGE W. NOBLIT

It is probably unfortunate that educators are held accountable for school desegregation, for it is hardly an educational issue.[1] Rather, it is better understood as an issue of the political economy of this country. For example, the constitutional justification for school desegregation assumes that the real issues are not educational ones but issues of access and opportunity in the world of work. Were it otherwise, equal educational opportunity would not be a major public policy debate but an aesthetic discussion of academicians. Nevertheless, public schools are more vulnerable than the economy and, given the interface of schooling and employment in this country, are destined to be the vehicles of public policy, albeit indirect, to amend the political economy.

Further, the political economy analysis has great credence on the local level. A close analysis of local desegregation controversies suggests that, at least in the South, the debate centers more on the political and economic implications than upon educational issues. Blacks and whites alike understand southern school desegregation to be closely tied to the

---

[1] The research upon which this article is based was performed pursuant to Contract 400–76–009 with the Field Studies in Urban Desegregated Schools Program of the National Institute of Education. It does not, however, necessarily reflect the views of that agency.

65

DESEGREGATED SCHOOLS
Appraisals of an American Experiment

development of political power. Though some have maintained that desegregation threatens the political self-sufficiency of blacks (cf. Hamilton, 1968, and Chisholm, 1975), others see desegregation as a major vehicle to reapportion the availability of socioeconomic mobility relative to the races. One administrator for the school district in which this study took place argued that the public schools have traditionally been a vehicle for white mobility both to the city from rural areas and to the middle class. Desegregation of school staffs opened this mechanism to blacks, and with limited school budgets the mobility of whites was consequently being limited.

Further, this same administrator and other school district personnel argued that school desegregation threatens to make each southern city "another Atlanta." This fate is ominous to whites inasmuch as it signifies the loss of political dominance by whites as well as the loss of control over public funds and employment.

Although school desegregation may not be properly conceived as an educational issue, it is the schools and the school systems that will be held accountable for its implementation and success. This creates a significant problem for school administrators, since "success" has various meanings. To satisfy the courts, a numerical balance must be maintained. To satisfy federal policymakers, a boost in the academic achievement of minorities, or at least a possibility of such, seems to be required. To satisfy the local community, however, quality education and discipline must remain sacrosanct, and this accountability falls largely on the individual schools and principals.

As a result, the individual principal is largely left to manage a complex set of pressures and forces. Principals, however, are hardpressed to find guidance for their response to the challenge and threat of school desegregation. Normative texts like Lipham and Hoeh (1974), for example, ground the principal's role in existing social theories but only hint at the notion that the individual principal in a desegregated school setting will have to manage the vested interests of the local political economy. Of course, some would argue that this is not an impossible task, since schools have always served the existing political economy well. Katz (1971), Karier, Violas, and Spring (1973), and Rist (1972) all point out that the practices and procedures of American education have historically perpetuated the stratification of our society. Nevertheless, desegregation has the potential to redistribute educational rewards and skills and in the long run could affect the local political and economic order, and local communities understand it in this way.

Seemingly, then, a school principal has a massive task with desegregation. He must manage the challenge of desegregation to the local political economy, integrate desegregation as a major educational goal (even though it is not an educational issue), and ultimately integrate immediate desegregation into an existing logic of education that is based upon notions of stratification and long-term assimilation.

Patience and Prudence

Wolcott (1973) has portrayed the school principal as a "man in the middle," buffeted about by superiors, the demands of the educational setting, and the various participants in the school. Coupling this with a noteworthy lack of role clarity on the part of principals, Wolcott sees the school principal vacillating between "patience" and "prudence" in responding to the challenges that must be faced. Patience represents a concern with the normative, ethical and moral, and prudence represents a concern with the practical and functional.

In the eternal searching for an "improved" role, patience, in Wolcott's terms, is "the one possible hope in which most of them are willing to invest energy as well as concern [p. 296]," even though there is little expectation that it will ever be achieved. This preoccupation with the changing role of principals has two components. One emphasizes the historical changes in duties and responsibilities. The other reflects a more normative upgrading of the principalship in quality and as a profession. As Wolcott notes for this latter component:

> This quest was echoed constantly in the recurring rhetorical question that principals ask: What *should* we be doing as principals [p. 297]. [Emphasis in the original.]

Prudence, on the other hand, is described as "how to survive the principalship," and "survival does not seem to entail doing the job outstandingly well—no one can persistently satisfy so many individuals representing so many divergent interests—but rather doing it well enough to remain in the position at all [p. 306]." Further, Wolcott notes:

> The school principal is successful in his work to the extent that he is able to contain and constrain the forces of change with which he must contend as a matter of daily routine; whatever force he exerts on the dynamics of the school

67

contributes to its stability, even when he wants to act, or believes he is acting, in a way that will encourage an aura of change [p. 304].

Nevertheless, Wolcott reflects upon the principal's prudence and con-
cludes, "his freedom was to make no serious mistakes [p. 306]," since
the principals serve "their institutions and their society as monitors for
continuity [p. 320]."

In short, the principalship engenders both approaches, patience and
prudence, in everyday action. However, each principal must strike his or
her own balance between these approaches without any concrete knowledge of the implications and consequences of any specific balance. Desegregation dramatically affects the efficacy of the balance, since, as
noted earlier, it requires the school principal to manage the school in
the face of its new implications for the local political economy and
populace.

Ethnographic Study

Data from an ethnographic study of a desegregated high school in
the South [2] provide an opportunity to better understand administrative
styles and their consequences in a qualitative manner. On occasion,
natural sequences of events that are the substance of ethnographic
studies also allow unique research experiences. In the high school
studied, Crossover High School, the dynamics of desegregated schooling prompted a change in principals during the 2 years of data collection. Each principal had his own administrative style. The first man,
dedicated to the "improved" and humanistic role of the principal, em-
bodied Wolcott's definition of patience. The second was more practical, more prudent. His goal was pragmatic—survival. A comparison of
these two styles and their effects will reveal the dynamics of desegregation and provide some direction for school desegregation policy.

The Demise of Patience

As is obvious even to those unused to school routines, principals
play a major role in the dynamics of schooling. To the students, parents,
and teachers, he or she is both a threat and a protection. He is em-

[2] For more detail on the setting, please see Chapter 3 by Thomas W. Collins.

powered to make decisions that can almost destroy a student's or a teacher's school career, while concomitantly serving as a moral and behavioral guardian responsible for the inculcation of appropriate values and skills in children. He is responsible for an orderly instructional and educational setting, which has become the hallmark of quality education, while knowing that such order is not necessarily educational or responsible behavior. Nevertheless, the principal's charge is to manage the career development of parents' children and the teachers, and he is empowered to act as both an advocate and a police officer.

School desegregation makes the resolution of the principal's charge even more problematic. It was with this realization that the white principal of CHS retired prior to the beginning of the 1972–1973 school year. The central administration turned to the black assistant principal of the former black high school that was to become the feeder junior high school to CHS, and offered the principalship to him with the provision that his decision be made within 2 days. He accepted the position.

From the outset, it was evident to him that he was potentially a marked man. The central administration regarded CHS as a showcase for desegregation.[3] Further, the news media chose to use CHS as a "barometer" of desegregation and regularly invaded the school. As the principal related it to the newly desegregated student body: "We are living in kind of a fishbowl on how desegregation can work."

The primary problem as far as the central administration was concerned was to keep the lid on—no matter what. The principal recognized this and further realized that one faction of the student body and one faction of the teachers were particularly influential within the community. The "honor students," as we call them, came from elite families within the city who, while being liberal enough to "try" desegregation,[4] were not above using their influence. The "old guard" were the remains of the faculty who had served this elite class and, given their recognized reputation as the best teachers in the system, were capable of mobilizing influence in the community as well as within the school system.[5]

[3] This, in fact, was one of the major reasons why this site was suggested to us. We asked for a "good" school and they gave us the one they thought was the best at that time. The central administration has since amended this assessment.

[4] *Try* seemed to have two simultaneous meanings of "attempting" and "putting to the test" to these parents. Thus desegregation was at risk for these parents.

[5] As will later be shown, the principal actually underestimated the power of these groups.

69

Recognizing the power of these factions and their allegiance to one another, the principal allowed them considerable influence within the school. The old guard received the better classes (populated by the honor students) and were the last to receive the additional teaching assignments that later became necessary. The honor students were allowed control of student government and student honors. Whenever possible, both whites and blacks received awards for "best dressed," "best student," etc. The selection of representatives for the student council was controlled by minimum grade and behavior requirements, teacher approval, and, finally, student elections—all of which gave the elite white students an advantage over the other students.

For about 3 years, the lid stayed on. The school and the principal maintained their showcase designation. Further, although white enrollment dropped dramatically in the system and fewer and fewer students were promoted to CHS, the white students were not leaving CHS in any large numbers. Desegregation, a cause in which the principal believed fervently, was seemingly being accomplished. However, it should be noted that desegregation meant the retaining of white students—not black. Black students were regularly suspended for offenses for which whites were merely reprimanded. The lack of discipline exercised toward the white students was commented upon by both the teachers and the white parents. As one teacher put it: "When I send a student—white—down to the office, the student is right back in my class again." The disgruntlement of the school participants was evident; nonetheless, the lid stayed on.

By the time we began our observations, optimism was fading fast. Small enrollments had prompted the elimination of some advanced-placement and foreign language classes. The old-guard teachers had begun to transfer to suburban schools. Black students and parents had been and continued to be alienated from the school. White parents complained about a lack of discipline within the school.

In this setting, the demise of the "marked" principal was effected. The white female social science teacher, a member of the old guard, transferred to a suburban school and was replaced by a black female who had been in a professional development program at the central administration offices. Though no one knew it at the time (except possibly the principal), this teacher had been administratively transferred a number of times and was regarded as incompetent by at least one of her superiors in the central administration.

Almost immediately, the honor students became dissatisfied with her teaching. She assigned homework, required them to pay attention in class, and chided them for their laziness. Though her competence may have been questionable, it appears that what caused the students' disgruntlement may well have been her "standards." Their performance on her examinations was poor; they rarely completed their homework, and she was unyielding to their demands. Nevertheless, she was lax in returning homework and examinations and was reluctant to take class time to go over basics and errors the students had made. She maintained they should already know such things in order to be in the advanced classes or, at the very least, should be able to sharpen these skills on their own.

Many of the honor students were angry and complained directly to the principal, who decided to support the teacher. After continued complaints to the principal were met with support for the teacher, the majority of the honor students declared war. They went to the old guard, whose allegiance would seem to require a sympathetic response. The old guard began to complain but were reluctant to confront the principal, even though they made it known whose side they supported.

The honor students had not previously mobilized their parents for support. In fact, parents had all but ceased to exist as far as the school was concerned. The P.T.A. had not yet met that year. The Principal's Advisory Committee, consisting of parents, had been essentially recruited by the principal and rarely met. To this point, parents had been successfully "cooled out." The honor students had been so secure in their power that even though they might complain at home, they requested their parents to stay out. One mother related her daughter's response to an offer of intervention: "Mother, I can handle it."

With their influence stunted, however, the honor students initiated the mobilization of their elite parents. The parents were concerned. They called the principal, came to the school, and talked with both the principal and the teacher. The teacher wavered but little in the face of the onslaught, and the principal stood firmly in support of her—after all, "standards" were at stake and the old guard had repeatedly demanded that standards be maintained. Unfortunately, in retrospect, it appears that only their standards were to be immutable.

The elite parents were in a dilemma. As they had originally viewed it, their liberal ideology supported desegregation even though it might result in some possible educational costs to their children, but were the costs now too high? With the support of their children, they decided that the teacher incident was an indication of the ineptness of the prin-

71

cipal. They recounted the discipline problems and the principal's low-key response to their complaints. They noted the erosion of the academic program as fewer and fewer accelerated classes were offered.[6]

It seems that the development of these two issues was a major determinant of what further action, if any, was to be taken. Being influential people in the community, the parents were not going to take on the school just to resolve the incidents their children brought to them. The result of their search for the "basic issue" was that there were significant quality-of-education problems at Crossover. Of course, this conclusion was based largely upon the reports of the honor students to their parents.

The parents went to the area superintendent with their complaints instead of to the principal. They interpreted his response as protecting the principal. The area superintendent explained the course offering problems, recited his faith in the principal, and promised to look into the situation further. As a result of this action, the only P.T.A. meeting of the year was called. It was hoped the meeting would result in once again placating the parents. Both the principal and the area superintendent spoke about the problems, actions that had been taken, and the recalcitrance of some problems. The parents, black and white, were not convinced and left still disgruntled.

The elite white parents decided to use their influence. They utilized their social networks and developed a direct "white line," as the principal was later to term it, to the central administration and the school board. In most instances, they began to bypass the principal and the school and went directly to the sympathetic ear of a school board member. Finally, however, the school board member convinced the parents that for their concerns to have a proper hearing, they would have to go through channels and appeal through the lines of authority within the bureaucracy.

At the school level, the principal and parents understood the problems in the same way, although the principal argued he was powerless to make the necessary changes. When the white elite parents worked their way up the bureaucracy to the school system's central administration, they were pressed to define precisely what they meant by "quality

[6] School system policy specified minimum enrollments for classes to be offered. The small number of white honor students when distributed across the desired number of accelerated classes, and the "active blacks'" desire for higher grades, which led them to enroll in "standard" classes, conjoined to eliminate accelerated classes from the curriculum. Nevertheless, the principal was held responsible.

of education." The parents were certainly ready to agree that the principal was a problem, if not the major problem, and the central office administrator argued that what was needed was a principal who could enforce the bureaucracy and thereby guarantee "quality" education, or, in other words, someone who represented prudence over patience.

The parents left the central office meeting with assurances that something would be done. Their impression was that the principal would be removed, probably by transfer to an elementary school.

Toward the end of the year, the old guard became aware of the possible transfer of the principal. They began to realize their influence had persisted through the desegregation process only because he had allowed it. The old guard was aroused and circulated a petition to retain him. They maintained they had not anticipated the transfer outcome; they had only wished for the principal to be more susceptible to their influence.

The honor students showed only slight remorse. The lower-class black students who had been disproportionately subject to the principal's discipline were, in many cases, glad to see him go. The principal was transferred during the summer. He was not even officially notified. He learned of the transfer from his secretary, who obtained the information from the secretary who wished to transfer to CHS with the newly assigned principal. A call to the superintendent confirmed the transfer.

The reputation of the new black principal preceded him. He was known to be a "tough cookie" who ran a "tight ship." The coaches had heard through their network that he was a "student's principal." Other schools began to recruit the old guard teachers, hoping to "skim off the cream." A few transfers resulted, and the new year began with apprehension.

The pragmatic new principal believed the problems at CHS were twofold—discipline and quality of education. His strategy was to attack the former immediately and develop the latter. His discipline was strong, which, in his mind, was what the school participants had demanded.

He cleared the halls of students. He dismissed a guidance counselor after declaring her "surplus" and then replaced her, even though the impropriety of this action was noted by many of his staff. Although the first principal had lacked dramatic community support, he was at least well connected in the black networks within the school system and in the black neighborhood that CHS served. The second principal, while having achieved great administrative success in the past, lacked the

73

support of networks in and out of the school. He was not as much a part of the black school system network and not part of the black neighborhood network, lacked immediate teacher support, and quickly lost the support of even the honor students by eliminating their preferred status within the school. However, the elite white parents were full of praise, even as some of their children transferred to other schools for a higher-quality education and for access to student honors. In any case, these problems were not attributed to the new principal but to desegregation, the past principal, and the school system. The new principal reassigned the coaches from study hall duty to large sections of social studies classes, and he increased teaching loads, even to the point of assigning each of the two guidance counselors two classes a day in addition to their guidance responsibilities. He was very visible within the school and very coercive. He said he would eliminate anyone, teacher or student, who was "not on the program," and he did.

The school became uneasy, quiet, and closed. Students initially feared him, as did the faculty. No allegiances could be counted on for protection against possible punishment. Student assemblies were patrolled by teachers as the principal chided the students for misbehavior and noise. His assembly dismissals were dotted with paternalistic praise for their cooperation. If control was lacking in the past and the previous principal had "failed" because of it, the new principal was going to succeed by establishing order.

As the year progressed, the new principal received tacit support from most networks, since their interests required at least some support from him, although, once again, the halls were not clear of students during classes. Teachers put in for transfers and students transferred, withdrew, or were pushed out, even though some students did develop friendly ties with the new principal as they became accustomed to his procedures. One teacher even commented that "things were fine," but he also noted that he had been unaware of the problems attributed to the former administration.

Rules and Enforcement: Elements of Administrative Style

In order to understand the two administrative styles and their consequences, it is necessary to define what actually changed over the 2-year period. Each principal had a distinct personality; each also perceived and had a somewhat different setting and context in which to act. Nonetheless, the similarities outweigh the differences. What varied was the philosophy required.

An analysis of the two styles must be grounded in the observations and accounts that constitute our data. The analysis and an assessment of what changed in the setting are best captured by developing characterizations of "order" as engendered in the administrative styles of the two principals. A consideration of the rules and their enforcement in Crossover High School will help ground these characterizations and provide the basis for an assessment of most direct effects of change on the school participants.

In any school there are rules that attempt to prompt "appropriate behavior." As with most rules in our society, school rules are based on the assumption that penalties will deter illicit behavior. Unlike much of the research on deterrence, which reveals it to be a complicated issue (Tittle and Logan, 1973), the rationale for deterrence in schools is rather simplistic. Each principal of CHS argued that order is necessary for learning to take place in the classroom and that schools should be safe places for students to attend. Yet they varied in how they saw rules and in their understanding of "deterrence."

These differences between the patient and the prudent principals can be elucidated somewhat in an analysis of rules and rule enforcement. In any setting for which rules have been developed, there appear to be at least two distinct sets of rules. One set of rules is more or less universalistic and impartial, considered legitimate by most of the constituents, and when it is enforced the offender will display more vexation at being discovered than at the existence of the rules. The second set of rules is negotiable. The legitimacy of these rules is challenged by some body of constituents, usually on the basis of unfair discrimination against a constituent group or against youth in general. Moreover, the administration sees it as in its best interests to withhold enforcement selectively so that the offender is indebted to the administration. In this way, nonenforcement of these negotiable rules is intended to elicit students' commitment to and compliance with school authority.

Thus, for both principals, deterring illicit behavior through rules and rule enforcement involved two levels of understanding of deterrence. On one level, and for the impartial rules, it was argued that deterrence was promoted by strict and universalistic enforcement of rules. The invoking of penalties for the infraction of these rules was believed to reduce the likelihood that students would engage in illicit behavior. On the second level, the negotiability of some rules was allowed so that commitment to the school could be fostered by the students' personal indebtedness to the administration for the nonenforcement.

It is now possible to better understand the implications of the two styles for the everyday operation of the school. The second principal is characterized by more reliance on impartial rules (which we will call bureaucratic order), and the first is characterized by more reliance on negotiable rules (negotiated order). The styles of each type of order are distinct, but they have many similarities and are bound by the parameters common to all public schools. As seen in this school, bureaucratic order assumed both the legitimacy of the principal's authority and the recognition of that legitimacy by all constituents, and thus, overall, rules were enforced with impunity. Negotiated order, as we observed it, did not take that legitimacy as given, but rather as something that had to be developed and cultivated, even as rules had to be enforced.

The types of order were characterized by different enforcement strategies. Bureaucratic order was enforced by the principal himself. He administered discipline and patrolled the halls. Further, the bureaucratic principal developed an informal record-keeping mechanism. He allowed students three "unofficial visits" to his office, which he recorded on cards in a file in his office. By and large, these visits dealt with infractions for which the informal administration of discipline would have been difficult, since evidence of the infraction was lacking or not collected. Thus, an "informal" disciplinary talk occurred. After three of these visits, the student became subject to suspension for an infraction for which evidence was present. Generally, without three unofficial visits, a student with a similar offense would not be suspended.

The negotiable principal enforced order through a network. He, the vice-principal, and the administrative assistant were all responsible for administering discipline. Usually, however, the principal would not make the discipline decision. The vice-principal and/or the administrative assistant would do so, and they would call in the principal only when there were extenuating circumstances. Conferences among the three were frequent, however, as discipline decisions were made. Both principals patrolled the halls, but the negotiable one put more emphasis on the teachers' enforcing order in their classrooms and in the halls. Further, he gave the athletic coaches responsibility for maintaining order in the halls, a practice that was discontinued under the bureaucratic principal. The coaches under the negotiable one were informal disciplinarians. They would "prompt" movement on to classes, the removal of hats, and the elimination of jostling in the halls. Their approach, by and large, was to cajole students into compliance; only rarely would they actually refer a student for formal discipline. In practice, they engaged in supervision but not in disciplinary behavior. Thus, the negotiable principal attempted to enforce rules informally through the wider network of teachers and coaches, as well as through the formal discipline meted out by the administrators.

The styles, then, differed in some crucial dimensions: the degree to which authority was vested in the principal and the way in which informal discipline was managed. The bureaucratic-order principal was the disciplinarian of the school and managed both formal and informal discipline. The negotiated-order principal delegated his disciplinary authority and separated formal from informal discipline by asking the coaches to manage the day-to-day supervision and enforcement of minor rules and by allowing them discretion on enforcement. In essence, he delegated negotiable as well as bureaucratic authority.

The Dynamics of Power and Order in a Desegregated High School

School desegregation in the United States found many educators unprepared for a multicultural educational setting, regardless of the educational rhetoric of the late 1960s and early 1970s. During the 2 years we observed CHS, both principals had to face the issue of student power, and each responded differently.

Desegregation meant a dramatic transformation for CHS. Not only had the school previously been all white, but it also had a history as a public "prep" school for the middle- and upper-class youth of the city. To the new negotiable black principal, the school represented both a threat and a promise. The promise was that if desegregation went smoothly at CHS, he would gain the publicity and reputation that would bring further advancement in the school system and prestige in the general community. The threat was that if it did not go smoothly, both he and desegregation, a cause in which he believed fervently, would be criticized.

The influx of black students and some school flight by the middle- and upper-class whites led to the development of four large student

77

groups that were, for practical purposes, networks of students. We have termed these networks honor students, blue-collar whites, active blacks, and lower-class blacks. Each network was relatively distinct as to racial and class characteristics. The honor students were middle- and upper-class whites who, by and large, populated the accelerated classes offered at CHS. The blue-collar whites demonstrated less commitment to success in school and more to the street; some were middle-class but most were from working-class homes. The active blacks were a small group of students relatively committed to success in school, and some were in the accelerated classes. These students were from higher-status families than were the lower-class blacks, yet their social class was more akin to that of the blue-collar whites than to that of the honor students in that they came from essentially working-class homes and had parents who were stably employed. The lower-class blacks were from the housing projects in the neighborhood and were poor. They had a relatively strong commitment to behaviors and attitudes and styles that are common to the street.

In short, three variables differentiated the students: class, race, and commitment (school versus street). Blacks have been, and are, a numerical majority in the school (approximately 60 and 70%, respectively, for each year of observation). However, as noted earlier, the first black principal was in the spotlight to make desegregation work, a task that entailed satisfying the educational and order requirements of all concerned. As a result, he, in his patience, established a system of negotiated order whereby each of the groups could have influence. But the honor students were from highly politically influential families whose loss from the school would demonstrate the failure of desegregation; thus, the principal felt obligated to grant some additional influence to the honor students. This influence ended up guaranteeing them essential control of student activities and honors. In those arenas where control was not complete, most notably sports and elected honors (best dressed, etc.), the honor students either withdrew (as they did for most sports) or were guaranteed equal representation with blacks (elected honors had black *and* white victors). The honor students were able to maintain their support by mobilizing the teachers (who "respected" these students), the blue-collar whites, and the active blacks (who were attempting to gain admission into the honor student network). The lower-class blacks were the contenders in the student power confrontations and on occasion were able to pull some support from the active blacks, usually through ridicule ("You've been eating cheese," or

"You're a Tom"). However, many of the active blacks felt it was necessary to maintain their street skills so they would be able to use that option if the school denied them access to success in academics and the world of work.

Thus, negotiated order and patience permitted issues of race to be salient to the process of schooling. Racial and cultural differences could be discussed, and tolerated to some extent, although the street culture was not tolerated to any significant degree. This carried over into the discussions of school crime and disruption; that is, it was allowed and common for each group to see the other as perpetrators and themselves as victims. Disagreements could be phrased as racial in origin, and the groups were allowed to segregate themselves in informal activities if they chose. The annex to the school was the "recreational study hall," which quickly became a black area; the library was the scene of the "nonrecreational study hall," which was largely white. An overly simplistic view perhaps, but two schools did seem to exist under one roof, a school for blacks and a school for whites. Each style was respected in the school.

Under the negotiated order, students seemed to perceive the rules as legitimate inasmuch as they were the product of the peace bond that had evolved to keep the lid on the desegregation of the school. The bond was continually evolving as the constituents of the school vied for influence. Thus, though there was no formal mechanism for students to participate in governance, their role in rule formation was evident. Further, since enforcement of rules was largely informal, the offenders rarely needed to consider whether to question the legitimacy of the rules, and thus they never developed a stance of defiance. Put simply, the penalties were rarely severe enough to cause a reconsideration of commitment to the rules of the school.

Of course, some students were forced to face that decision and were essentially uncommitted to the school. For students exhibiting a street style of behavior or an obvious lack of respect for "appropriate" school behavior, formal authority was quick to be imposed. Further, a student exhibiting such behavior and/or attitudes was not permitted the range of negotiability of enforcement that committed students had. As noted before, one teacher put it this way: "When I send a student—white—down to the office, the student is right back in my class again." Teachers commonly complained of a general leniency on the part of the negotiable principal. Conversely, one black student commented on what she thought was overly harsh treatment of the streetwise black youth: "They do all the dudes [in the housing project] like that." Although these accusations of discrimination are alarming, most persons familiar with schools will realize that they are not really unusual. But there is something significant about the accusation in this case: School participants under the negotiated order felt free to lodge complaints in the company of other participants, regardless of whether they shared the same network. Negotiated order allowed participants to express their opinions quite freely.

In many ways, it was this freedom that damaged the first principal's credibility and led to his transfer. The second was led to believe that the failure of his predecessor was due to lack of order. Since desegregation had thus far failed at CHS, and since that was believed to have resulted from a weak administration, the new and prudent principal centralized authority in his own hands and began to formulate and enforce rules. His concern was to "turn the school around" and increase the quality of education at CHS. Success in these endeavors seemed to require the opposite of what was assumed to have caused the failure. Therefore, rule enforcement was to be less negotiable and more impartial. The principal ran the ship. His administrative assistant (a black female) and the vice-principal (a white male carry-over from the former principal) were assigned to curriculum development and attendance, respectively. Teachers and students alike were held accountable and were disciplined for infractions.

The same networks of students were evident, although some of the faces had changed. Overall, the white population had decreased, even though the new principal brought in four classes of multiply handicapped students in what seemed an effort to boost the white enrollment. This white loss was most evident in the number of honor students, who suffered the greatest loss in terms of the size of their network. Seemingly more important than the shrinking size of this network was the power loss the honor students suffered under bureaucratic order. Because rules were impartial, the quotas for white representation in elected honors were no longer in force. The honor students at first were not dismayed because they felt that the blacks, who were even more in the majority this year than last, would continue to respect them and in the end vote so that both whites and blacks would receive honors. However, the blacks did not vote for many of the white candidates, and in the eyes of the honor students, the elected honors of the school no longer went to the "best" students.

Though race was no longer a salient issue as far as the bureaucratic principal was concerned, the school's identity became more firmly black in the eyes of the students. Whereas under the first principal it had been easy to discern the variables that differentiated the students—that is, class, race, and commitment—it now became more difficult. These variables continued to be important to the teachers, who used them to refer students to the principal; and with the centralization of authority, the referrals of students by teachers increased. Note, for example, the following episode:

> A black male entered the room wearing a stocking cap. The teacher (a white female) ordered him to remove it, which he did. However, as he removed the hat, he assumed a stance with his shoulders held back, arms falling straight down a little behind his sides, his chin thrust forward, and sauntered back towards his seat. The teacher, at the sight of this, ordered him to the office. Within 1 minute a white male entered wearing a baseball cap. She said in a stern tone, "Robert, your hat!" He responded by whipping his hat off, and turning his head to show the sides and rear of it, said, "See my new haircut." The teacher responded, "Yes, it's very nice." He strutted to his seat triumphantly.

Thus, life in the classroom still granted more negotiability to the higher-status, white, and committed students, and, as had been done during the negotiable principal's reign, these students continued to use, or "hustle," the discretionary interpretations of their behavior in the classroom. Further, students were quick to discern, but did not openly or freely discuss, that grades, achievement scores, and conduct history (another indicator of school commitment) were the crucial factors in the disciplinary decision the new principal made for any particular infraction; that is, the punishment decision depended not so much on the actual infraction, but on the student's history. Though corporal punishment continued not to be the policy of the school, the bureaucratic principal did introduce a form of punishment that previously had not been used. The academic and conduct history of a student beyond the age of compulsory attendance determined, in large part, whether a rule violation would result in suspension or being dropped from the rolls. For example, a student guilty of fighting who had low grades and a history of at least three unofficial visits to the principal's office would simply be withdrawn without official expulsion from public schooling, whereas a student guilty of fighting who was a good student and did not have three unofficial visits would receive a short suspension.

As a result of the more formalized enforcement of rules, prompting of acceptable behavior by school staff was replaced with action and punishment by the principal. Students were more and more often faced with the decision of whether or not to comply willingly with school rules. They had to face and evaluate the costs incurred by remaining committed to the school. They had openly complained about racial discrimination under negotiated order but now did not openly complain about the injustice they felt from the new principal's unilateral discretionary power. They saw the bureaucratic principal as having discretion, but they were not allowed to attempt to negotiate it. As he himself put it:

> No one can argue with me . . . when I have all the cards [records of unofficial visits] in my hand. I don't kick them out of school, they do.

Under bureaucratic order, students seemingly did more questioning of the legitimacy of rules and the principal's right to enforce them. The student role was passive and weak. The increased severity of penalties (withdrawal from school) and the relative lack of negotiability under bureaucratic order seemed to lead to the emergence of an unofficial front challenging the school. In general, street-type clothing styles were worn more often within the school, and hats, particularly hats that connote "pimp," became more common. Further, open defiance of rules was more prevalent and organized. Male students, black and white, from the vocational school behind CHS refused to wait in the auditorium for the bell indicating time to change classes. Whereas students under negotiated order would skip and hide, they now stood at the doorway in the center of the hall that the classrooms opened upon, wore their hats, and glared down the hall. They did not scatter or move back as the principal approached; they stood quietly and defiantly. In one of these encounters, witnessed by the author, the principal demanded, "Why aren't you in the auditorium? Don't you know the rules?" One student responded, "You weren't there." The principal retorted, "You mean I have to be there for you to obey the rules?" There was no response from the five males, except quiet and emphatic defiance. The bell rang and the principal shook his head sadly. The students went on to class.

In short, under bureaucratic order the rules of the school became "his rules"—the rules of the principal. Their legitimacy was not established, and the students responded with defiance.

Although principals are hardly omnipotent in defining the school milieu, it does seem that, within the limitations of school system policy and expectations and "good educational practice" as defined by staff and others, the principal does negotiate order and decide how to conduct the school. It could be expected that a change in style of order would most affect students, since they usually are not permitted to place strict limits on the principal's behavior. We have seen how the first principal allowed students to set limits because he believed that to be the only way to retain whites and keep the situation under control, and seemingly this plan worked. The controversy that had erupted led the second principal to believe that the problem was one of too much student freedom. He saw discipline as the answer. Each attempted to manage the political economy of the school as each saw it.

We would expect the change in style of order to have less influence on the teacher and parent networks. Teachers are insulated somewhat by the principal's need for the support of the staff, unionization, and other sources of power available to lower participants in an organization. The parent network is obviously independent of the principal and therefore represents a source of threat to him, particularly in the case of Crossover High School. Nevertheless, the change in the style of order did have some effect on both networks.

The teachers, like the students, were subject to a new bureaucracy within the school. Impersonal rules were applied to them as they were to the students. Teachers were required to be on time for work, to have more class preparations, and to submit lesson plans, which they had never been forced to do at Crossover. They argued that until the second principal took charge they had been respected as professionals who did their jobs with minimal supervision. They were disgruntled at this encroachment upon their professionalism and saw it as an almost personal affront. The coaches were moved from study halls and hall patrol to large social studies classes in which their teaching effectiveness was observed and reported to be minimal. Faculty meetings became nothing more than forums in which the principal addressed his teachers without any expectation of feedback. The staff became reluctant to be seen talking informally in the halls for fear that he would charge them with abdicating their responsibilities.

However, the bureaucratic rules that were newly imposed upon the faculty did not bind the principal himself. At the beginning of the school year he confronted a black female guidance counselor who seemingly did not keep the records demanded of her position. He declared her "surplus," since enrollments had declined (first principal's request to dismiss a counselor on that basis had been denied by the central administration), and after her reassignment replaced her with a new

83

guidance counselor. The teachers were miffed but were obviously threatened by the action and therefore were silent. This event seemed to prove to them that rules were something by which they had to live but by which their principal did not.

The teachers began to see that there was a totalitarian element to the new bureaucratic order, and at first they sought only to maintain a low profile in order to avoid ridicule and punishment. As the year progressed, however, the situation was not as well tolerated, particularly by the old guard. Transfers were sought and retirements taken, all seemingly with the tacit approval of the principal. The teachers who initially did not seek transfers were somewhat repressed, but they also believed that the tightening of school rules was beneficial. However, some of these faculty were later reported to have wished they had put in for transfers early enough so that they would have been able to seek an acceptable position in a different school.

The parents, white and black, who had complained about the school were quite happy with the change. The school was the tight ship that in their eyes marked a quality educational program. The other parents, as they had done before, stayed out of the school except for the occasions when the principal invited them to come and meet with faculty.

On one such occasion, report cards were withheld until Parents' Night, when parents were to pick them up from the homeroom teacher and discuss their children's progress. Although many parents, particularly white parents of at least moderately good students, were glad to participate, the black parents felt somewhat affronted because the black community had had a Parents' Night tradition of turning out the entire family with an element of celebration. Turning the evening into a long series of teacher–parent conferences was thought inappropriate.

In his opening remarks the principal chided the parents for not enforcing their children's attendance, and for their lack of respect for time and thus punctuality. The principal took on the black neighborhood, and the uncomfortable and disgruntled black parents had no recourse.

Numerous black families with children who received low marks responded by picking up the report cards and embarrassing their offspring by using this forum—with the homeroom teacher and other parents and children as witnesses—to demand that they promise to shape up. These confronted students acquiesced, but resentment was high.

Though the white parents who had demanded the change were

happy with the new principal, they did not wait for the new situation to develop fully before pulling their children from the school. The number of honor students dwindled with transfers to private schools and other city schools with better programs. Intriguingly, many of these transfers were the result of the new principal's style. Although the lack of curriculum flexibility and accelerated courses was the chief reason that white parents continued to withdraw their children, a new reason emerged a few months into the second school year. White parents reported that their children were quite unhappy at the lack of social life at the school because the honors that CHS had to offer were now going to the undeserving. By removing the stipulation that awards were to have black and white recipients, the new principal allowed democracy to prevail in a majority black school. Whites were rarely elevated to office or to rewards. The rewards of being a white honor student at CHS had disappeared, and the honor students and their parents began to seek alternatives at other schools.

Conclusions

It is not the intent of this study to report two tales of failure, for neither principal actually did fail. Given their goals and conceptual frameworks for understanding the situations they faced, they were indeed successful. The first upheld his humanistic orientation as he searched for his proper role, and the second developed a functional system that reduced the complaints of parents.

Different administrative styles seem to create distinct school climates. Further, school desegregation seems to heighten emotionally the pressures a principal must face and may well heighten the consequences of any particular approach to the principalship. Since school desegregation is understood by both blacks and whites to be a political and economic issue, school principals will be challenged on more than the educational justifications for their decisions and therefore must understand educational stratification not as an objective reflection of a student's aptitudes and motivations, but as a preselection mechanism for the labor market and ultimately as an agent of power maintenance by society's elites. Desegregation has the potential to challenge the maintenance of this power by the existing elites, and ultimately may be the primary vehicle to alter the economic disadvantage of minorities.

There is an alternative implication of this study that needs some discussion. The first principal fostered something like cultural pluralism as the goal of desegregation, and even though he attempted to make it politically acceptable to the whites by allowing them disproportionate influence, it was ultimately unacceptable to the powerful whites: It did jeopardize their control. On the other hand, the second principal embraced assimilation as the goal of desegregation, a policy that ended up allowing the black student majority more control. This, as it turned out, was also ultimately unacceptable to whites—even as they praised his middle-class emphasis on orderly schooling. Further, the alienation of the somewhat disaffected students seemed to increase. In short, our previous suggestion that principals need to better understand the political economy of schooling as they face desegregation may be a moot point. Inasmuch as desegregation challenges white supremacy, it may not be possible to make it acceptable to whites who understand their status to be based on the control of a limited economy.

Some Policy Considerations

This chapter has attempted to be policy-relevant even in its emphasis upon one school and two principals. Let us examine some of the policy implications that can be extracted. First, it is evident that desegregation when seen as a district-level phenomenon will not necessarily promote equal educational opportunity. The federal courts have usually assumed that equal opportunity between whites and minorities can be achieved by placing whites and blacks in the same school, and therefore by implication blacks will receive equal opportunities. There is great variety in how school systems, schools, and principals can respond to desegregation. As we have noted, though system desegregation has occurred in the city in which this study took place, the first principal established two schools under one roof, and the second allowed a black majority-controlled school that led to more school flight by whites. In either case, resegregation resulted. Desegregation needs to be monitored in individual schools as well as at the district level.

Second, existing school system practices (e.g., levels of instruction and minimum enrollments) and beliefs concerning the limited potential of minority students play a large part in the resegregation of students, and furthermore are highly political. That is, parents and students will define quality education as segregative, at least by ability, unless other models are available and convincing. Without such models, it may be impossible for schools to meet the challenge of desegregation, since it seems that desegregation is at odds with quality education as it is currently defined. Such mainstreaming models and justifications need to be developed, and school systems, principals, and teachers need to be able to defend them when the local political economy challenges them as ineffective.

Third, negotiated order and bureaucratic order are but two possible organizational formats in desegregated schools, and cultural pluralism and assimilation are but two possible models for integration. Other models and combinations of models need exploration and evaluation, particularly in the face of desegregation.

Fourth, regardless of the years of research and rhetoric, parents and schools are still at odds. In fact, parents are probably the main threat to the principal and the school. It would seem that desegregation might even exacerbate this problem. Since even after desegregation schools have a specific clientele, further consideration of community involvement and control as a vehicle for effective desegregation is needed. If parents and community are committed to making desegregation work, it is more likely to succeed.

Fifth, academic standards as currently defined seem to be a major roadblock to desegregation within a school. Logically, it would seem that standards, like laws, are meant to be discriminatory in that they are invoked only when one does not behave in ways more powerful people would prefer. As a higher authority to define quality education, standards promise to be a thorn in the side of principals who must manage a multicultural setting. Nevertheless, teachers seem to need guidelines, and alternative standards need to be developed.

Last, there are implications for policy formation in general. We have revealed that a desegregated school is a complex social setting; however, it is more than complexity that is at issue. In human settings, multiperspectival realities are common (Douglas, 1976) and difficult to analyze, so that clear and specific policy implications are problematic. Maybe in the end what the two principals in this study have demonstrated is that social research can best inform policy by delimiting the many perspectives and viewpoints of a setting or issue.

References

Chisholm, S.
    1975   "Desegregation and national policy." *Integrated Education* 13(1) 122–126.

George W. Noblit

Douglas, J.
1976   *Investigative Social Research*. New York: Sage Publications.
Hamilton, C. V.
1968   "Race and education: A search for legitimacy." *Harvard Educational Review* 38(4):669–684.
Karier, C. P. Violas, and J. Spring
1973   *Roots of Crises: American Education in the Twentieth Century*. Chicago: Rand McNally.
Katz, M.
1971   *Class, Bureaucracy and Schools*. New York: Praeger.
Lipham, J., and J. Hoeh
1974   *The Principalship: Foundations and Functions*. New York: Harper and Row.
Rist, R. C.
1972   *Restructuring American Education*. New Brunswick, N.S.: Transaction Books.
Tittle, C. R., and C. H. Logan
1973   "Sanctions and deviance; Evidence and remaining questions." *Law and Society Review* 8 (Spring): 371–382.
Wolcott, Harry F.
1973   *The Man in the Principal's Office*. New York: Holt, Rinehart and Winston.

Chapter 3

From Courtrooms to Classrooms: Managing School Desegregation in a Deep South High School

THOMAS W. COLLINS

Introduction

In 1972 the federal district court ordered the Memphis city schools to desegregate.[1] The reaction in the white community was expectably negative. Although the parents were nonviolent, they reacted swiftly and withdrew nearly 35,000 white pupils of a population of nearly 120,000 to private academies. In the past 5 years the system has been attempting to recover from this loss and to make every effort to stabilize the social relationships of those students remaining in the system. During the years 1975–1977, the processes of desegregation were documented by an ethnographic field study of one racially balanced (60% black, 40% white) high school (population 500) within the Memphis system. The purpose of this chapter is to report the extent to which the court decision has affected new social relationships between black and white students in this Deep South high school and to describe how racial boundaries are maintained.

[1] The research upon which this article is based was performed pursuant to Contract 400–76–009 with the Field Studies in Urban Desegregated Schools Program of the National Institute of Education. It does not, however, necessarily reflect the views of that agency.

DESEGREGATED SCHOOLS
Appraisals of an American Experiment

Generally the data support the proposition by scholars such as Burnett (1969), Kimball (1974), Scrupski (1975), and Waller (1965) that a school system is crosscut by at least three subsystems: the administrative, the academic, and the student. By means of observational and interview techniques each of these subsystems was analyzed. Only the student subsystem will be described in this chapter.

Rather than describing cultural or subcultural factors conflicting in the student subsystem, this chapter will focus on those boundaries separating the races. As Barth (1969) and others have found, by contrasting boundaries it is possible to gain a fresh approach to race–social class dialogue, since the goal is not to assess the relative effects of each, but to understand primarily the interaction of ethnicity and stratification processes.

As important as academic achievement may be considered by all three subgroups, extracurricular activities become the chief focus of a great deal of effort and manipulation by students (Burnett, 1969). These activities are an important source of reward and self-esteem in which the participants invest a considerable amount of time and effort. As Scrupski (1975:165) reasons,

> That adolescent peer groups would exist without the institution of extracurricular activities is certain. However, it seems almost equally certain that these activities give added visibility to those who participate, indeed, allow a distinction to be made between those who do and do not participate and in that the activities tend to be ranked with respect to prestige, affect the sociometric standing of participants and nonparticipants.

The competition for rewards and the building of boundary-maintenance systems in this case study were carried out in a formerly all-white high school we shall refer to as Crossover. After nearly 2 decades of litigation for school desegregation, Crossover (CHS) was paired with a black high school called Feeder (FHS) located across the tracks, some eight blocks away. As was the pattern throughout the South, the black school was converted into a junior high and the students were ordered to attend Crossover. However, the reaction of the students and the rules created in the informal subsystem are more fully understood in the context of the social and economic conditions of the wider community and review events preceding federal court directives for school desegregation.

Background of School Desegregation

Memphis, located on the Mississippi River in the extreme southwest corner of Tennessee, historically developed as a commercial and banking center for the highly productive agricultural region of the Mississippi Delta. Over the years vast quantities of cotton, soybeans, and hardwood lumber, the major products of the region, were shipped from Memphis to national markets. Service industry, headed by a large regional medical complex, and an extensive warehousing industry provided employment for a large unskilled and nonunionized working class.

However, the post-World War II economic miracle that swept much of the nation and several southern urban areas provided few benefits for Memphis. The city suffered a series of economic setbacks. For example, the Ford Motor Company chose to move its automobile assembly plant elsewhere. Faced with intense competition from carpets and plastics, one of the city's primary industries, hardwood and cabinets, slowly disappeared. The local wholesale grocery industry, made obsolete by the rising supermarket corporations, became a shadow of its former self.

By the late 1950s manufacturing facilities in Memphis were quite limited. Most large plants, such as those operated by Firestone, International Harvester, or General Electric, contained no corporate (or divisional) business functions within the city, and other manufacturing facilities tended to be relatively small. City and regional leadership was dominated by local banking and real estate interests, which were very powerful in the area's economy but without influence in the national economy.

The city had been ravished by several yellow fever epidemics in the late 1870s that either killed or drove off its foreign-born population of German, Irish, and Italian Catholics, and hence much of the social and cultural diversity common to other cities was lost. Taking its place were migrants from the rural delta, predominantly from economically poor counties within a 100-mile radius. These migrants were of two types. Members of land-owning families invested their surplus capital in Memphis commercial and banking enterprises, whereas the untrained and the poorly educated sons of sharecroppers and tenant farmers filled the low-paying positions in the developing service industries. Many of the latter moved on to the northern urban centers over the years, but they were always replaced with other rural folk eager for wage labor up through most of the 1950s. The social-class structure of Memphis nearly duplicated that of small rural delta towns as described by Davis, Gardner, and Gardner (1941) and Dollard (1937). Opportunities for interclass mobility were limited for both blacks and whites.

This unique economic and demographic situation gave rise to a political environment that was somewhat of an anachronism for large U.S. cities. All political power rested in the hand of one man, Boss Crump, for nearly the first half of the twentieth century. The Baptist church, the dominant religion, did not serve a particular neighborhood or geographic area that could be identified as a political unit. Twenty years after Crump's death, grass-roots political organizations are just now beginning to assert themselves and take a role in decision making. Unfortunately, however, a strong community leadership during the controversy over racial desegregation of the 1960s and 1970s was conspicuously lacking, and for that reason school desegregation has suffered. Most of the advantages the city had going for it at the outset of the litigation, such as integrated neighborhoods where children would not have had to be bused, have been lost. Extreme animosity now reigns where once some racial tolerance existed.

The unique social structure of the city and the lack of socioeconomic mobility have had their effect on the Memphis city school system. The system has consistently been one of the few major sources of professional employment for the sons and daughters of children from the lower class of the region. The common saying that a college-educated black could only teach or preach was not far off the mark up to the time of the Civil Rights Act of 1965. Moreover, it was also true for whites of the same socioeconomic background. In an earlier unpublished survey by Collins, of 162 public-sector employees, nearly 100% of the blacks came from within Memphis and a correspondingly high number of whites came from rural areas within 100 miles of the city. The demographic characteristics of the Memphis city school system teaching staff indicate a similar pattern. The result, first, is an insular attitude among the staff that is reflected in the values espoused within the classroom. Effective socialization for rapid change is thereby minimized. Second, the staff is defensive about outside influences such as unionizing activity. Third, it encourages effective, informal (schoolboy) networks that can develop in the administration of the school system. Decisions therefore do not follow regular hierarchical lines of authority. Fourth, the presence of a closed occupational career ladder, both black and white, can create strong vested interests that distort the real educational issues. In other words, school desegregation may threaten access as well as open new routes of mobility. As such, the regionalism of school system staff (and the implications of that regionalism) suggests that school desegregation in Memphis may be unique when comparing it with other large urban systems.

Litigation and Confrontation in the 1960s

The massive desegregation of the 1970s arrived only after a long agonizing decade in which the city was rocked with severe racial and labor strife followed by street confrontations and riots, and finally the tragic assassination of Dr. Martin Luther King. A description of this conflict can provide a sense of the state of affairs that preceded court-ordered desegregation in 1972, and it sets the stage for the character of interracial education as it currently exists.

The first actual attempt by a black parent to enroll a child in the Memphis city school system came in the first week of school in 1958 but was successfully thwarted by the city fathers. Three years later (October 1962) the school system began its "Good Faith Integration Plan," under which 13 children enrolled in four separate, formerly all-white elementary schools. On the same day, the names and addresses of all their parents were printed on the front page of the local newspaper (*Commercial Appeal,* October 4, 1961). The following year (1962) 40 additional black elementary students entered all-white schools, a year when the court of appeals ruled that the desegregation plan currently used was not adequate. The board of education was following a 1957 "Tennessee Pupil Placement Law where Negro children had to apply for transfer to another school." The court argued that the board was not demonstrating good faith.

In September 1964, out of 112,000 students (54,212 black, 52,852 white) only 732 black students were located in formerly all-white schools; a number of black teachers were being hired, but nevertheless all 24 high schools in the system remained segregated. By 1965, there was a new awareness that the courts and even the federal agencies were not going to relent in their efforts to carry out the law as interpreted in *Brown.* As a result, the board of education saw fit to prepare teachers and staff for desegregation by sending a few of its members to a meeting in Chattanooga under Title IV of the 1964 Civil Rights Act. (Six million dollars had been provided nationally by the federal government to aid districts in desegregation.)

Black frustration was beginning to build in other areas and institutions over economic problems and the slow progress in achieving equal rights. The black middle class had gained some concessions in the early sixties: Libraries, recreation facilities, and public accommodations had been integrated. In 1963, blacks had been instrumental in helping elect what they had anticipated to be a liberal mayor. These expectations proved to be false, particularly in the policy of desegregation in industry and schools. Frustration reached the boiling point in 1967. According to Collins (1974:4):

> Actually, little progress was made. Frustrations began to mount in the late 1960s. When a tough-minded mayor . . . was elected to office in 1967 without the support of any segment of the black electorate, the mood of the blacks changed to one of greater militancy with an emphasis on direct confrontation. The black middle-class organizations were waiting for an issue when the sanitation employees walked out on strike February 12, 1968. This time the employees were not ready to back down. They had organizational support, a militant union, and a city mayor who was capable of unifying the blacks.

This strike continued for 65 days with some street action occurring nearly daily, along with a crippling boycott by blacks of downtown business establishments and a number of severe clashes between the police and young blacks. The end of the strike came only with the tragic death of Dr. Martin Luther King, who was in the city to lend support to the sanitation employees. Needless to say, the focus of the national and world press following the assassination was not kind in its assessment of race relations in the city. The image Memphis created in 1968 has been difficult for the city to overcome even now, after nearly 10 years.

In the following summer, black groups, who were now solidly unified, were obligated to pursue the action that the sanitation workers and Dr. King had begun. The all-black city employees union pushed for further unionization of hospital service workers. In what union leaders called their "spread-the-misery campaign," attempts, or at least threats, were made to create havoc in the suburban shopping centers (e.g., rumors were circulated in July that rats were going to be trapped in black residential areas and set loose in East Memphis). Black youth were recruited in the hospital strike action to keep the pressure on the city. When the students returned in the fall, the NAACP elected to carry pressure into the schools in a final attempt to end desegregation and win its "struggle for dignity." An effective action was carried out where the black students (65,000 pupils) walked out of school each Monday for 6 weeks in September and October. This protest was aptly called the "Black Monday Boycotts." On October 20, 600 black teachers voted to stay away from school in support of the students. For the next 2 weeks nearly 2000 city employees, mostly sanitation workers, walked off their jobs on each Monday. The coalition of black groups directing the protest made the following 15 demands on the board of education (*Commercial Appeal*, October 16, 1969):

1. That the school system be decentralized into three or four large, racially mixed districts with Negroes actively involved in the preliminary planning for decentralization, and once it has been accomplished, at least half of the top positions to be filled by Negroes.
2. That schools be "paired" so white children will be sent to formerly all-black schools and vice versa.
3. That two or more school board members resign, so that vacancies can be filled by Negroes.
4. That the personnel department be taken out of administrative services, and that a Negro be made assistant superintendent of personnel.
5. That the director of human relations be made an assistant superintendent.
6. That Negro coordinators be appointed to the departments of administrative services and of plant management.
7. That Negroes in substantial numbers be placed in administrative positions in classified personnel and in plant management.
8. That twice as many black recruiters be hired to recruit from other areas.
9. That at least 75% of new teachers hired be Negroes.
10. That at least 80% of new administrative personnel hired this year be Negro, with a majority placed in predominantly white schools at the level of principal.
11. That courses in black culture be introduced in high schools immediately.
12. That textbooks "which do not reflect the racial composition of America or which minimize the Negro's contribution to American society" be eliminated.
13. That important books on black life and culture be placed in school libraries.
14. That the school board finance a comprehensive program to provide free lunches for every child of a poverty level family.
15. That all school board meetings be open to the public and televised.

It should be noted that nearly half of these demands focused on the issue of increased opportunity for black teachers and administrators. Equal education for children continued to be just a part of the wider problems perceived by the black coalition. In a region of limited access

95

to white-collar jobs, the Memphis school system was a critical source of employment for socially mobile individuals, both white and black.

By the end of November, the city had been in almost constant turmoil over desegregation for 2 years, and although there was still support for a hard-line attitude against black demands from the lower-middle-class segments of the community, many leaders were willing to concede to the demands. A nine-member, biracial committee of prominent citizens was formed to attempt to work out a solution to the school issue. This was followed by an order of the NAACP to send the students back to school on November 17. In part, this decision broke up the unity of the black coalition, since black union leaders wanted to continue the effort to gain more economic concessions. The NAACP broke with the union two days later, and the NAACP president resigned. The black community has not been able to present a solid front since that incident (cf. Collins and Schick, 1977).

In the following year, the school board was reorganized by expanding the number of members to nine. And to assure representation of black neighborhoods, six of the members are elected by districts and only three "at large." Moreover, the federal district court directed the board to rezone certain districts and pair a number of all-black schools with some predominantly white schools. Massive reassignments of teachers had already taken place in the two previous summers to enable desegregation of most school staffs. Moreover, the federal district judge was not considering student ratios as a necessary criterion for desegregation.

After nearly 11 years of litigation and continuing confrontation, the students who finally came together at Crossover High School must have had some grave expectations of their future in education. For most of these 11 years the major topic around the family table was school desegregation. The many pronouncements by the radical fringe of the community had been well publicized for youthful consumption. The only exposure most whites had ever had to blacks was through blacks' subservient roles. Most blacks had never even driven through white neighborhoods. For the middle-class blacks the opportunity to attend an all-white school presented a hope for better employment and improved education. However, there were many students from low-income families who never understood why their high school was being turned into a junior high and they had to attend a school that was not "their own." As one graduating senior said after attending Crossover High School for 3 years, "I don't know why they closed our school, it was good. It is just another way white folks have of messin' over us, I guess."

Two Communities

Since the turn of the century, Memphis has been expanding east from the banks of the Mississippi. The Feeder community is one of those small towns that became engulfed in this urban expansion and was annexed by 1919. Located at the intersection of two railroads, the community developed several small manufacturing firms, warehouses, and a foundry. Even after annexation, the Feeder area has been able to maintain a viable image as a community largely because of the working-class character of the people. As new residential neighborhoods, mostly upper-income, sprang up in the cotton field around Feeder, this working-class area became more insular in character. Before World War II, several black migrants started to move into areas just across the east side of the tracks. After the war several single-story housing projects were built to accommodate the greater flux of displaced tenant farmers predominantly from Fayette County, less than 40 miles east of the city.

While the white area west of the tracks has been displaced by mostly business and warehouses, the black residential area has remained a highly viable community with a stable population of home-owning (single unattached dwellings) citizens. Moreover, it is a community in the sense that there is a high degree of consensus over territorial boundaries. In a survey of residents, there was disagreement only about where to place the east boundary, and this was due to the fact that some white flight is occurring in the area of former blue-collar whites. Otherwise, the black area is a tight, stable community surrounded on one side by industry, one side by business, and two sides by white neighborhoods, the boundaries to which have remained stable for nearly 30 years in the southern urban tradition of residential desegregation (i.e., blacks living on the alley but not on the same street).

When first entering the Feeder neighborhood, one is struck by its rural character. Residents are friendly and concerned about what is taking place on their street. Small garden plots are common in the yards of single-unit homes. As is the case in most low-income black communities in the south, the extended family and the church continue to be a major institutional strength for the residents of Feeder. The extended kin provide constant social interaction for adults and

97

play groups for the children. For example, members of many of the small cliques within the high school are cousins or other distant kin. These informal mutual aid groups provide vital support for important areas such as information on employment, the exchange of consumer goods, and support when legal problems occur. It is not uncommon for these networks to maintain ties with rural kin and to maintain membership in country churches. In fact, children will return to the country to live with an aunt and attend school there for extended periods of time (see Collins and Schick, 1977:136).

A large part of the working force is employed in service industries such as the city sanitation department and as maids and janitors in hospitals, schools, and other institutions (Collins, 1973). Low wages are the norm for this type of employment; according to the 1970 census data, 25.4% of the residents have income below the poverty level. The work, however, provides a stable income, also reflected in the 1970 census listing, that has made it possible for 395 out of 815 black heads of household (or 48%) to own their own homes.

In addition to single-family houses and a few older one-story duplex-type apartments, other housing in the neighborhood consists mostly of an apartment complex erected in the early 1970s by a private contractor who was heavily subsidized by federal monies. This is a high-density, three-story brick complex of 300 units that is designated as low-cost housing. The rear of the complex backs up to a chain-link fence that serves as a barrier between it and the single-family houses on the next street. Residents of these apartments are, by definition of the federal government, low-income, with the families receiving some type of welfare payment, either as the sole source of income or as a supplement to low income from unstable unemployment. A man who is familiar with many of the families said, "These people are working just to survive."

The neighborhood school of Feeder was a strong unifying force in the Feeder community. The school had gained a reputation for outstanding athletic teams and marching bands. (Many of the alumni from the athletic teams of the 1960s are now playing professional football and basketball.) Business and parent groups such as Band Parents, Booster Club, and P.T.A. were active, and ball games drew capacity crowds (Noblit and Collins, 1977). The staff of the school and the community had a good relationship with each other. A former teacher in the Feeder school described the neighborhood in this manner:

There is a good sense of community there and a great deal of stability. People tend to marry within the community and do not move out. I have come a full generation with the students and now teach the children of students I had when I began. I used to take students home with me overnight and on weekends.

The former principal also remarked on the close involvement between the school and the community:

I used to take "A" students out to dinner and to places around the city they had not seen as a reward for their good work. My wife used to say I was married to the school because I kept the gym open on weekends and holidays. It was a good neighborhood. People in the community would call me when they saw children cutting class and I would go out into the street and bring them back to school. You don't get that kind of cooperation any more.

In 1972 the school of Feeder (K–12) was desegregated and paired with Crossover, a formerly all-white high school in an affluent neighborhood, and Crossover became the high school for the area. Crossover had historically been considered a college prep school with high academic standards and some of the best teachers in the Memphis public school system. Many families who might otherwise have sent their children to private schools chose instead to enroll them at Crossover. The assistant principal from Feeder, the guidance counselor, coaches, and several teachers, mostly black, were transferred to Crossover, with the assistant principal being promoted to principal of the newly desegregated school.

Race and Ethnicity at CHS

When different ethnic groups attend the same school, they must contend with the established right of usage assigned to the dominant ethnic group. Each school "belongs" to a particular ethnic group (Suttles, 1968:58).

Schools . . . are consigned to ethnic groups on multiple criteria: location, precedent, ethnicity of staff, and ethnicity of student body. Where all these criteria coincide, the minority group students may take on the ingratiating manner of a humble guest. With this behavior they can survive and sometimes even advance. . . . If they do not accept this status they must fend for themselves.

99

In contrast to the relative homogeneity that characterized Feeder, the Crossover community was and is a larger, more mixed population in socioeconomic status. Though primarily middle-class, the homes range from extremely modest small two- and three-bedroom bungalows to extremely wealthy, rambling mansions complete with large lots and often servant quarters. Generally the children from the families occupying the affluent section have always attended private schools. The families occupying the modest homes once represented a striving, socially mobile population of lower-management types and small shop owners. They were not the moneyed families, but given the wage rates for general labor in the local economy, even these families were able to afford some of the accoutrements of affluence, such as service workers to clean their houses and care for their lawns. Although this group attempted to emulate the people in the upper-class sections, the class lines were nevertheless rigidly maintained.

Crossover High, the school that served the area and which was destined to be paired with Feeder High, was located on the border of the community, just across the tracks from the Feeder community, roughly two blocks away. Built in 1948 with facilities to serve a school population from first through twelfth grades, or 2000 students, it graduated its first class in 1951. Much to the chagrin of the city fathers, including Boss Crump, the school was more elaborate than any in the Memphis system up to that time. Sitting in the center of a rolling hill, surrounded by a large park area, the school had many extras, including large stone columns at the entrance, marble halls, large classrooms, and a modern cafeteria. In fact, construction costs overran allocations, and the school board had to wait for the next budget year to complete the auditorium. An addition called the "annex" was provided as the school enrollment rose, but was more in keeping with the modest interiors of other schools. Needless to say, the structure and decor of the school were in keeping with the affluent residences of those it was built to serve.

Neither the superintendent nor the school board ever made any attempt to include any population other than pupils of the white middle class. Both the white and black working-class populations from both sides of Feeder were discreetly zoned to other schools farther away. Students were permitted to transfer from other high schools in the city to take advantage of the competitive academic program that developed at Crossover. For example, children of Jewish families who were categorically denied entrance to private academies found their way into the

Crossover program. The exclusive nature of the attendance policy provided a strong competitive system that other schools in the system lacked.

Over the years, beginning in the mid-1960s, the character of the school changed. Families occupying the smaller homes in the district moved to the newer suburbs and were replaced with working-class families as part of the usual "trickle-down" of housing from the more affluent to the less affluent. Jewish children transferred to new high schools or began to attend private schools as discrimination against them lessened. This is not to imply that the academic program was slipping, for the small graduating class of 1968 still managed to draw nearly $250,000 in college scholarships. There was, however, a greater heterogeneity, and the competitive nature of the academic program was changing even before Crossover was paired with Feeder in 1972.

The blacks turned to their neighborhood schools to secure their entertainment and recreational needs. They identified with their neighborhood schools in spite of the fact that they had little representation on the school board. Moreover, since most blacks did not attend college, they identified strongly with the high school from which they graduated. Schoolboy ties remain strong even today among older blacks. It is common for adults in their forties to reminisce about the high school teams, the assemblies, the personalities of particular English teachers, the severe discipline, and the high school antics of the "dudes that are making it locally and nationally in politics." A similar folklore does not exist among the white adults; they prefer stories of activities at "their" regional college or university.

Another factor that has to be considered as a special influence on the desegregation process is the low tax levels. The city has always emphasized low taxes to attract northern industry. Instead of increasing property tax or enacting an income tax, the city and the state legislatures have opted for more taxes such as liquor taxes and higher sales taxes.

With this tax structure, it was not difficult for most middle-income families to send their children to private schools created in or by their own churches in the early 1970s. The traditional upper class already had its children in high-status private education programs. Thus, it was no surprise that over 35,000 white students withdrew from the public schools when mass desegregation was finally ordered by the federal district court in 1971.

Since leaving, these families have subsequently attempted to lower the status of public schools by directing frequent innuendos at those parents who have elected to keep their children in public school for philosophical or financial reasons. Hence, these white students and parents suffer status deprivation, which has remained a critical factor in continued "school flight."

In sum, the character of the city and the general attitude about race have strongly preconditioned the general structure of the interaction taking place within Crossover High School. The litigation process and the many confrontations produced strong feelings and tempered the possibility for success in the formal administration of the school.

The Student Subsystem [2]

When the pairing began, most of the white students then in school chose to stay rather than transfer to a private school. It was the group of students who were bused to the Feeder Junior High who left the system. By the end of the 1975 academic year, when this research project began, the original students had graduated. From 1975 on, the white school population declined rapidly each year, indicating that all but those who were dedicated to desegregation or too poor to afford private school had left the public school system rather than attend the formerly all-black school of Feeder. Thus, it must be kept in mind that competition in extracurricular activities, as described in the following section, has continued to evolve in favor of the black students as they have expanded numerically over the whites (from roughly 50–50 in 1972–1973, to 72% black, 28% white in 1976–1977).

Moreover, the white students already enrolled at Crossover had an early edge in the beginning of desegregation: They knew the territory, so to speak. There was a clique of students who had been together from first grade on, and they were well organized. Even the white students who arrived from a different junior high school had difficulty gaining any prominence in the subsystem. This group, referred to as the "Crossover 12-year club" by the outsiders, made it especially difficult for the black students.

The formal organizations and activities analyzed here are sports

[2] Some material in this section is reproduced by permission of the Council on Anthropology and Education from the *Anthropology and Education Quarterly* 9(4), 1978. Pp. 248–257.

and cheerleading, student government and clubs, music, band, ROTC, and school publications. Each activity area has a separate set of rules and is assigned varying degrees of prestige in the system. A schematic presentation is shown in Fig. 3.1.

The four cells in the diagram represent student groups, each identifying with separate racial and socioeconomic family backgrounds. The activities carrying the greatest reward in the system are located across the vertical line to indicate interracial competition. The arrows point out the directions from which cell the competition is most active. As we shall demonstrate in the next section, major sports has become controlled by students from the lower socioeconomic cell. The under-class white cell shows only interest in ROTC activity.

SPORTS

The most important student activities in terms of prestige and status position are usually focused on and around the sports teams and inter-high school competition, particularly football and basketball. Related activities are cheerleading, homecoming activities such as the selection of a homecoming queen and her court, dances, and fund raising. Crossover High School was no exception. Before Crossover was paired with Feeder School, its athletic achievements were limited, but games were well attended and teams were particularly well funded by the adult community through direct donations. On the other hand, at Feeder High School, athletic teams received support, and a great deal of attention was focused on those individuals achieving athletic success. Feeder School had an active parent booster club, and the black adult community took pride in the fact that this small school was able to produce state-level championship teams on a regular basis. Basketball and football teams provided the community with a great deal of community entertainment, pride, and identity.

Immediately after the two schools were paired, the new combination of athletic talent produced outstanding football teams. This provided both the white and black students with some identity in Crossover. However, as white athletes became less prominent as standout players, making the team became less important. Only those who could achieve a regular starting position would remain on the team after the first few days of each season. By the 1975 season there were only three white students out for football, all of them in regular positions. In 1976

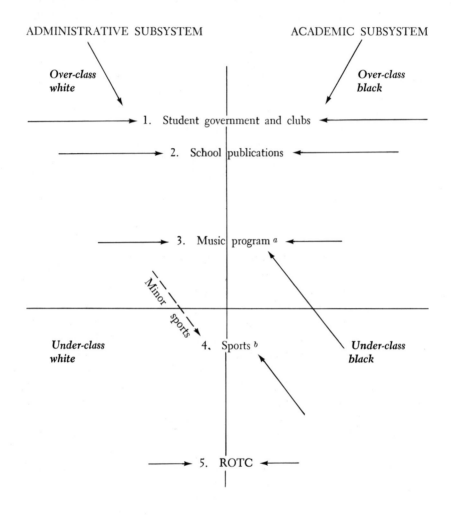

FIGURE 3.1 *Research model of school student subsystem. Superscript a designates least ethnic competition. Superscript b designates dichotomy between major and minor sports with addition of cheerleaders.*

the entire team was composed of black students. Basketball was controlled by black athletes from the beginning. The white students who could compete in these sports chose to participate on all-white church-sponsored teams in the City Park League.

The athletes would never discuss openly why they chose not to play for their high school. Usually they gave a weak excuse to the coaches that they had jobs or were busy with school work. Privately they stated that "if you're the only white on the team it just isn't any fun. The blacks play a different type of basketball. They do not learn to play as a team. All they want to be is a pro and make the bucks, the standout star. They talk about being a pro all the time." The white players who played on the 1975 football team would interact with other players only in practice or during games. When off the field or even taking a break during practice, they usually stood with their own racial group.

The black athlete, on the other hand, saw sports as the one possible means of gaining recognition in an institution where he was generally ignored. Moreover, the slim possibility that one might receive a college scholarship was a lucrative alternative to the menial job or unemployment that followed high school for most black males. Other students viewed the athlete who did gain a college scholarship as one who was "gonna make those long green beans." Thus, the motivation to excel as an individual was evident. Frequently, the black student players would say, "I got to make the yardage tonight," or "score a lot of points in this game; there may be some scouts out there tonight." They were not worrying about how well their teammates were doing, white or black.

Given this change in composition of the team, the white students said outright that they could not identify with the teams and now considered major sports "a black thing." In the same manner, neither the black nor the white community identified with the new situation. The black community, almost from the start, considered the loss of their Feeder School a critical setback and a loss to community life. Crossover was dismissed simply as "the white school, not theirs." Moreover, white business and community leaders stopped attending games. Private contributions fell off to zero. Immediately after the two schools were paired, one white businessman informed the principal of Crossover that although he had given $2000 to the teams in the past, he would be able to contribute only $200 in the future. The principal refused the offer out of pride. Attendance at football games over the last two seasons ran from roughly 400 on a good night to maybe 40 or 50 persons, depending upon the opposing high school. Since the athletic program was supported directly from the gate receipts and from outside contributions, this change of events left the coaches and the athletic director with little option but to scrape for additional funds in many directions. Fund raising was centered around after-game dances and selling candy during and after school. This latter task took more than a small amount of the coaches' effort to keep the program functioning.

White students simply withdrew, for the most part, from attending athletic events. During basketball games it was unusual to have as many as 10 white students. Generally only 20 or 25 white students attended football games. The removal of local status of sports did not, however, reduce competition activities associated with games. The 12 cheerleading positions were divided equally between white and black girls through 1976. This balance was officially maintained by the first black principal to encourage "good race relations." Nevertheless, the black girls for most of the first 4 years tended to have lighter skin and straight hair. The choice of cheers or yells was evenly balanced between black and white styles. When the second black principal took over the high school, the recommended "balance" was discontinued as an official policy. Hence, only 2 white girls out of the 12 were selected for the squad. These girls were hard-pressed to deal with their minority status. They offered a number of reasons why they were "not really interested in the squad this year." However, they were aware that they could not control the style of the team. When they were informed by the new black team captain that they no longer needed any "white type" cheers, the white girls quit the squad. Thus, the athletic teams and the cheerleading squad became completely black.

The football homecoming is a traditional activity in which many students are able to participate. A homecoming queen and five female attendants are chosen by the athletic teams. In 1975 the white faculty sponsor of this event insisted that three of the girls be white and three black. Again, when the policy of forced balance was discontinued, the black athletes chose only black candidates for homecoming queen.

White students remained competitive in only the minor spring sports such as cross country, golf, and tennis, in which few blacks were willing to compete. Moreover, white boys had sought competition in the all-white chess club. Thus, after 5 years the Crossover student body had sorted out the various sports-related activities for ethnic control.

STUDENT GOVERNMENT AND CLUBS

The most intense area of competition between the two upper cells of white and black students is over the elected offices of student council president and senior class president. In a recent survey of the entire district carried out for the board of education, white parents and students named these student offices as the most important status positions in the school. It was considered critical to be associated with the students who held these positions if one wished to attain even a moderately high social status. Although the white students at Crossover High had always been in the minority, they had effectively outmaneuvered the blacks and maintained control of these elected offices and many key elected positions in school clubs. It was only in the 1977–1978 school year that a black student was finally elected student council president. There are at least two reasons for the previous control by the white minority. First, the white students from the Crossover 12-year club were effectively organized. They knew when to bring in certain black students in order to maintain legitimacy with the student body and school administration. Second, blacks as a group hurt their own positions in obtaining these offices by not voting for black students in the upper cell. This attitude may, in part, have been a deliberate sanction by the under-group black leaders toward the upper group, who they felt were either "acting too white" or who were in some way "copping out for a white thing." Black males who were capable and possessed the leadership skills were aware of this attitude and hence were reluctant to put their names in nomination for the higher offices out of fear of being ridiculed. As one put it, "If I ran for president, what would the [other] dudes say?" Thus, the more capable black candidates did not run for office during the first 4 years after pairing. Black girls were less sensitive to this peer pressure and did become candidates, but they had been successful only in taking over the secondary positions such as treasurer or vice-president or sergeant-at-arms. Black males expressed their attitudes about girls in these offices by saying, "They only screw things up." However, the overall explanation can be attributed to the fact that most of the under-class black males simply did not see any payoff and had little interest in these activities. Many felt there was no point in voting, since the whites rigged the elections anyway.

The whites had used the student offices to maintain control over activities they considered important. For example, the president of the senior class always appointed the planning committee for the annual spring prom. This committee then selected the music group, which directly influenced the style of music that would be played. The location of the prom also determined its accessibility to students. Thus, whether the prom would be accepted by either the white or the black students was guaranteed by the planning committee.

In planning homecoming activities, the committees catered to white aspirations and activities. They tried to maintain the traditions of the school "before it was desegregated." Until 1976, black students were brought into these activities, but only as workers and not as decision makers. When black students failed to put forth the effort in decorating or other work assignments, they were chastised by the whites as being unwilling to participate in school activities or as not displaying the "proper school spirit." A black girl was placed in charge of the prom committee in 1977, but she had been one of the few who had attended Crossover elementary before pairing. Hence, she was held in high regard by the white leaders.

If the over-class blacks participated in these school activities, it was necessary to cooperate with the over-class whites as a group. Those who were encouraged to participate had to display a commitment to white group norms—that is, they wore moderate clothing and hairstyles, used standard English, and showed some aspirations for future achievement, such as getting a college education. The black students who effected these norms were included. Others who gained access to elected positions but were not willing to emulate these behavior patterns eventually became categorized as "deadwood" or "not caring." Moreover, students who did cross the boundary rarely gained access to decision making.

Some black students of the upper group had adjusted to these norms but were privately bitter about their high school experience. As one expressed it:

> After 3 years of this, I am just now learning how to deal with these tricky devils [white students]. Even in petty things they will use trickery if need be to get their own way. The whites have taught me how to smile and at the same time be able to stick them in the back as they do me. I'm now able to play their game of smiling on the front and having no-good intentions in the back. I'm not bitter about desegregation, and I do not hate all white people. But it distresses me that

*they have to treat people like they do. Any time you get a white friend
you just cannot trust them.*

Student clubs that were sanctioned by the administration were
similar to the student government in terms of participation. Where
white students controlled, they promoted activities that minimized participation by the economically poorer blacks. For example, club activities such as overnight trips were too expensive for blacks; quite often
activities were deliberately held at night, sometimes in the homes of the
white students, to which most blacks lacked the necessary transportation. One club member stated, "Many of us really love to participate in
club meetings, but the majority of meetings where you really have fun
or really get into something are held at white students' houses far from
the school. Usually they are held at night and black students don't
have the rides to go. They know we can't make it out that far anyway."
The black students perceived these activities as a ploy to keep them out.
At the same time, the whites were critical of the blacks for their lack
of willingness to participate in projects or shoulder responsibility.

In sum, the white students from the upper segments continued to
control student government and many club activities and hence exercised an inordinate amount of influence over most student activities for
nearly 5 years while they were a minority group.

MUSIC PROGRAM

The music program was subdivided into band and choral groups,
both with separate directors and sets of activities. In contrast to all the
other activities, the band appeared to be a unique case in terms of student relationships. The band organization attracted a particular type
of student who set himself apart from other members of his own ethnic
group and appeared to be more genuinely interested in those who
shared his music experience. Although the members mixed with students outside the program, relationships within the band were friendly
and easy and, for the most part, without dissension. There always
seemed to be room for one more, and the greater number ensured con-
tinuation of the band program. The joking relationships and communication were different from the other school activities, and competition
was minimal. Primary relationships were carried into other areas of interaction. For example, in the lunchroom, the only racial mixing of
tables on a consistent basis was done by band members. Students in

109

one ethnic group readily accepted members of the other group as leaders without any apparent signs of distrust or apprehension. Moreover, the band parents' association was, until recently, the only viable parent group willing to cross racial lines. As late as 1975, black and white parents joined together in a fund-raising activity to buy band uniforms. It is now defunct.

The choral group in the music program, however, had not achieved the same relationship. It was composed completely of black students and was identified as a "black activity" by the white students. Prior to desegregation, the Crossover High choral group each spring put on an elaborate musical production complete with elaborate costumes and scenery, rented from New York agencies. This tradition was discontinued after 1974 because of the lack of community support, which was essential since funding for this event depended on the number of tickets sold. Thus, performances became limited to single or group performances by choral members. Community attendance became minimal, usually 300 as compared to the 2000 tickets that would have been sold prior to desegregation.

Students in the choral program were drawn from all segments of the black student population; membership was limited only on the basis of vocal talent. However, the largest number of students came from the upper cell of blacks, and most of these participated in a variety of other student organizations.

SCHOOL PUBLICATIONS

An additional important mark of status in the high school was a position on the school paper or the yearbook (as editor or assistant editor). These positions provided high status for students while in school and promised greater mobility in the labor market in later life. In particular, participants determined what classmates would receive the most publicity and thus the greatest validation of their campus popularity. The yearbook staff tended to be the most selective of the white upper group; specifically, they were the students who came through the accelerated track of the academic program. For the past 3 years, the editors had been the chief power brokers among all white students. Very few activities took place without their immediate involvement. Only those black students who met "high" standards were permitted access to the staff. The rest of the black students saw the yearbook as "a white thing" and chose to ignore it. Thus, the yearbook staff was hardpressed to sell the requisite number of books to ensure its publication from year to year. A number of activities were held to attempt to raise funds and generally support the yearbook, but very few of these had much success.

The black upper group had been able to gain control of the newspaper, but as they carried out the preparation of the prescribed copy and editorial requisites of the administration, the black staff members became aware that they were channeled into areas of interest only to the white upper group. The under-class black and white students, again, chose to ignore this publication. Several indicated they would have liked to see or read about themselves, their own network groups, and what was going on in them. Hence, the number of editions steadily declined each year until 1976–1977, when none were published, since sales of the paper were so low that they did not cover the costs of publication. The adviser explained, "No one was interested in working on the paper."

ROTC ACTIVITIES

The ROTC program included both boys and girls and represented a major focus of involvement for a significant percentage of whites from under-class families. These students tended to be drawn from that segment of the white school population that was the least competitive in the academic tracks. Their outside school orientation was distinctive from that of the over class. It was not uncommon for them to wear hunting clothes and caps and to refer to themselves as just "good ole boys." Over-class students applied the pejorative reference terms *grits* or *country* to these students. Several admitted they remained in the program only to participate in the rifle matches. The rifle team was made up of all white students. The white students enjoyed the company of the veteran army staff instructors. Both were rough-talking men of the world, with backgrounds similar to the white under-class students. The teacher–student rapport in this situation was perhaps more intense and more satisfying to under-class white males than it was in any of the other high school programs.

For the black students, ROTC represented an extension of the many credit course options to be taken in lieu of academic solids. As in other courses, the under-class black males tended to ignore the instructors and paid little attention to the program. Cutting class was frequent, and not wearing the uniform when required was common.

111

There were, of course, exceptions, particularly among those students who saw a career in the military as a good alternative to the lack of opportunities in civilian life. An ROTC graduate could enlist in the army at the rank of corporal, making it worthwhile for these students to strive for the promotions as cadet officers. But thus far, no blacks have been able to achieve the two highest positions of commander and executive officer in the program. This imbalance may have been due to the fact that ROTC was the last place where under-class white males were still in a competitive position. They competed rigorously for their rank in the program as a way of gaining prestige.

Racial mixing in ROTC carried the greatest potential for violence. Both the under-class white and the under-class black segments were socialized in acting out their aggressions. Indeed, in a period of 18 months, the only fist fights observed between blacks and whites began with incidents in the ROTC drill sections and continued outside or in the halls later on in the day. In both cases the controversy started when a white cadet officer reprimanded a lower-ranking black cadet for not obeying rules and for goofing off in the ranks.

At times the racial interaction was amiable in the ROTC quarters, but the black students were frequently the butt of jokes. It was not uncommon to hear such remarks as, "Stop picking the lint out of your hair and get to work." Outside the quarters, and away from the staff instructors, the black and white cadets were distant with one another. For example, there was rarely any verbal exchange in the halls and very little in the classrooms. When isolated by race, the whites openly expressed their animosity toward blacks, occasionally using the term *nigger* and quietly cursing desegregation for having changed "their" school. In sum, the ROTC program was the only remaining formal activity in which under-class white students could assert themselves and compete for status positions with blacks. The undercurrent of resentment toward blacks by the whites in this segment was the most pronounced of anywhere in the school. It seems likely that if the ratio balance had been roughly even, the conflict would have been even more severe and open.

Conclusion

Court-ordered desegregation paired two high school populations but did not erode the racial boundaries in the student subsystem. The whites, largely because they had been attending the school prior to desegregation, had been able to maintain their control over many student activities. As the blacks took over areas such as sports and cheerleading, the status of these was refuted by whites. The whites were able to control areas such as student government, clubs, ROTC, and the yearbook, although desegregated, and most of the activities sponsored by them. This control, for the most part, came through the rigid maintenance of the boundaries separating blacks and whites. Students who crossed these boundaries were sanctioned by their own groups. For example, only those blacks who modified their style of dress, speech, and general deportment were accepted by the whites. On the other hand, this modification was interpreted by other blacks as a "cop-out" (or "acting white"), and thus those blacks who were accepted by the whites were excluded by members of their own ethnic group. Correspondingly, those whites who crossed over the boundary in the opposite direction were denigrated by whites.

Therefore, what we have observed is a rigid boundary-maintenance system between the two groups. As one insightful student observed, "Desegregation has only brought blacks and whites together under one roof, but segregation remains." Had the school been able to hold whites, as Barth (1969) suggested, it might have changed the maintenance model to a generational one in which the blacks and the whites in the two upper cells could have merged their boundaries to share the system of rewards and resources. But after 5 years, the upper whites chose to withdraw from the school, since they had lost control of the student subsystem.

References

Barth, F.
  1969   *Ethnic Groups and Boundaries*. Boston: Little, Brown.
Burnett, J. H.
  1969   "Ceremony, rites and economy in the student system of an American high school." *Human Organization* 28(1):1–10.
Collins, T. W.
  1973   *Regional Migration in the South: A Case Analysis of Memphis*. Paper presented at annual meeting of the American Anthropological Association, New Orleans.
  1974   "An analysis of the Memphis sanitation strike." *Public Affairs Forum* 3(6):1–8.
Collins, T. W., and R. Schick
  1977   "Bargaining climate for Memphis sanitationmen in 1975." In R.

Schick and J. J. Couturier (eds.), *The Public Interest in Government Labor Relations*. Cambridge, Mass.: Ballinger.

Davis, A., B. Gardner, and M. Gardner
1941   *Deep South*. Chicago: University of Chicago Press.

Dollard, J.
1937   *Caste and Class in a Southern Town*. New Haven: Yale University Press.

Kimball, S. T.
1974   *Culture and the Education Process*. New York: Teachers College Press.

Noblit, G. W., and T. W. Collins
1977   "Order and disruption in a desegregated high school." In G. W. Noblit and T. W. Collins *Theoretical Perspective on School Crime*. Hackensack, New Jersey: National Council on Crime and Delinquency.

Scrupski, A.
1975   "The social system of the school." Pp. 141–186 in N. K. Shimahara and A. Scrupski (eds.), *Social Forces and Schooling*. New York: David McKay.

Suttles, G. D.
1968   *The Social Order of the Slum*. Chicago: University of Chicago Press.

Waller, W.
1965   *The Sociology of Teaching*. New York: Wiley.

Part 2

The Northern Experience

Chapter 4

Color, Class, and Social Control in an Urban Desegregated School

JACQUELINE SCHERER
EDWARD J. SLAWSKI

In 1971 Pawnee [1] became one of the first northern cities to be required by court order to institute a program of busing to achieve desegregated schools. This research took place 6 years later at one of the two high schools in the district, Pawnee West, and represents a case study of one of the "oldest" desegregated schools in the northern United States. The experience provides an example of some of the problems and promises that the implementation of a social policy brings to dedicated and concerned people. By understanding the events and processes in Pawnee and Pawnee West, educators and community leaders in other cities may be able to avoid some of the pitfalls experienced in this one urban desegregated school, as well as recognize the positive factors that made the policy workable.

Introduction

This account focuses upon the strategies of control that characterize Pawnee West. The emphasis upon control seems to have resulted, at least in part, from an increasing pressure to desegregate the public

[1] Pawnee is a pseudonym for the city in which this research was conducted.

DESEGREGATED SCHOOLS
Appraisals of an American Experiment

Copyright © 1979 by Academic Press, Inc.

schools. At the most general level one could interpret the entire control apparatus that developed at West as the only manageable mechanism for implementing the court order, given the difficult situation in which school leaders had to function. However, one of the assumptions of this control strategy is that desegregation is an episodic event: one that could be considered accomplished once the court demands had been satisfied. As a result, it has been extremely difficult to view systematically the long-term, continuous nature of race relationships within the school and in the wider community surrounding the school. Control strategies have also produced unintended consequences in terms of educational experiences of Pawnee children both black and white.

Control—or more accurately, efforts to control events and their interpretation—is a dominant theme in many kinds of social situations at West. Black and white parents at various times during the past 10 years have tried to control school developments, a major share of teacher effort is devoted to controlling student behavior, and students continually attempt to gain some measure of autonomy or self-control over their school experiences. The negotiations over control at Pawnee take place in many different areas, including in classrooms and during extracurricular activities. The issue of control is important in considerations of schedules, lunch hours, and the physical location of the building site. The tactics used are also varied and include voting, participation, and rhetoric.

The control issue is characteristic of school controversies that have had complex political and historical roots in American education. Desegregation is particularly important because it is a manifestation of larger social issues engulfing this society, involving demands of blacks and other minorities for more control over all aspects of their life experiences. The struggle for control at Pawnee West is but one instance of the larger societal struggles and debates over power, opportunity, and freedom that have concerned Americans throughout history.

The City of Pawnee

Pawnee is a medium-sized city (population 85,000) located on the northern fringe of a major industrial area. A large proportion of its residents are relatively poor despite the wealth of the city government, which draws upon a large industrial tax base that provides 60% of the city's revenues. Since the factories in Pawnee provide high-paying jobs for families within a 30-mile radius of the city, a superficial view of Pawnee sees the town as a busy, working factory center. The reality is that Pawnee residents do not get the well-paying jobs in industry, or for that matter, the "good" city jobs. It is estimated that about one-third of all Pawnee families receive some form of public assistance. "Official" unemployment in Pawnee is almost always among the highest in the state, ranging between 14 and 24%, and the Pawnee school district qualifies for almost every major federal supplemental education program on the basis of need.

A second characteristic of Pawnee is that the industrial base is restricted to one particular form of manufacturing, and the long-term prognosis for growth in this segment of the economy is not good. Although the industry may remain stable for several years ahead, there will be fewer jobs and little possibility for expansion, thereby providing few economic opportunities for the disadvantaged.

Third, Pawnee has a southern, rural quality. In a recent school district survey of parents, 69% of whites and 83% of blacks reported that they were not born in Pawnee. Of these, 19% of the whites and 54% of the blacks had moved from the South. Although the southern, rural atmosphere seems to be slowly changing, it is still important in understanding Pawnee culture. The city is a small town in outlook and rhythm: Leaders are locally attuned and influence is still expressed in personal ways.

Finally, the minority population of Pawnee has consistently increased over the last 30 years. At the latest census, the black population was approximately 23,000 (from 3000 in 1940 and 7000 at the end of World War II); the Latino population, a mixture of Mexican-Americans, Puerto Rican migrants, and other Spanish-speaking groups, is estimated at 10% of the total population of the city. The percentage of families below poverty level differs by ethnic group: In 1970 19.3% of black families, 6.3% of Spanish-speaking families, and 10% of white families received public assistance. Pawnee's relative poverty, the shrinking industrial base, the southern, rural ties of the residents, and the increasing minority population are important in understanding the general community response to efforts to desegregate the public schools in Pawnee.

Desegregation took place during some of the lowest points in Pawnee's development. The bitter busing controversy was aggravated by the small-town atmosphere in which long-standing racial attitudes rose to the surface. But the publicity, the infusion of federal monies, and the emerging political power of black leadership contributed to an important transformation in local leadership. By 1970, black voters could not be ignored; federal regulations had to be enforced and official policies had to be enacted, in spite of "old guard" reluctance to share influence. One can now find black representatives in almost all divisions of the city government, although not usually in key policymaking positions. In 1976, four black representatives were elected to the school board, thereby putting blacks in the majority for the first time in city history. Federal funds have enabled departments to buy expertise in specific areas, crime has been reduced substantially, and for the first time one finds expressions of optimism about urban renewal and a growing confidence that Pawnee can be restored.

In summary, desegregation was introduced into a turbulent social environment in which major political, economic, and social changes were taking place. Desegregation was both a result of those changes and at the same time a stimulant for even more change.

Pawnee West High School: Planning a New Building

For over 50 years Pawnee West High School was housed in a rambling red brick building located on 4 acres of land about 1 mile due west of the geographical center of Pawnee. The campus is atop a small rise, fronting on the main east–west traffic artery that divides Pawnee. The old building was a landmark in the community and directions are still given with reference to "Old West." Increasing student enrollments and the inadequacy of existing facilities demanded expansion. Remodeling could not repair the serious structural flaws. Therefore, the school board decided to construct a new facility to house West.

The decision to build a new facility took place at the same time that the school district was involved in the desegregation controversy. Logically the two issues were separate and distinct, but in the minds of many people in Pawnee, they were closely interwoven. The new West building housed a student body and staff that included blacks and whites, but it was included in the court-ordered busing decree program. The effects of the building and the dynamics of desegregation simply were not separated in the minds of many in the school and community.

120

Of the two sites proposed for the construction of the new high school building, one was an inner-city location in a severely depressed area; the other, recommended by the board of education, was on the western boundary of Pawnee on state hospital grounds. The inner-city site was favored by predominantly black groups of citizens, since it was located closer to the largest concentration of black families. The whites in Pawnee were in favor of the hospital site, which was in a "safer" section farther away from the poor southside. As it turned out, a coalition of citizens and urban planners forced the board to compromise on a location that was almost midway between the inner city and hospital sites, adjacent to the existing high school building.

The issue resolved into one not simply of community control but of control by which community (i.e., black or white). Many members of the black community view the outcome of the site selection battle and the broader desegregation order as a victory—as evidence that they have wrested some control over "the system" in Pawnee. The importance of control is also realized by parents in both the black and white community. For blacks, success in the battle for control represents chances for integrated education. One black parent, herself a West graduate, told the interviewer:

Well, up until not too long ago, there was only one high school. That's why the high school has always been desegregated. That's why we fought so hard to keep the high school where it is because at one time that was the only high school that was here. . . . The elementary school and the junior high school had all black students but when students were ready for high school, they went to the only one we had.

According to this parent, "integrated education" means her child will get a better education. Some white parents also say that the situation is better as a result of the fight to desegregate the schools. A very active white mother, also a graduate of West, stated:

Before there were trouble spots. Puerto Rican and black neighborhoods and schools. But now every school is integrated with 30 to 35% black and I feel very positive about that. It has definitely improved the whole system.

In the opinion of these parents and many others, the successful battle to eliminate predominantly white or black schools has improved the overall quality of education in Pawnee. However, the fragile quality of desegregation and the necessity to protect the gains accomplished are clear to many residents.

121

Jacqueline Scherer   Edward J. Slawski

Conditions in the New Building

The new building housing Pawnee West is starkly modern—a low, sprawling, gray concrete structure. On first view, one notices an apparent absence of windows, which gives the building what some informants have termed a prison-like appearance. In fact, there are windows around the outside walls of the third and fourth levels, but very few classrooms are on the outside walls. A curved driveway gives access to the front of the high school, and parking lots are adjacent to the other three sides.

More recently, the old building has been torn down and the southeastern corner of the campus has been converted into a park and recreation area with tennis courts and a short running track. The result of the building project is a modern high school building located on an attractive and spacious campus. Classrooms are plain rectangular rooms with large wall clocks, bulletin boards, wall phones, loudspeakers (for morning and afternoon announcements), and brightly colored carpets. Each contains, in addition to several modern student desks, a teacher's desk and a supply cabinet, which is usually locked. In general, despite the bright colors, the appearance of the classrooms is austere.

Many of the concerns about conditions in Pawnee and the quality of race relations in the city are reflected in the ways in which students and residents react to Pawnee West. The symbolic value of the new building surfaces in how people talk about West and how the physical plant is treated.

One of the most striking features of West is the absence of vandalism. There has been almost no problem with this since the new building was opened: The walls are clean and without markings. Visitors are struck by the cleanliness and newness of the facility, and the excellent condition of the building is a source of pride among building staff. When one compares West to other secondary schools in surrounding communities, often located in the most affluent areas, the absence of vandalism and destruction is even more dramatic. Clearly, the fact that so little damage has been done to the facility is an observable statement about student and staff pride in the facility.

A concern with safety and social control is incorporated in many aspects of the physical layout, leading to an oppressive, military-like atmosphere in some instances. For example, student lavatories have no doors. For both male and female students only a wall perpendicular to the outside hallway provides some modicum of privacy. There are very few "legitimate" places where students can experience a sense of privacy. However, there are an almost unlimited number of places where students may hide, causing teachers and administrators considerable effort.

The entire area is patrolled regularly. Even then, there is no guarantee that student behavior can be effectively monitored. Teachers have hall duty and at appointed times are visible in the halls. Unfortunately, the halls are not where the action is. The stairwells at the corners of the building abound with secret places where illicit activity (for example, smoking dope) can be carried out with relative impunity.[2]

Many agree that the traditional techniques for controlling student behavior are ineffective in the new West building. Another staff person, an old-timer white male, says much more is at stake in the failure to control behavior in the school.

> *It's like Rome and the provinces. You know after a certain point Rome got too big to control. Well, this building is too big to control. There are too many places to hide. It's not a closed campus any longer. It's just a matter of time before the whole thing explodes. There are two teachers watching each floor but that's not enough. I take hall duty just so I can keep in touch with what's going on. I'm telling you that things are going to explode. They have to close the campus. Otherwise . . .*

What this teacher is referring to is a time when West was torn by violent episodes. The memory of the earlier period of violence is forever close to the surface and gives particular meaning to the issue of control in Pawnee West.

The campus is technically "closed" and elaborate gatekeeping procedures are supposedly in operation; however, students can easily be observed leaving West at all times of the day and returning at the

---

[2] The stairwells are the scenes of much of the residue of violence in the building. Students tell us of many minor skirmishes that take place in the corner stairwells. These may last only 30 seconds, but to the students who are victims, they are frightening. This fear may account for the overcrowding of the central staircases in Pawnee West. Students seem to prefer the pushing and shoving of the crowds to being "punched out" on one of the stairways. In an attempt to reduce some of the illicit activities that occur on the stairs, monitors were chosen from among the junior and senior students. Equipped with armbands, they stand on the landings for a few minutes before and after the breaks between classes. This program reportedly has been successful in reducing some of the more blatant activity in those areas.

123

end of classes in time to catch the bus home. Many students quickly learn how to subvert the elaborate checking procedures so that they have free movement in and out of the building.

The reactions of members of the community to the new building are mixed. They range from admiration to disgust toward the appearance of the facility. Even among those who admire its newness there seems to be a hint of ambivalence. One white female parent who is very active at Pawnee West commented:

> *Well, I'm glad that the sign [saying Pawnee West over the front entrance] and the flagpoles are finally up. You know this is a lovely building but it's hard to tell what it is. People driving along the street [past the front of the school] can't tell whether this is a school or an office building.*

This same parent advised the administration to "plant more trees and shrubs around the outside to make it look less stark. One older white female teacher recalled more negative reactions from the students as they watched the progress of construction from the old building.

> *The students were negative. They watched the thing go up from over there [the old building] and it looked like a pile of stones. They called it Alcatraz High.*

On the other hand, the absence of vandalism and frequent positive statements about the building by students suggest a strong reservoir of positive feeling. Clearly interpretations of the building are varied: It is impressive, large, modern. Some see it as a progressive step forward toward comprehensive and sophisticated housing for new educational opportunities, whereas others view it as an impersonal, overwhelming, and forbidding structure that represses humanness.

TEACHER ISOLATION

Several unintended, and apparently unanticipated, consequences occurred as a result of the move to the large, multilevel building. One of the most serious was the isolation of the teaching staff. In the old building, it had been possible to look down the long halls on each floor and see a substantial portion of the entire facility. Short walks around the building would bring one in contact with the entire staff. Moreover, certain groups, such as the male faculty, appropriated special spaces to meet. The most remembered is a basement room known as the "The Hole" in which male faculty regularly congregated for discussions. Although women faculty members recall their exclusion from this place somewhat bitterly, most admit that the institution of The Hole was an important part of the informal social structure of old West and fostered camaraderie. Such an institution is almost impossible in the new building, where teachers are restricted to exchanges with those who teach in the classrooms adjacent to their own. The absence of a lunch hour reinforces the isolation: Most teachers remain in their rooms for the 2 hours immediately following the close of class at 1:00 P.M. and only a few get together regularly.

VIOLENCE

A second characteristic of the new building is the result of an almost accidental link to violence. There were more violent incidents in the old facility prior to the actual busing order, but once again, in the perceptions of many, violence is tied to the new building and colors the general discussions of the building. In our observations we found relatively few instances of overt violence and do not believe that West is any more violent than most other high schools.[3] But West has a reputation that includes violence.

The late 1960s was a time of turmoil in the country and in Pawnee. The emerging awareness of racial discrimination provoked more response from the Pawnee community than there had been previously. Issues like the site selection controversy produced demonstrations. The suspicion that forced integration was close at hand tended to intensify longstanding animosities among blacks and whites in Pawnee.

---

[3] It is difficult to get a count of the incidents of violence that occur at Pawnee West. In the initial phases of desegregation, there was a consistent attempt to count these incidents. They were generally defined as "confrontations between groups of students of different races," and there were several. However, recently virtually none of these types of confrontations have occurred. There were fewer than six during the 2 years of our field work, and all were relatively contained. In an attempt to cooperate with a national study of safe schools, building staff counted only four events that remotely qualified for the 1-month period of the study. All these were incidents involving single students.

Organized resistance to the court-ordered busing may have served as a catalyst for the violence that erupted.[4] As one white student vividly recalls:

> *Well, back in '71 it was a general sign of the times. There were a lot of high school dropouts and gangs of blacks. . . . I remember the black guys lined up on one side of the street and the white guys on the other. They would fight. Gang war. The school [Pawnee West] was just opened then; there were no hall monitors or anything. Finally one of the gangs came in at lunch hour and just started ripping it up. I guess we joined in, too. . . . If you got into the corner—an individual in the corner—it might be bad news, but just there out in the open in a group it was a lot of fun turning the tables over and going crazy. They didn't do it because they just didn't want to have to go to school.*

The residue of the violence of those times still haunts Pawnee West.

One white female teacher who witnessed one of her students stab another outside her classroom told us what those times were like for teachers.

> *Those were the days when you would come in the morning and wonder if you were going to make it through the day. It was a war zone. Friends in other districts would run up to you when you met them to find out the latest from Pawnee. When people found out you worked in Pawnee, they would be amazed and ask how you could do it. I sometimes wondered myself.*

The experience of those difficult times has created a bond among staff members who survived it—"we went through hell together." [5]

---

[4] Despite the somewhat dramatic quality of the violence that did occur in the early years of desegregation, the actual amount of that violence is reported to have been small. As one police officer reported:
> *the busing situation caused a lot of tension, very little conflict, contrary to a lot of reports that you read regarding it. There was a lot of verbiage but there wasn't all of the physical problems that the media portrayed there to be. It was a tense situation for a period of time but through the combined efforts of community people both black, white, and brown [sic] they calmed it and they quieted it right down.*

[5] Sharing the experience of the violent times at Pawnee West is a bond only for those teachers who were there at that time. The younger members of the faculty are, of course, excluded from this relationship. This fact may contribute to the separation between newcomers and old-timers, which we are told is a significant split among West's faculty. We note that this is not the only distinction or even the most important one for teachers. There is some evidence that the male–female division is also quite important.

EXTRACURRICULAR ACTIVITIES

One result of these events was the attempt to limit the large groups of students who would congregate, since these seemed to offer greater opportunities for confrontations. The lunch program was eliminated, and there were severe cuts in the number of extracurricular activities that were held.[6] A member of the parent club explained:

> *Music programs, some of the school dances, pep assembly . . . things like this that they had to cut for a while . . . because you know for a while things were so bad up there the kids would be so unruly during the assemblies and pep assemblies and things that you couldn't hear the groups that were performing or anything, you know, so they just completely cut out **all** of that. And now, the kids have asked, you know, to have this put back and things are going well. [The kids] are handling themselves beautifully and there is no problem.*

Staff members at West also notice the change in conditions and have attempted to modify their reaction to student requests for more activities. Another white Pawnee West staff person talked of the change of the lessening of restrictions on activities.

> *I think that we're nowhere near what we were 4 years ago. We can do things that were impossible then. For example, 4 years ago if somebody had suggested having a dance, it wouldn't have been seriously considered because of how we thought the climate was out there in the community. But I think that has changed. We are able to defuse incidents.*

How many or how few controls need to be applied to student activities is a matter of some continuing concern. Some vandalism resulted after a girls' basketball game held shortly after the homecoming dance—at least one parent was seriously injured and over $3000 worth of damage was done. The staff person continued:

[6] A student-produced film by Pawnee High School students focused upon the concern that administrators have for "control." The film, entitled "A Day Without Incident," portrays the high school atmosphere in Pawnee as if the building were a prison. Although the producers state that the message of the film applies to both Pawnee High Schools, it was filmed at West. A screening of the film before a group of parents led to numerous supportive statements from the audience about the veracity of the portrayal of West. This would seem to indicate the pervasiveness of this view of the school. It seems that if school officials are changing, they are not changing fast enough.

127

You know [the girls' basketball game] was an open admission policy. Anybody could come in from the outside. There weren't any tickets. Maybe that's too open. Clearly we cannot have $3000 worth of damages done every time there is an activity. We can't support that kind of thing.

Many people who are concerned about preserving West as a "quality high school" work very hard to keep the violence at the school in perspective. There is a very real attempt to dispel the image of Pawnee West as a violent place because it detracts from the kinds of attachment (i.e., "school spirit") needed to maintain West as a "good school."

ACADEMIC QUALITY

Another feature linked to the new building is the apparent decline in academic standards, in comparison with what was taught at the old West. Academically, Pawnee West High School had had the reputation of being "the best high school in Pawnee," the school "where the good kids went" to get their education. Although this academic glory has paled somewhat in recent years, it is still recalled by two white female teachers.

T 1: *Old West was an old heap of a building but it had a very good reputation. You realize that when you get away from this place how good a reputation it has. Whenever you go to meetings, you hear people say what's happening in Pawnee. There is a new program they have in Pawnee. Flexible schedules—they're doing that in Pawnee. Electives—they have that in Pawnee.*
I: *Is that the way it used to be? Or is it still true?*
T 1: *No. It's still true. We still have a good reputation for innovating, for doing new things.*
T 2: *Well, it certainly used to be true but I would disagree with her [Teacher 1] about now. I don't think our reputation is as good as it once was.*

This comparison with the past is not restricted to teachers. One black parent sees a deteriorated situation at West compared with when she was a student there.

Things seem to have been different back in those days. I don't remember thinking of West as a particularly bad place to be, but now that my kids are there, I think it is pretty bad. Things have changed so much though, you know.

Other parents and staff point out how much easier it is now for students to get through West. The new building symbolizes the change for many people.

ATHLETICS

In one area, however, the old–new comparison breaks down, and that is in athletics. West has always had a reputation as an athletic powerhouse, and this continues to be a significant factor in the reputation of the school. It is not uncommon to see entire families at the games, including three or four generations. The small-town quality of Pawnee [7] intensifies this pattern.

You don't know, but here in Pawnee that's all there is here in Pawnee for them to attend. I bet you never go to your high school football game or basketball game in [the big city]. But here in Pawnee everybody goes.

In sum, the changes associated with moving into the new building led to reorganization of major elements of the social structure of Pawnee West. The daily routine of West reflects many factors: bus schedules, the need to control students in the large building, student choice, and bureaucratic regulations. The routine might have been changed in the old building, but the fact is that the changes are associated with the new West.

[7] We noted several things in the course of our research that indicated the smallness of Pawnee, but this perception was most clearly stated by one of the residents we interviewed:

Pawnee is so small you just know everybody. [Turning to the interview] I know you're not from Pawnee because if you were we would know you. We would know exactly where you were from and all about you because we know about the people we like, we know about the people we don't like, we know about those we can stand, and anything that goes on in Pawnee, somebody, somewhere knows about it. We could even tell you where everybody's family is from. . . .

Jacqueline Scherer   Edward J. Slawski

Desegregation and Social Organization

The social organization of Pawnee West can be understood as attempts of actors to control an ambiguous social environment. In Pawnee, efforts to remove racial discrimination against blacks have heightened the levels of ambiguity that surround several institutional areas of city life, especially education. Pawnee schools were, and continue to be, the target of intense scrutiny and pressure to reduce racial discrimination. Local educators, who in their own view had been doing a conscientious job of educating Pawnee youth, both black and white, were subjected to a great amount of implicit and explicit criticism. The result of the confrontation has been a degree of ambiguity that individuals need to define, order, and control.

Space and Time—the Currency of Control

The elements of social organization most susceptible to control are the physical spaces set aside for certain activities and the time allocated for participation in them. The authorities of Pawnee West—administrators, teachers, and supporting staff—believe it important to control space and time in order to manage student activities effectively and maintain a "safe" social environment in the school. The major technique for establishing and maintaining control of internal spaces involves controlling time: When students are where they are supposed to be, fewer problems are likely to result. Therefore, school authorities enforce a rigid time schedule.

Time and space control were important features of the social environment at Pawnee West. As a result of the threat of violence that was part of the early phases of desegregation, the high school schedule was drastically changed: The school day was shortened by eliminating all times when large numbers of students could congregate in any one space, such as study halls and lunch hours. The attempt was to structure the student use of space through the mechanism of "official time." For our analysis we will distinguish between "student time," which includes those periods during the school day when students can exercise some degree of autonomy over how and where they spend their time, and "official time," the schedules imposed by staff at West. Most of the participants in Pawnee West do not consciously make such a distinction, but it is clear that student time often dictates quite different uses of space than does official time.

It is important to note, again, that the ways in which space and time are perceived at West are probably not very different from those found in other American schools and are not unique because Pawnee is desegregated. Racial factors may add to the complexity of some of these social negotiations and influence the outcomes in some instances, but this is because race is a "dominant status" in the society at large (Curtis and Jackson, 1977), and no school walls are hard enough to screen out dominant social attitudes. Of more interest is the extent to which schools may be able to modify social attitudes to some degree.

THE STUDENT'S DAY—OFFICIAL TIME AND SPACE AT PAWNEE WEST

The official day for students begins before 8:00 in the morning when the first school buses discharge their passengers at Pawnee West. Most teachers are already at their stations in their classrooms, and a few have been in the building to monitor the activities of early-arriving students since shortly after 7:00. Grade principals have been in their offices or patrolling the halls since 6:30 or 7:00 getting ready for the day and taking care of business that could not be completed the previous evening. The doors to the high school are open and the monitors are in place as the first busloads of students stream through the corridors. From that time on, the time of students is rigidly scheduled.

Upon arriving, the students may go directly to their lockers in the commons areas or stop off for a "couple of drags" in the smoking areas. There are a few free minutes before homeroom, and many students use this time to socialize or to retrieve their class materials or books. The area outside the building, including the large parking lots that extend to the rear of the school, is an important place for social activity, often illicit.[8]

---

[8] In effect, this area is a no man's land, since the staff cannot adequately patrol it and it is not routinely watched by the city police. The parking lot offers a special refuge for "skippers." If an open automobile can be found, students can use it for making out or smoking some dope instead of going to class. An observer was offered several opportunities to engage in these activities once the ninth-graders learned he had an automobile. Routine sweeps of the parking lots are made by school staff, but most offenders manage to avoid detection.

Groups of white students often are seen sitting in their cars and smoking. On the east side of the building groups of Latinos and blacks, predominantly male, lean against the school walls. On occasion one sees an interracial group, often smoking marijuana. There are fewer groups of females than males and almost no loners. It is not uncommon to see small groups of two or three students, or boy–girl combinations, talking intently outside the building even during class time.

The official start of the daily routine is homeroom, a 15-minute period that provides a time anchor for students at West. This period is used to provide continuity to the student's career at West; the student keeps the same homeroom for the entire stay at West. During homeroom, attendance is taken, official school notices distributed, and announcements read over the loudspeaker concerning daily events or major upcoming activities. Students recognize that homeroom is not a time for organized activity and engage in various other pursuits during that period: Many simply rest by putting their heads down on their desks; others catch up on the news with friends; several play cards or stare aimlessly off into space; a few do their homework. For still others, homeroom provides an opportunity to complete the morning grooming. For example, it is a mark of high status for some black males to have their hair combed out by girlfriends.[9] Rules are more relaxed generally and it is relatively easier to get a pass to go "to the lockers" or "to the bathroom" during this time. Moreover, students often arrive late because of late school buses or because they know "nothing's going to happen" and "homeroom is boring."[10]

Classes are scheduled for the entire school day with five 50-minute sessions and 5-minute breaks between. Student behavior in class varies greatly depending upon the teacher and the subject matter. Observers noted that in advanced classes or in more difficult subjects, the level of student attention was generally higher. In lower-level classes, espe-

[9] It is particularly important for black males to have their hair combed out early in the school day, since males are not allowed to wear hats in the school building. Black males often wear caps to cover their braided hair and complain that the no-hats rule is unfair since it applies only to them. We note that this rule is enforced differently depending upon the particular teacher. In general, black teachers seem among the most consistent enforcers.

[10] The belief that homeroom serves no useful purpose is shared by many members of the Pawnee West staff, who notes that the period is not long enough for the teacher to get to know the student very well or to allow sufficient time for club meetings or counseling sessions. Teachers seem generally to tolerate most activity during homeroom as long as the noise level does not become unreasonable.

cially those in ninth- or tenth-grade required subjects, student interest is lower and there are more instances of disruptive or inattentive behavior. Students in several classes pay little attention to the lesson for most of the class time. This seems to be tolerated by the teacher as long as the student does not disturb others. Students can sleep but not talk to one another in these classes.

After fifth hour, most students return home. Bus transportation for late activities is limited, and students who participate must walk home or have other transportation.[11]

The daily schedule is an attempt to control the social environment by effectively using official time. However, the management of time and space at Pawnee West is more complex and subject to more negotiation than the description of official time suggests.

STUDENT TIME AND SPACE AT PAWNEE WEST

Many students at Pawnee West accept the limitations official time places on them. For them, student time is restricted to the few minutes after the buses arrive in the morning and before they depart in the afternoon and the 5-minute breaks between classes.

For these students, student time is organized around the constraints of official time. They give a personal meaning to the routines of official time by seeing their friends. Several students more actively seek to expand the amount of time during the regular school day that belongs to them. Students are anxious to obtain some degree of autonomy over their lives and to break the monotonous routine that official time constrictions impose on their activities. This was well expressed in essays describing a utopian school. As the black female teacher who assigned the essay noted:

> *I've noticed that when they [the students] wrote these things most of them ask for more freedom, they want to be able to go to the bath-*

[11] We were interested in discovering what most students do after classes are dismissed at 1:00 P.M. Many upperclassmen have part-time jobs, and the active students participate in sports and clubs that meet until at least 2:30 P.M. A few students take a sixth-hour class. The overwhelming majority, however, go home, eat, and watch television. They often may have some domestic responsibilities (baby-sitting, cleaning the house, starting dinner), but watching television is the major activity for most of them between 2:00 and 6:00 P.M. Yet students generally are in favor of the tight scheduling and, although complaining of hunger, prefer to get out at 1:00. Most believe that the free time provides them with more opportunities to do what they want to and have little desire to stay at West any longer than necessary.

133

room, walk around, you know. But you couldn't run a school like that. You can't have people walking around—they'd be in the bathroom all hours.

West students are not different from other secondary school students (see Cusick, 1973; Freidenberg, 1963), nor, for that matter, do they differ from subordinates in most complex organizations (Etzioni, 1961). The desire for autonomy is a powerful one and becomes particularly acute when rewards for conformity are in the long-term and distant future. Many students fail to see the payoff to them for tolerating the dictates of official time and subvert them for their own ends.

For those students who seek more freedom during the school day Pawnee West offers many avenues of escape. Attempts to increase student time seem to make use of two major techniques: negotiations and avoidance. Which technique is utilized seems to depend upon the bargaining capital of the student involved and the space where time will be spent.

NEGOTIATIONS FOR TIME IN THE CLASSROOM

Negotiations for time usually occur in the classroom. The 50 minutes allocated teachers is seldom spent entirely on instruction, the proportion depending upon the outcome of the negotiations between the teachers and the students. Students try to restrict the official time in the classroom by many strategies: talking, opening and closing books, being restless.

Time is so deeply involved in the structure of social interaction that one observer reported a breakdown in activity when the school clocks were out of order. Students appeared to be disoriented, frequently asking one another and the teacher, "What time is it?" Students delay the onset of class, as one observer notes:

The teacher didn't really start class until 5 or 7 minutes after the bell rang. There is a settling-down time in which the kids are allowed to talk and to roam freely. The unfortunate thing is that they don't slow down those 5 minutes—they speed up during the 5 minutes.

Students in another class try to shorten class time by ending early.

With 3 minutes to go in the class there were at least 10 kids crowded around the door waiting to leave; that is, the kids are aware of when IT IS TIME TO GET OUT.

Students can negotiate more time for themselves by delaying the actual start of teaching in class and by signaling the end of class by packing up their books when they have had enough. Teachers must constantly protect teaching time from student incursions.

More subtle techniques are apparent during the actual time of instruction. Students can resist official time constraints by tuning out the teacher, by withdrawing from the classroom activities, by coming to the class without papers, books, and other materials, and by causing disturbances. Classroom etiquette seems to imply that a teacher should not bother a student who has put his head down on the desk to sleep or because he is not feeling well. One student reprimanded for sleeping in class was offended, saying, "You know, I wasn't bothering anybody."

From the teacher's perspective, this behavior indicates unwillingness to follow directions and prevents learning. As one white male teacher explained to a class:

> The most important thing you have to learn in school is how to follow directions. If you cannot follow directions, you haven't learned anything.

The students' refusal to follow directions or pay attention might better be understood, however, as a technique for gaining control over their environment.

One arena in which teachers and students have complex negotiations concerns homework. Students resist the infringement on after-school time. Most teachers resolve the situation by allowing students to begin the homework in class, and those who work quickly usually finish. Students have so many ways to defend not working during student time that most teachers make sure there is official time provided.

> [One teacher] reports real difficulty in the area of homework. She assigned 20 problems, 10 of which were completed by a student by the end of the class period. This teacher told this student to complete the assignment at home. The student told her, "I don't work at home." She told him that he was supposed to. The next day he came to class without his book and the 10 problems that he had done the day before.

Our data indicate that, in the complex, never-ending negotiation process over control of official time in the classroom, students are able effectively to limit the constraints of official time and to accumulate more student time in their day.

Jacqueline Scherer   Edward J. Slawski

SKIPPING—AVOIDANCE OF OFFICIAL SPACE

Official time at the high school defines the legitimate use of space at West. There are prescribed times when students may go to their lockers, walk the halls, or stand in the smoking rooms. One way in which students attempt to expand the amount of student time is by completely ignoring the constraints of official time by "skipping." The hard walls of West are simply not powerful enough to hold the students inside. Students report that the important thing is to know when to "cut," or skip. The essential element in this knowledge is not missing important deadlines or examinations that would put the student in serious jeopardy of failing the course.

Skippers will make it a point to see the teachers or other students in the parking lots to find out when tests are being given and attend class that day. Students selectively cut some classes and attend others, partly in response to how rigid the teacher is in enforcing rules against absences, how easily they can obtain legitimate excuses, or how severe the consequences appear to be. For the bright student, lack of attendance does not appear to be a problem, as one white male staff member complains:

> You know, I don't know if I've told you this before but I think a kid shouldn't pass unless he's there at least 50% of the time. I think that if a kid does well on a test and he's not there you're not teaching him. He shouldn't get a good grade unless he does something. He should produce something every hour of every day. This idea of passing them if he passes a test even if he doesn't come to class I think teaches them bad habits. They should know that they don't get anything for nothing.

Students give many reasons for skipping: boredom, defiance, dislike of a particular teacher or class. One informant explained what students do when they skip and why they avoid classes:

> R: Most of the kids just leave here all day. Go up to X Junior High, come back here and catch the bus. If you get caught you get kicked out.
> I: Why do you think kids skip?
> R: Boring, classes boring.

They also have many places to go inside the building when they skip, as another student explained:

> R: First I was in the bathroom until about 10 minutes after the hour waiting for the hall monitors to leave. Then I was on the fourth

floor, went down the back stairs to the third floor, and went to sit in the bathroom for the rest of the time.

Another suggested the following places to go:

All the students have to do is wait 5 minutes after they [hall monitors] leave and walk around until they see a teacher coming and then leave and they go to the back hall or to the stairs because the teachers never go to the back ones. It's very easy. They keep saying they are going to stop us but they cannot stop us unless they put a person in every hall, every stairs, and every bathroom.

One white male staff member noted that some of the skippers never even come into the school:

I'd see the school buses arrive and the kids get off and some kids take off across the fields; and then at 1:00 when the school buses were loading up, the same kids would come back across the field and get on the school bus. They had never been in school all day and what they did, we don't know—we can only imagine. They weren't in their classes.

Data provided for the ninth-grade class indicate that fully one-quarter of all discipline referrals and class closures are for truancy.[12] This proportion must be seen as a conservative estimate of the actual incidence, since so many offenders are not caught. According to one teacher,

On any day about half my students are absent. Not the same ones every day.

[12] Records of offenses yield the following breakdown:

Percentage of Discipline Referrals by Category

Class disturbance	26
Truancy	25
Not dressing for PE	11
Insubordination	19
Tardiness	12
Fighting	4
Smoking	1
Miscellaneous	2
Total Percentage	100
(Number)	(899)

(Footnote continues on the bottom of page 138)

Since state laws mandate compulsory attendance, the responsibility for attendance is seen as a legal obligation of school authorities. Any student absent is either excused or truant, and serious consequences can follow the latter. A white female staff member responsible for attendance explained district policy in these words:

> A registered letter goes home after 15 absences in one or five classes. If you miss 15 days a teacher can deny credit. That's the board policy. If the kid is willfully truant and under 16 and if the parent is out of control, then we can refer to the court. However, there's no backup for kids who are over 16.

Considerable administrative and teacher time is consumed in matters of attendance: Teachers call the parents after 5 absences; after 10 absences a counselor calls; after 15 the grade principal confers with the parent, and they are to develop a program to maintain attendance.

Both formally and informally the student is told that attendance is linked to "making it"—that is, staying in school. But many students ignore the message. They are able to accumulate more student time for themselves by avoiding official space. It is important to repeat that this kind of behavior appears to occur in most secondary schools, according to the educational literature, and is not a special phenomenon of West. Since it is virtually impossible to quantify the extent to which it takes place, it is not possible to argue definitively whether or not it is more of a problem at West than at another school. We can say with

---

(Footnote continued from previous page.)

Percentage of Class Closures by Category

Smoking	3
Insubordination	32
Class disturbance	8
Truancy	25
Not dressing for PE	4
Fighting	17
Abusive language	3
Tardiness	3
School incorrigible	4
Miscellaneous	1
Total Percentage	100
(Number)	(158)

some degree of confidence that skipping is a common phenomenon and that many students are expelled on this basis alone. Black parents maintain that black students are "pushed out" of the school more often than whites; some also believe the attendance policies are enforced arbitrarily and are prejudicial to black students. We cannot support or deny these allegations because such data were not available for systematic analysis. Staff members deny these claims strongly.

One parent describes her ideas as follows:

> *The [school officials] want them out of there. They want it that way but they aren't getting rid of my kids—I know what their rights are. Even if they don't do as well as I want them to do, I want them to follow some of the rules at least and make an effort of their own. But just because they get in a fight or they skip school, I'm going to stand by and make sure that they don't get put out of school, because when that happens that's the end of everything.*

Parents on the whole, however, accept the legitimate responsibility of the staff to regulate the use of space and time within the building. As one black parent noted:

> *They make the kids mind, they won't take any stuff. They sent this note home saying what all they'd do with the kids if they were caught doing anything. I know they don't stand for no fighting.*

AVOIDANCE IN STUDENT SPACE— SOCIALIZATION INTO THE CULTURE OF VIOLENCE

Most parents applaud the efforts to provide a safe environment for their children, but they recognize that all places may not be equally safe. What seems to be important is that their children find at least some places where they will not be bothered and that they find these places quickly. One white female parent shared her son's experience:

> R: *Oh, sure he knows where to go and where not to go, he won't go into the john, but they learn quickly, they catch on what's safe and what isn't safe. But look even I walk around all the time and I'm not afraid. You know, if you can get parents into the place, into the schools, they find out it's not nearly as bad as they thought it was. You know, they think it's a jungle in here and it's really not like that at all.*

139

An important part of student learning is to know what are safe places—and when. We find that avoidance mechanisms function at Pawnee West to organize social environments during student time. The understood rules for behavior are mind your own business and avoid risks. One white female student explained it as follows:

> I heard a little about fights—my sisters told me. It didn't really scare me. I am just cautious and make sure I don't get into any trouble. I mind my own business. My mother always told me just mind your own business and you won't get in no trouble.

Older students and siblings frequently warn new students not to go to certain places alone, and importantly, to mind one's own business if trouble starts:

> Well, I just don't start trouble. I don't like to fight. I just talk— I walk away.
>
> Yeah [there are rules about what to do and not to do]. Get in class before the bell rings. Try not to get two referrals, you might be kicked out. Don't skip and stay away from fighting—you know—people who like to get in trouble.
>
> I heard different things [about West before I got here]. Like I heard how Pawnee West is always having fights and how much trouble there is and how you're going to get approached by people selling drugs—really that much hasn't happened. Occasionally you see one [a fight] at the back stairwells or something but not that bad.

The fact that expectations of how bad it will be outstrip the reality of the students' actual experience does not diminish the importance of the avoidance of violence in a student's life at West.

Avoidance is made more necessary and more difficult by the crowding that occurs at certain times and places. The halls are seen as troublesome areas because of the crowding; the main stairs are particularly congested since students avoid the back stairs and more secluded parts of the building. One student vividly described the risks that may be involved in using out-of-the-way spaces in West.

> But when the black dudes came after [Bob] he took off and one of the other black dudes started fighting him and hit him in the back and they beat him with a billy club. Bob's friend just run and Bob was pretty mad about it and he said he was knocked out for a couple of minutes—he was sore and that. . . . I didn't see him come to school for a couple of days.

140

Although these incidents are not frequent, students hear of them and avoid such places to reduce the risk of harm to themselves.

In trying to explain what happens in crowded halls students frequently used the term *hassle*.[13] To hassle someone is to annoy or provoke the other purposefully; it is somewhat related to the concept of teasing but includes more actual physical pushing and persistent annoyance deliberately intended to upset the other person. This behavior is often directed at someone of the opposite race. One black female student told us how this process works:

R: *When you walk down the hall and there are a lot of people they just push you out of the way. You just keep going.*
I: *Is it more likely to happen if you're black or white? Or does it matter?*
R: *Mostly happens to white people.*
I: *Why is that? Do you know?*
R: *I don't know. Like if a black hits another black they know they will get hit back but if they hit a white they just keep on going. . . .*
I: *So if a black pushes another black person they are liable to get hit?*
R: *Yeah.*
I: *If a black person pushes a white person—they will kind of let go?*
R: *Yeah.*
I: *Is that how it seems?*
R: *Yeah.*
I: *Why do you think that white people let it go?*
R: *I don't know. [The blacks] ought to get smacked if they push . . . [the whites] look like they are mad but I don't know. . . .*

Students reported that there was considerable hassling in the halls, sometimes with definite racial overtones. Our observations tended to substantiate the student testimony above that black students usually

---

[13] Students are not the only ones subject to hassling, and feats of mild provocation of teachers can enhance a student's status with peers. One observer noted this in a classroom interaction.

He then went up and opened the teacher's desk up and grabbed a pen— looked like the teacher's red marking pen out of the desk and proceeded to use that for the entire class period. . . . At the end of the class to conclude this relationship the pen needed returning PF put it back in the teacher's desk and then came over to George and said, "I just put the pen back in the teacher's desk and he didn't say nothing." He seemed proud of the fact that he took something from the teacher's desk and the teacher didn't catch him for taking it, I guess. He was very proud of himself and he reported that to George.

141

provoked these instances and most whites ignored them, continuing on their way. Black students volunteered the observation that most white students would not respond to hostility on the part of blacks but tried to avoid confrontations.

> *I have never been hassled. It's especially the white kids. You know they are really scared. There was an assembly for Black Awareness in the fieldhouse, and there were some white kids that got out of their class to go to the assembly but when they found out there was just going to be blacks there, they skipped class.*

A similar phenomenon was noted between younger students, both black and white, and older students: The higher-status upperclassmen had more freedom to invade space, and the underclassmen were less likely to respond in kind. Avoidance of such occasions for hassling seems to be a general response of white students, who are mystified about the motivation for black behavior:

> *[The blacks] think they are really bad and they think they can beat up anybody they can. I don't know why they act like that. If you don't mind your own business they will kick you down the stairs. This morning when I was in the smoking room, this one black girl flicked a cigarette at my girlfriend Carol for nothing, just to be smart. I don't think that's right. I don't know why they do that.*

Crowding and consequently more opportunities for being hassled or getting into fights also occur in two areas where students are allowed to smoke. Many students avoid these areas because the risk is too high.

> R: *Well, I don't go into the smoking room. You know there's sometimes trouble in there. But I don't know. Other than that I haven't really thought about it. You know I go where I have to go for my classes and I haven't thought about it. We don't usually have fights in here [Pawnee West]. Sometimes people beat up on each other like a couple of blacks against whites or a couple of whites against blacks. Sometimes the smoking room gets too crowded and fights start in there. Everybody gets in. Locker rooms—everybody gets on top of lockers, throwing chairs when they fight. I just keep away from there.*

Another student told us:

> *I never hear until they start fighting. I don't go to the smoking room. I don't smoke so I just don't go there. Probably a lot of things [happen] down there. I was walking down the hall one day and a whole*

142

bunch of dudes started running down the hall and I moved out of their way. They all ganged up on this one dude. Teachers tried to break it up but they all got away.

By staying away from the smoking room, the student can minimize the risk of being hassled or getting into fights.

In its yearly Senior High Student Attitude Survey, the Research and Evaluation Department asked a random sample of almost 1000 ($N = 922$) students about the relative safety of different locations in the school building. Almost half (45%) responded that there was at least one place that students avoided "because someone might hurt or bother them there." Almost one-third (32%) of students listed two or more such unsafe places.[14]

Habitués of the problem areas also develop defensive strategies

[14] For Pawnee West students the distribution of responses shows a consistently higher avoidance rate for whites than for blacks.

Places Avoided by Pawnee West Students

(Percentage "Yes" to question "Do you stay away from any of the following places because someone might hurt or bother you there?")

	TOTAL	WHITES	BLACKS
Smoking area	27	28	26
	(412)	(209)	(203)
School restrooms	23	33	12
	(419)	(209)	(210)
Hallways or stairs	21	25	16
	(417)	(210)	(207)
School parking lot	17	17	18
	(414)	(210)	(204)
School commons	16	21	12
	(419)	(209)	(210)
Any school entrance	12	13	11
	(416)	(210)	(206)
Shortest route to school	7	7	8
	(420)	(210)	(210)
Other places	21	25	16
	(415)	(210)	(205)

We note that significantly more whites than blacks avoid school restrooms, hallways, and stairs, and the commons areas—the latter two are high-risk hassling areas, according to our informants.

143

against the more violent forms of hassling that may occur. One student described her behavior in the smoking room:

> I: *But in the smoking room is there a particular place where you usually go? When you go in there is there a kind of spot that you go to?*
> R: *Against the wall.*
> I: *Is there a particular reason for that?*
> R: *If you stand in the middle, in the center of the room, you would be pushed down and knocked down. If you go to the wall, they just bump into you and you won't be knocked down.*

In addition to these spatial accommodations, white students also learn that certain affective accommodations are more tolerable than others. In the student world of Pawnee West, a "low profile" pays off in aiding the student in avoiding trouble. A white female told us how one asks for trouble:

> R: *By fooling around and being boss; if you act higher and push, then you ask for trouble. You must not be better than anybody else.*

Staff members at Pawnee West also observe the patterns of hassling that occur frequently within their sight. They see the acceptance of this behavior by whites as one of the consequences of desegregation. However, some see changes occurring in the pattern.

> *I tell you one thing—white kids aren't taking as much guff. You know I had a black girl stand up in one of my classes. She turned around and said, "Why do you honkies take stuff from us? You don't have to. You know that if someone takes your pencil, you don't have to put up with that. You wouldn't if it was a white person."*

Avoidance, then, seems to be an important process in dealing with the student social environment at Pawnee West, in expanding the amount of student time during the regular day beyond the constraints of official time, and in dealing with complex student-to-student interactions.

AVOIDANCE AND EXTRACURRICULAR EVENTS— THE SOCIAL ENVIRONMENT OF INFORMAL STUDENT TIME

We have described in some detail the mechanism of avoidance as it applies during the regular school day. Our observations indicated that such avoidance mechanisms do not end with classes. Traces can be found throughout the entire range of school-related activities.

In both formal and informal arenas, the established pattern seems to be for students of different races to remain separate. Our informants indicated that strong pressures are exerted by peers to limit "crossing over"—that is, acting as if the person is a member of a different race. We found very few instances of attempts to resist this pressure among students.[15]

Student perceptions of the racial composition of various athletic teams produce dramatic separations in student activities. Several students told us that certain athletic teams were the domain of particular racial groups. For example, "everybody knows" that the basketball team is black. The one white player on the team was introduced at pep assemblies as "the Great White Hope." Likewise, swimming and golf are "white sports." [16] Wrestling is integrated, with about equal numbers of blacks and whites participating. Football is also a sport with about equal umbers of students of both races, but there are more subtle differences by position. In general these patterns are seen by students and some others as reflecting the inherent abilities and interests of particular racial groups. In contrast, one of the most integrated activities at West is band. Students in band seem the most relaxed in interracial contact even though much pride is taken in the "black sound" that West's band has.

Seating patterns at athletic events and pep assemblies also reflect the avoidance mechanisms of students. It is not uncommon for the stands to be segregated informally into black and white sections. Students who attend with their families may be more constrained by the presence of family members whose sensibilities would be offended by too open contact with members of a different race. We do not believe these patterns indicate that school staff members are primarily responsible. The avoidance that maintains racial separation of Pawnee West students at an interpersonal level seems to be part of the social structure of Pawnee. Public events are occasions during which the strength of the separation is manifested.

Pressures for avoidance and separation are also felt at a more individual level. Many informants reported the difficulties involved for

[15] Our classroom observations revealed that interarcial student contact occurs only around some specific, time-limited task.

[16] A count of the numbers of students of different races in team pictures in several past yearbooks reveals that there is some validity to these perceptions. What is more difficult is the assignment of direction of causality in these patterns.

students who are friends with or date members of another race. A graphic example of this phenomenon appeared as part of a student-produced film that addressed the experience of integrated education in Pawnee high schools. In this scene a black cheerleader is shown talking with four or five white cheerleaders. She is "discovered" by a group of black students who ridicule her for "wanting to be like them." Reluctantly the black cheerleader turns her back on her fellow black students and returns to her discussion with the white students. The message is clear. This black girl has been forced to choose, and either choice has its costs. The film's producers see this as an unfortunate consequence of integrated education that they hope students will eventually outgrow.

It is significant that a cheerleader was chosen to illustrate this point, since such "cultural maximizers" are least likely to be bound by the avoidance mechanisms that govern most students. The high levels of interracial contact in the band are possible because of the high status that band members have at West and because the band constitutes a closed society within West that supports its own norms. More typical is the experience of a white male senior at West who reported that he rigidly avoids any contact with his black girlfriend at any school-related function. He is able to see her only at times completely removed from student time.

One event early in our field work threw the operation of avoidance mechanisms among students into sharp relief. The event was the first homecoming dance to be held in several years. Student avoidance mechanisms created, in effect, two separate dances—one for whites and another for blacks. Students alternately used the same space but almost never interacted.

The pattern was clearly defined, with blacks at one side of the fieldhouse, dancing occasionally and exclusively to the "black band," and whites at the other side dancing to the "white band." One black male ninth grader was observed standing at the door to the white side of the fieldhouse, hesitating over his decision where to sit. He stood a few moments looking things over, shrugged, and made his way to the black side of the gym. The message seems to have become clear to him—each group had its well-established space. The vast expanse of fieldhouse floor seemed small in comparison to the social-structural gap that separates the races in Pawnee.

THE CONSEQUENCES OF AVOIDANCE

Using space and time avoidance mechanisms does reduce uncertainty and assist persons in managing their social environments. However, these mechanisms are dysfunctional to the extent that they limit opportunities for growth and development. They allow one to avoid challenges to personal order that facilitate growth: Fear restricts inquiry, and seeking and learning experiences are made less effective and exciting. Teachers who use space to keep a safe social distance between themselves and students contribute considerably to the routine character of many classroom experiences. Students are expected to approach the teachers for assistance. Because moving about is such rare teacher behavior, it is often considered patrolling by students. Our records contain many instances of observer surprise when a teacher walked around a classroom and actually smiled. Students who avoid others have fewer biracial contacts, and the ones they have are essentially undifferentiated. We have noted that biracial contacts increase when students have a common task to perform in a classroom or are on a team together with a group purpose. For many black and white students at West, the motivations of their fellow students remain mysterious or are explained by simplistic generalizations gathered from partial understandings borrowed from the adult world in which they live.

Since many students avoid making the initial moves to stimulate informal associations during student time and in student spaces, the actual amount of biracial contact is limited. Ordinary classrooms at West provide a few structured opportunities for ongoing biracial contact because many of the control mechanisms require rigid time and space ordering. Those students who do not avoid these experiences regard them as the most successful part of their education. For example:

I: *What do you like most of Pawnee West?*
R: *Different people in general. If you can meet other people you can better cope with them.*

POSITIVE COPING STRATEGIES

It would be a mistake to view the management of space and time as strictly negative coping mechanisms. Even avoidance may be useful at times because it allows students to pick and choose occasions for meeting that they judge to be more positive. We found many instances of a student's selecting one person from the opposite race as a person to know better. By dealing with desegregation on a limited one-to-one basis, the student tried to understand the person in a more manageable and personal framework. Almost every survey of student behavior showed that a white student had one black friend and vice versa, but such statements were unreliable because the term *friend* could mean a casual acquaintance or a deep relationship. In our observations and discussions, however, we frequently encountered the latter as a deliberately maintained strategy for coping with desegregation.

Biracial contacts increased significantly when students shared not only time and space, but also common activities within these dimensions. For example, students in the college preparatory programs reported many more biracial contacts than those in less demanding academic programs. We observed these students sharing homework problems, studying together, preparing assignments, and sharing the classroom experiences. Athletic activities on mixed teams also led to many biracial contacts.

But for many students, school is not an exciting and stimulating experience. They do not find either classrooms or the official school culture of clubs, athletics, and sponsored activities interesting, and they do not participate in anything. As long as they do not cause disciplinary problems and put forth a minimal academic effort to pass, they are left alone. One could say the official school system avoids them, and they, in turn, follow the same avoidance and noninvolvement strategies with the school. Biracial contacts among these students are low. In simple terms, then, coping strategies that deal most successfully with race are byproducts of dealing with other concerns at school. Successful students are more successfully desegregated.

Since time and space management are the ways in which school organization is maintained, those students who do not understand the importance of career tracks, scheduling, school rules, and the unofficial etiquette observed in everyday interaction are highly disadvantaged in terms of surviving in the school environment. Efforts to run the school smoothly and to avoid disruption in the routine may have long-lasting educational consequences, not the least of which is teaching students avoidance, conformity, and passive acceptance.

Control and Rhetoric

Another strategy for controlling uncertainty in a turbulent environment is through rhetoric—the ways in which particular words are used to describe a position or viewpoint, particularly if this is designed to influence others.[17] Rhetoric often takes on the quality of ritual: "[Rhetoric] says something about the speaker, the spoken-to, and the situation, which goes beyond the surface message [Parkin, 1975:114]."

At West, rhetoric is used as a means of control to bring about consensus, reduce conflict, and provide a framework to unify participants of diverse persuasions. It is a style of speaking that provides an umbrella to encompass differences. Often the use of rhetoric is totally unconscious: The ideological underpinnings that form the source of the ideas are almost never examined. And it is ambiguous in order to encompass a wide variety of interpretations and perspectives. Parkin (1975) summarizes the features that make rhetoric effective.

> The surface messages contained in the verbal pronouncements . . . are conspicuous for their lack of specificity; their ambivalent and sometimes contradictory exhortations; and, by offering a wide-range of interpretations, their communicability to otherwise disparate elements in population [p. 117].

At West there is an important rhetoric associated with desegregation. It is based upon the view that desegregation has been successfully completed. In this view, in spite of serious obstacles and notwithstanding a period of violence and uncertainty, Pawnee West has accomplished the desegregation goals ordered by the court. West is an example of school desegregation that has been achieved and maintained.

The view of desegregation as an accomplished fact at Pawnee West obscures the persistence of racial concerns in high school interactions. People at the school are generally reluctant to talk about race. They will answer direct questions and occasionally volunteer a comment in connection with a specific topic. For example, most students know the race of the school symbolic student leaders and will offer an opinion about

[17] It is more common to use rhetoric to apply to a formalized manner of presentation. However, our data indicate that although the manner of presentation varies, substantially the same content appears throughout the range of messages. The quality of this speech, which relies upon accepted "recipes" that are unquestioned, is what we hope to capture by calling this language rhetoric.

the appropriateness of the boy's being black and the girl's being white. But most often we are told that "people get along well now" so that there is no need to talk about the subject of race. This reluctance is understandable given the negative publicity that previous racial confrontations brought the school. Most participants believe that the notoriety was distorted and grossly unfair and wish to avoid a similar experience. Avoidance of discussion of the issue of race relations, however, gives talk about desegregation a rhetorical quality.

Today, desegregation is ritualistically used to emphasize the ethnic diversity of the student body at Pawnee West and in Pawnee, an "all-American" city. Students of all races and cultural backgrounds are pictured as sharing a common educational future. "Caring" has triumphed over the destructive forces that opposed busing and a few short years ago threatened to rip Pawnee in two. Students of all races now find themselves in a stable educational environment that offers many unique learning opportunities, not the least of which is the experience of a multiracial setting. In short, the people at West are proud of their record on desegregation: They have successfully accomplished mixing black and white students to the point that racial confrontations are a thing of the past.

By being relegated to the realm of rhetoric, desegregation is no longer dealt with in a realistic way at West. Concern with the problems of race has effectively ended. A black teacher disagrees with the rhetoric and questions how useful the effort to desegregate the schools has been:

> What it's done, busing that is, is to have effectively taken the life out of us. There is no more fight left in us. No one cares anymore. It seems as though we have all just sort of accepted the fact and there's a trend not to oppose the voices that are against us. What you may not understand is that busing is a "tool." Busing has been used to not integrate or what they call desegregate us, but busing has served for even more segregation . . . there was a time when white students were interested. They did want to find out about the life of black students and black people in general. Busing has been used to take that away. Busing brought out all the hostilities.

Black students describe their positive memories of "almost all-black" junior high school. One student expresses his recollection in the familiar terms of the rhetoric of concern:

> It was almost all black back then and we had a good school. We worked together, we cared—the teachers cared. Everyone cared. But

now I feel as though no one cares. I feel as though I could drop dead right in this spot and no one would care what happened to me!

For these students, much of this quality has been lost as a result of desegregation. As another student comments:

There is all this talk about equality of educational opportunity but all I can say is that I've got a bus ride.

Many people at West resent the emphasis that desegregation has placed upon noticing what color a student is. They assure us that they were previously colorblind and now dislike having to worry about how many whites or blacks are involved in a particular activity. Our observations tend to support the contention that many staff members are not primarily concerned about the race of their students. However, the conditions at West are such that consideration of race is important in providing equal educational opportunities to all West students. Our data reveal situations approaching colorblindness taking place only when the students were so intently engaged in some common enterprise that they forgot about themselves. Biracial contact among students seems to be directly related to the degree of involvement students have in academic work, athletics, clubs, drugs, or social events. Many students have little involvement in any of these or other high school activities because of their fear of biracial contact. To the extent that colorblindness prevents the school organization from recognizing these students and providing them with alternative experiences that break down their pattern of fear, ignoring the race of a student may be a disservice to his or her education.

By treating desegregation as if it has been accomplished once and for all, the continuing racial problems at Pawnee West can be denied, avoided, minimized, or categorized in ways to prevent them from being recognized, confronted, and improved. Furthermore, racial tensions are forced underground, and the violence that may be associated with these tensions in the students' minds is not perceived as any longer a serious issue. The concerns many students have about violence become identified as isolated and individual problems and the student must deal with them as best he or she can, often by avoidance.

Finally, a rhetoric has grown up around desegregation at Pawnee West that includes the statement made over and over again by students, parents, teachers, and administrators: Students who have learned to cope with others who are different from themselves have learned an important social skill. The experience of attending a desegregated

151

school is believed to give the students a "taste of real life" that more than compensates for any academic deficiency. One student explains it this way:

> *In a school like ours with so many different people, you got to cope with people who are different. I think they finally realize that you got to cope with people in different ways. You can't treat everybody the same way and I think they have come to realize this in our school.*

Our observations and discussions, however, convince us that this experience is not as widespread at West as many believe it to be. Many of the social learning experiences of students are not consistent with the view that contact will lead to increased understanding and acceptance of different people. Students are affected by desegregation differently. Some whites are isolated, afraid to venture into unknown places and reluctant to face new challenges. Some groups of black girls, on the other hand, appear to enjoy the new opportunities that are open to them at West, such as cheerleading, homecoming contests, and club activities. The emphasis on athletic success at West has made it possible for some black males to receive recognition both inside the hard walls and outside in the community. But the black males not actively engaged in athletics or academic activities often try to bask in the reflected aura of the "brothers," unrealistically assuming that they too will be able to obtain social rewards with the hard work and disciplined participation required for these achievements. As a result, we found many unrealistic expectations among some of these students. Despite the varied and individual responses of students to the same event, many would like to perceive the desegregated experience as a uniform, monolithic event with the same consequences for all.

Postscript: Race Relations at Pawnee West

One could argue that West's experience is indicative of the desegregation controversy as a whole. The debate over busing has obscured the more complex issues of poverty, unemployment, and economic discrimination that affect equality of opportunity, just as efforts to preserve neighborhood schools from busing obscure the more difficult issues of residential segregation. To the degree that desegregation is viewed independent of such basics as learning, developing competence, and fostering trust in school relationships, it is given over to rhetoric, having the appearance of solution while leaving basic issues untouched.

The elimination of predominantly black and predominantly white schools has not diminished the importance of race as a factor in the education of Pawnee youth. No school walls are hard enough to keep out the widely accepted community assumptions. The dominant cultural perceptions of race in the community are carried into West and influence the students' understandings of the world that guide their behavior. Second, many of the problems associated with poverty are automatically attributed to race, whether or not the two are related in any given situation: There is no doubt about the level of poverty in Pawnee but not all poor people in the city are black. Third, there is a widespread belief, in spite of evidence to the contrary, that desegregation has caused a decline in academic achievement. Although achievement patterns throughout the nation show decline, even in segregated schools, many believe that this is a special condition in Pawnee. Finally, there is still a strong tension in American society about race, and many people express a deep-seated fear that racial conflict could erupt at any moment, whether or not there are immediate grounds for such a concern.

Desegregation was simple in concept, but the notion has proven extraordinarily complex in practice. By itself, racial balance in the schools cannot bring about educational equality, integration, or improved race relations. These are the goals for which desegregation is one strategy. Until these goals are recognized as valid and accepted as the agenda for American education in West and throughout the nation, we have no yardstick by which to measure the effectiveness of desegregation.

References

Curtis, R. F., and E. F. Jackson
    1977   *Inequality in American Communities.* New York: Academic Press.
Cusick, P. A.
    1973   *Inside High School: The Student's World.* New York: Holt, Rinehart and Winston.
Etzioni, A.
    1961   *A Comparative Analysis of Complex Organizations.* New York: The Free Press.

Freidenberg, E.
  1963   "The modern high school: A profile." *Commentary* (November): 373–380.
Parkin, D.
  1975   "The rhetoric of responsibility." In M. Block (ed.), *Political Language and Oratory in Traditional Society*. London: Academic Press.

Chapter 5

The Social Context of Learning in an Interracial School

JANET WARD SCHOFIELD
H. ANDREW SAGAR

The *Brown* v. *Board of Education* decision was based on the constitutional principle of equal protection (Read, 1975; Wisdom, 1975). However, many social scientists and educators were quick to point out the possible beneficial effects of desegregation—in particular, that school desegregation could lead both to increased academic achievement by minority group members and to improved intergroup relations. A tremendous amount of research has attempted to assess the effect of desegregation on the academic performance of both white and black children (St. John, 1975). Much less attention, however, has been given to the social experiences of children in interracial schools and the impact of these experiences on intergroup attitudes and behavior.

Perhaps one reason so little attention has been paid to social learning occurring in interracial schools is that, for most people, traditional academic achievement is a matter of infinitely higher priority. The proportion of students going on to college and the way local students score on nationally normed tests of academic aptitude and achievement are typical of the indicators used to judge the performance of schools and school districts. The widespread resistance of whites and also of

155

DESEGREGATED SCHOOLS
Appraisals of an American Experiment

many blacks to desegregation suggests that they do not give high priority to interracial contact in schools (Clark, 1973; Goldman, 1970).

Some compelling arguments, however, favor giving more thought to the matter of intergroup relations. First, the fact is that social learning occurs whether or not it is planned. An interracial school cannot choose to have no effect on intergroup relations. It can only choose whether the effect will be planned or unplanned. Even a laissez-faire policy suggests either that school authorities see no serious problem with relations as they have developed or that they do not feel intergroup relations to be a legitimate concern for an educational institution.

Because of pervasive residential segregation in our society, students frequently have their first relatively intimate and extended interracial experiences in schools. Whether racial hostility and stereotyping grow or diminish may be critically influenced by these first experiences. Though there still may be considerable argument about the desirability of close interracial ties, there is a growing awareness of the societal costs of intergroup hostility and stereotyping. It is clear that under many conditions interracial contact can lead to increased intergroup hostility. Unless interracial schools are carefully planned, they can exacerbate the very social tensions and hostilities that they initially hoped to diminish.

A number of recent trends suggest the importance of turning from a narrow concentration on the academic outcomes of schooling and focusing on other nonacademic outcomes such as intergroup relations. First, the long-assumed relationship of academic achievement and occupational success has been seriously questioned, and studies have instead cited the importance of personal characteristics such as interpersonal competence (White, 1968) or system awareness (Tomlinson and TenHouten, 1972). The ability to work effectively with out-group members is an increasingly important skill in a pluralistic society striving to overcome a long history of discrimination in education and employment.

Second, intense concern over youth-related social problems in the late 1960s revealed that drug use, dropping out of "the system," and ideologies sanctioning violence were more prevalent on the elite than on the average college campuses, underlining the fact that high academic achievement is not necessarily synonymous, from society's point of view, with desirable individual development.

Third, Jencks et al. (1972) as well as others have recently suggested that more attention should be paid to structuring schools so that they are reasonably pleasurable environments for students. This line of argument suggests that even if positive or negative interracial experiences do not cause generalized change in interracial behaviors and attitudes outside the school, positive interracial relationships within the school setting may be of value.

Finally, social relations among students in interracial schools can affect their academic achievement (Pettigrew, 1975; Katz, 1964; and U.S. Commission on Civil Rights, 1967). Katz (1964) argues that hostility or even indifference from whites is likely to distract black children from their work and create anxiety that interferes with efficient learning. He also argues that black children's academic motivation will improve if they are accepted by whites who are performing better than they.

Because of the importance of learning more about the complex ways in which schools can influence intergroup relations, we spent a large part of the years 1976–1978 intensively investigating the development of intergroup relations in a newly desegregated school and analyzing the ways in which the school's policies and practices appear to influence the development of relations between black and white students. One very specific aspect of our research—the often unintended and unnoticed effects of teacher's attitudes and classroom practices on intergroup relations—demonstrates that although most teachers are generally not aware of it, their everyday attitudes and decisions have a major influence on the relations that develop between black and white students.

The Research Site: Wexler Middle School [1]

Wexler Middle School is located in a large industrial northeastern city that will be called Waterford. The city contains a rich variety of ethnic groups. Just over 20% of the population is black. A large majority of the black population lives in heavily segregated and economically depressed neighborhoods.

Forty-two% of the students in Waterford's schools are black. However, over half the city's schools have heavily segregated enrollments (over 90% black or white). Waterford has been under some pressure from the state government to desegregate since the late 1960s. Nevertheless, the city has not come up with a plan acceptable to the state. Although the racially mixed board of education has strongly emphasized its commitment to desegregation, it has also consistently opposed

[1] The names of the school, all staff, administrators, and students are pseudonyms.

any desegregation plan involving large-scale busing of students. Given the residential patterns of the city, desegregation cannot likely be achieved without considerable busing.

In 1974 the board decided that Wexler, then in the planning stages, would have a racially balanced student body obtained through open enrollment of students graduating from 24 elementary schools in the northern third of the city. Although the opening of this school obviously could do relatively little to relieve the pervasive segregation in the city's school system, it was hoped that it could serve as a model of high-quality integrated education.

Integration or Desegregation

In the last decade, a number of researchers have stressed the importance of taking seriously Allport's (1954) argument that intergroup contact in and of itself is not an instant panacea for interracial stereotyping and hostility (Amir, 1976; Cohen, 1975; Schofield, 1978). Indeed, intergroup contact under some conditions appears to intensify rather than to mitigate racial tensions. Allport (1954) argued that intergroup contact is likely to improve intergroup relations only if the contact situation provides equal status for minority and majority group members and provides strong institutional support for positive relations. Allport also stresses the necessity of cooperative interaction aimed towards the achievement of shared goals. Building on Allport's work, Pettigrew has drawn a distinction between what he calls *merely desegregated* schools and *genuinely integrated* schools. Pettigrew, Useem, Normand, and Smith (1973:92–93) write: "Desegregation is achieved by simply ending segregation and bringing blacks and whites together; it implies nothing about the quality of interracial interaction." Integration, on the other hand, is achieved only when positive intergroup contact has been fostered.

CRITERIA FOR INTEGRATION

Equal-status Contact

Although Wexler has worked to provide equal formal status for blacks and whites, the disparities between blacks and whites in the society at large have undermined the school's efforts.

Typically, school desegregation involves sending black children to previously all-white schools. This immediately puts black children at a disadvantage because they are outsiders in the community surrounding the school and newcomers in an already established social system. Wexler is not located on traditionally white or black territory. It sits on a large tract of racially neutral land bounded by a factory with a racially mixed work force, a government building, a public park, and small stores that are on the periphery of one of the most desegregated shopping areas in the city. In addition, the school was interracial from the day it opened its doors in September 1975. Hence, children of one group were not confronted with having to make a place for themselves in an already functioning social system dominated by the other group and permeated with its attitudes and values.

Staffing at Wexler also fosters equal status between blacks and whites in the school. The administration and faculty are biracial. The faculty is approximately 25% black. It must be noted that the black faculty are not evenly distributed throughout the different types of teaching positions. For example, about 15% of the sixth-grade academic faculty are black compared with almost one-half of the faculty for certain vocationally oriented classes. This staffing pattern reflects the pool of teachers available within the school system. The school also has 10 teachers' aides, all of whom are black. Although clearly subordinate to the teachers, these aides do notably increase the number of blacks involved in the instructional process, since most of their time is spent tutoring students on an individual or small-group basis in the regular classrooms.

The nearly equal representation of blacks and whites in the student body also promotes equal status for black and white students. Moreover, at Wexler, the formal organization of students into teams and classroom groups generally avoids making distinctions among groups of students. For example, in the sixth grade students were assigned to teams essentially randomly with respect to their achievement test scores. Within each team, students were initially grouped into classes in a way that would guarantee moderate heterogeneity—that is, students with the lowest scores were grouped with students of average scores to form a class. Students with the next lowest scores were grouped with others who were slightly above average. Hence, the range of scores within each class was restricted somewhat, but there was no obvious "slow" or "fast" class.

Although Wexler does not use a tracking system, there are two highly segregated groups of students in the school. First, over 80% of the students in the eighth-grade scholars' program are white. Second,

159

nearly 90% of the children in educable mentally retarded (EMR) classes are black.

The racial composition of the scholars and EMR groups highlights a serious impediment to the achievement of the sort of truly integrated experience Pettigrew speaks of. Black children entering interracial schools are often noticeably behind their white peers in basic academic skills (Coleman, Campbell, Hobson, McPartland, and Mood, 1966). Tracking, a very common academic practice, is thus likely to lead to resegregation. The alternative—heterogeneous classroom groupings— virtually guarantees that, on the whole, black students will at least initially tend to do less well than white students. To the extent that informal peer status revolves around academic achievement, the average black student faces a challenge to his status that the average white student does not.

Cooperation toward Shared Goals

In addition to providing conditions that foster equal status contact between groups, Pettigrew argues that a truly integrated school must avoid fostering competition between blacks and whites as well as provide meaningful opportunities for individuals from both groups to strive cooperatively to meet shared goals. Wexler strives more than most public schools to avoid creating situations conducive to competition. The principal strongly discourages the use of academic honor rolls and is an ardent advocate of individualized instruction rather than more traditional procedures that foster comparison between students. Although there are some notable exceptions, a great many of Wexler's teachers share the principal's views, assigning amount and level of work according to the student's skill. Anyone who fulfills the weekly work contract gets an A.

A number of nonacademic activities have been instituted at Wexler precisely because they encourage children to get to know one another in a noncompetitive setting. In addition to sponsoring a very broad range of after-school activities, Wexler has two "directed activity" periods a week built into its curriculum. Students are offered a choice of activities ranging from decorating blue jeans to reading poetry and playing ping pong. Some of these groups are segregated, or nearly so, reflecting both prior friendship patterns and culturally influenced differences in interests between black and white students. Nevertheless, the clear majority of the groups show a significant amount of racial mixing (no more than 75% of the students are of one race). Although students work on individual projects in some of these clubs, the large majority have at least some activities in which cooperation toward shared goals is required. A notable example is the group that presented a production of the musical *Anything Goes* with leading roles filled by a white boy and a black girl.

Support for Positive Relations

The final criterion Pettigrew isolates as crucial to true integration is the support of the concerned authorities for positive intergroup relations. At Wexler, the school administrators strongly support positive intergroup relations. The usually mild-mannered principal said,

> *I have only seen one racial fight. . . . Two kids were fighting out in the hall during lunch time and the white kid ended up calling the black kid a nigger several times at the top of his lungs. He and I are the only two whites in the hall with about 50 black kids. . . . I got pretty violent with the kid. . . . I grabbed him by the throat. I had to do something very strong. I brought him in the office and talked to him. He was pretty ashamed about calling the kid a name. . . . He knew he was wrong for bringing names in. [February 1976]*

Teachers are virtually unanimous in agreeing that racially motivated negative behavior should not be tolerated. But their active commitment to fostering positive intergroup relations varies:

> *Being a teacher, I guess academics is more important [than personal or social development]. . . . I think we were told once that we shouldn't be concerned much in sixth grade with the academics of the children who aren't socialized yet. . . . It was presented to us that socialization, them getting along with each other, black, white, or from other areas, is the important skill development right now and the academic is secondary. . . . I think teachers say, "yea, yea, right, sure" and then they go and teach, try to teach [Mr. Don, February, 1976].*

THE "ACADEMICS FIRST" ORIENTATION

Although the school's principal, Mr. Reuben, often stresses the importance of the social outcomes of schooling, the administrators and the vast majority of the faculty in the sixth and seventh grades clearly see teaching academic skills as their overriding or even their only mission:

> *I really feel that the school is an academic setting. Quite frankly, I think that's what its primary function is. I think it is good for the*

children to interact socially . . . but . . . my emphasis is on academics. I believe a school should have an academic orientation. [Ms. Sharp, March 1977]

Teachers like Ms. Sharp believe that concentration on the traditional academic curriculum is the appropriate role for a teacher. Others emphasize academics because they view success in this area as important not only in itself but also for children's personal and social development:

I feel that many of the social problems that kids have are due to academic problems. . . . I think kids have to be taught study skills. I think they have to be taught essentially how to succeed. And once you have that foundation, then the social skills [will follow]. As he succeeds, the child's self-awareness becomes more positive. Socially he becomes happier and better. [August 1977]

Mr. James emphasizes the relationship of academic failure to discipline problems and sees academic improvement as a possible cure. Ms. Partridge sees emphasis on academic work as preventive medicine, too.

[We] keep them working constantly with the idea that if you keep them working that you will not have as many problems. [June 1977]

Because of the teachers' inclination to stress academic work, those teachers who want to foster more interracial interaction in the classroom are constantly pressured to focus almost exclusively on traditional, strictly academic materials. In addition, many teachers resist using nontraditional classroom procedures such as cooperative work groups because they are perceived as undermining academic progress for the sake of social goals.

Parents, especially white parents, react vociferously when they hear of practices that they believe do not promote their children's immediate academic achievement. For example, Ms. Partridge set up learning stations where students who had finished the regular math work could work on unusual and interesting extra-credit projects. The projects were clearly designed to promote social interaction on a relatively equal status basis between students with different achievement levels. However, some parents strongly objected to such projects. Ms. Partridge tells what happened:

I had several parents call Mr. Reuben and say, "What does this have to do with math?" They felt . . . that . . . an extra-credit assignment should deal with the basics or with getting a child prepared for algebra. Especially with the brighter students the parents were con-

cerned with getting them into the scholar's program. . . . There is a pressure there. . . . Last year I was really amazed that students who got a B+ were highly upset. They said, "My parents will kill me." [June 1977]

The children, too, are quick to react when they feel that their individual academic progress is being sacrificed to promote others' achievements or more general social goals. Students in one class resisted the teacher's efforts to set up project committees both because it made it difficult for them to sit with their friends and because some students felt it impeded their academic progress.

The tables are set up for committee work today. At one table sit David, Howard, and Keith, the only white males in the class today. Five of the six black males present are sitting together at another table. The sixth is sitting at a table with a black female. Two white girls and two black girls are seated at the only racially mixed table. Another table seats five black girls. . . . Mr. James announces a committee consisting of Eric (black), Fred (black), Howard (white), Stacey (black), and Leona (black). Howard says, "I don't get along with any of them. . . ." There are continued complaints from numerous children about the committee assignments. Mr. James says, "What's involved in a committee assignment? Am I asking you to hold hands? You don't even have to work together except to stand up and give a report." Howard and David object to being split up. Mr. James says, "You two have always been together." They answer, "And we've done good work too." Mr. James replies, "I'm not arguing with that. I need you separate this time." Now Mr. James has the committees go to their assigned tables. Howard sits with Sonya (black), Dave (white), Ted (black), and Lilian (black). Ted says sharply, "Mr. James, get him out of here. He doesn't belong here." Howard replies to Ted, "I know where I belong." Mr. James asks Howard to move. He objects. Mr. James says, "Howard, are you telling me you can only work with one person [referring to Dave]? I'm going to have to talk to your parents about this." As they argue Howard has moved so he's standing by the table where Lauri (white) now sits alone. Howard says, "You said we could work alone. Can't I work alone right here?" Dave grins at Lilian. He seems to be getting along quite well without Howard. Soon, however, he moves over with Howard, who finally sits down at Lauri's table. When class is dismissed, Howard is the last one out. He appears to have been talking with Mr. James about the committee assignments. As he leaves he says in a disgruntled tone, "I come here for my own education, not for somebody's else's." [May 1977]

It is not surprising that teachers heavily emphasize academics, given their personal inclination and the pressures from students, parents, school, and structural arrangements within the school. However, the extent of this emphasis is a bit surprising. In fact, teachers not infrequently break school rules or ignore the spirit if not the letter of school policies in their attempts to do all they can to promote the students' academic advancement. For example, in spite of Mr. Reuben's decision to eliminate academic honor rolls, some teams created team honor rolls and some teachers created classroom honor rolls. A great many teachers also went against the school policy of encouraging racially and academically heterogeneous classes by making informal changes in class composition to achieve greater homogeneity in academic achievement levels within given classes. These changes resulted in a marked increase in racial homogeneity within classes. For example, one group of teachers rearranged their initially very mixed classes into five new groups. The two "top" classes consisted of 64 children, 11 of whom were black. The "bottom" class of 18 had only 2 white students in it.

THE NATURAL PROGRESSION ASSUMPTION

The foregoing was not meant to suggest that teachers in any way actively attempt to subvert the integrationist goals of the principal. Rather, other considerations, especially academic considerations, are so vitally important in their thinking that other goals tend to be almost completely ignored. Also, most of the teachers believe that mere contact in and of itself will bring about improved intergroup relations—the natural progression assumption. Hence, they see little need to structure their classes in a way specifically designed to promote positive relations. Ms. Nobel, a white math teacher, states this point of view clearly:

> I don't know if you can do anything to make [students get together]. . . . I don't think it's something you can force. . . . I think it will come in due time. . . . Nobody can be forced to go with . . . if they are they will be negative. . . . So I think forcing them into a situation is not good. I think it has to be free and I've already seen some signs that the blacks and whites have gotten together . . . they are doing things together on their own now. They didn't know each other in the beginning of the school year. So, that was done very naturally. . . . There isn't going to be a race problem. [March 1976]

Two of the three teachers who disagree at all with the majority view are black women, Ms. Ireland and Ms. Partridge.

> Interviewer: Do you think that relations between black and white kids naturally become more positive as they spend time together or do specific things have to be done to encourage them . . . ?
>
> Ms. Partridge: I think they do need some planning. Some of these things will normally happen, but if more things were planned to bring the races closer I think we'd get there quicker, because with some of the students you'll never even get them together unless things are planned to force them together. [June 1977]

In addition to making the assumption of natural progression, many teachers hesitate to try actively to encourage more intergroup interaction. A number of teachers argue that strenuous efforts to promote new friendships generally disrupt old friendships and that any really vigorous efforts to promote intergroup interaction will backfire. Students, teachers think, demand autonomy in their choice of seating and working partners, an opinion born out by Mr. James's attempt to arrange seating according to committee assignment.

The few teachers who consciously try to increase intergroup interaction think that they must use subtle methods that will not create strong psychological resistance or outright revolt.

> Mr. Little: I don't think you can push kids to socialize [when] they don't want to. I think it is going to cause problems. . . . I try to do it in different ways, but I don't think the kids know it is happening. I think you can pull some tricks on them. . . . It is just basically a matter of moving tables around. [April 1976]

Although most teachers strongly believe that increasingly positive relations will evolve between black and white students, they see that the academic gap between the average white and the average black child poses a major impediment to this process. Indeed, when asked about it, most teachers qualify their initial ideas on natural progression, taking the position that positive relations will develop naturally between black and white children from similar backgrounds and with similar personalities or levels of academic performance. This sort of natural progression suggests a very different overall outcome of interracial schooling than a natural progression that operates in spite of

165

class and school performance barriers. Interestingly, a number of teachers seem to think it inappropriate for them to try to foster strong positive relations between children who are very different.

> Ms. Wire: *I don't like the idea of having a power to influence people to the point where they would become friends. . . . I mean, [it's OK to] point out people who have common interests or similar personalities. . . . But I really . . . just wouldn't want to be the person to fix up a friendship. . . . You could say, "You collect stamps and so and so does, too," or something like that. But beyond that I wouldn't feel comfortable. [March 1976]*

Students, in contrast, do not feel that time is sure to lead to increasingly positive relations between black and white students. Twenty randomly selected students were interviewed in the fall of 1975 shortly after they enrolled in Wexler and again in June 1977 as they finished seventh grade. Students' responses to the question, "How well do kids get along with each other at Wexler compared to your old school?" did not change significantly between October 1975 and May 1977. In addition, there was no statistically significant change in students' responses to the question, "How friendly are kids here at Wexler compared to your old school?" At the end of their second year at Wexler, the 20 seventh-grade students on our panel were asked whether they thought relations between blacks and whites were any different their second year at Wexler than in their first. The majority saw no change. The comments of a black male, Kenny, are typical.

> Interviewer: *Do you think that the black and white kids get along worse this year than last, or better, or about the same?*
> Kenny: *About the same . . . they get along the same 'cause they weren't really enemies last year and they're not really enemies this year. [May 1977]*

THE COLORBLIND PERSPECTIVE

Wexler's faculty tend to subscribe to what Rist (1974) has called a "colorblind" view of interracial schooling. This perspective sees interracial schooling as an opportunity for class assimilation. The purpose of schooling as seen from this perspective is to give all children a fair chance to learn the skills necessary for success in a basically middle-class society. Black staff members at Wexler generally appear to share this view with their white colleagues, as the following excerpt from an interview with Ms. Kent, sixth-grade dean (a black woman), shows.

> *I really don't address myself to group differences when I am dealing with youngsters. . . . I try to treat youngsters, I don't care who they are, as youngsters and not as black, white, green, or yellow. . . . Many of the black youngsters who have difficulty are the ones who . . . have come from communities where they had to put up certain defenses, and these defenses are the antithesis of the normal situation . . . they find in school. It is therefore [difficult] getting them to become aware that they have to follow these rules because [they] are here . . . not over there in their community. . . . I think that many of the youngsters [from the] larger community have a more normal set of values that people generally want to see, and therefore do not have [as] much difficulty in coping with their school situation as do our black youngsters. . . .*
>
> *[The black children] do have difficulty in adjusting because they are just not used to it. Until we can adjustively counsel them into the right types of behavior. . . . I think we're going to continue to have these types of problems. . . . [April 1976]*

From the colorblind perspective it is unfair or at least inappropriate to bring up race, since race is essentially irrelevant to one's needs and the opportunities that should be provided. Even taking note of race is seen as an indication of possible prejudice.

> *When I was arranging the student interviews I mentioned to Mr. Little that I thought there was only one white girl in one of his classes. I asked if I was right about this and he said, "Well, just a minute. Let me check." After looking through the class roster in his roll book he said, "You know, you're right. I never noticed that . . . I guess that's a good thing." [November 1976]*

The teachers' tendency to see race as a completely irrelevant aspect of an individual is reinforced by their perception that most children share this viewpoint. Thus, teachers argue, bringing up race or considering it will only create problems by raising a potentially volatile issue that is not otherwise a real factor.

> Ms. Monroe: *You know, I hear the things the students usually fight about. As I said before, it's stupid things like someone taking a pencil. It's not because [the other person] is black or white. . . . At this age level . . . I don't think it's black or white.*

167

> Interviewer: *You really don't see that as a factor . . . in their relation-*
> *ships?*
> Ms. Monroe: No. [*February 1977*]

Although the students rarely make overt reference to race in class-room situations, evidence does suggest that it is a factor in their percep-tions of and behavior toward one another:

> *Mr. James explained to me a regrouping of classes in his team that*
> *made them more academically homogeneous. . . . He said that the*
> *white kids in the slowest group complained. He said that a white girl*
> *was the ringleader but that a number of white boys went along with*
> *her. He went on to say that the white students were so upset that the*
> *teachers had to have a meeting with them. The teachers explained that*
> *students were grouped by achievement levels. He said after the ex-*
> *planation some of the white kids said everything was OK. But Nicki*
> *was very upset. . . . Her father came in and talked with Mr. Reuben,*
> *who said that a change would be made in the black–white ratio in the*
> *class. . . . [Later] Howard, a white male, leaned over to me and said,*
> *"You know, it just wasn't fair the way they set up this class. There are*
> *16 black kids and only 9 white kids. I can't learn in here." I said, "Why*
> *is that?" Howard replied, "They copy and they pick on you. It just*
> *isn't fair. . . ." [October 1976].*

The seating patterns in the school cafeteria suggest that race has a marked impact on students' interaction patterns. Systematic mapping of seating patterns showed that students clearly tend to sit next to stu-dents of their own race. On a typical day at the end of the school's second year of operation, 119 whites and 90 black students attended the seventh-grade lunch period. Of these more than 200 children, only 6 sat next to someone of the other race. Responses to queries about the cafeteria seating patterns show how important race is to the students at Wexler.

> Interviewer: *I have noticed . . . that very often white kids sit with*
> *white kids and black kids sit with black kids. Why do*
> *you think that is?*
> Mary (white): *'Cause the white kids have white friends and the black*
> *kids have black friends. . . . I don't think integration is*
> *working. . . . Blacks still associate with blacks and*
> *whites still associate with whites. . . .*
> Interviewer: *Can you think of any white kids that have quite a few*
> *black friends or of any black kids who have quite a few*
> *white friends?*
> Mary: *Not really.* [*June 1976*]

Factors Affecting the Development of Intergroup Relations in the Classroom

It is clear that a very large number of factors come into play in the development of intergroup relations (Cook, 1969). Five variables are discussed here which seem to have a major impact on the development of intergroup relations and are at least to some extent affected by the specific policies and practices adopted by teachers.

EQUAL STATUS WITHIN THE CONTACT SITUATION

Allport's original theory (1954), as discussed earlier, suggests that equal formal status within the contact situation should in and of itself be conducive to improved intergroup relations. According to this line of argument, equal status is achieved when members of all groups have equal access to basic formal roles, a position supported by recent research (Amir, 1969, 1976). Webster (1961) stated that Allport's criterion is met when blacks and whites are desegregated and both assume the role of student at the same school. But he says nothing about the racial composition of the school's staff or about internal arrangements such as tracking, which clearly affect students' status. On the other hand, Pettigrew (1975) goes much further than Webster's contact theory by emphasizing that all sources must have equal access to both formal and informal status to meet the equal-status criterion.

St. John (1975), Cohen (1975), and Armor (1972) have gone a step beyond Pettigrew, stating that it is difficult to achieve equal status when students bring with them very different backgrounds. After studying interaction between black and white students, Cohen (1975:294) writes:

> The inference may be drawn that even though blacks and whites might be brought together in a desegregated school in an "equal status" manner, it is still quite possible for the racial difference to act as a strong status differential triggering expectations for whites to do better. . . . If this occurs in the school situation, then the racial stereotypes that contribute to these expectations are only reinforced and confirmed by the interracial interaction.

Thus, the characteristics that the group members bring with them influence the development of informal status and consequent intergroup relations. The question of whether equal formal status will indeed

169

bring about improved relations when the personal status of the individuals involved is very different has not been conclusively answered.

Wexler School has come very close to meeting the requirement that blacks and whites have equal access to the formal roles of student and teacher. In addition, it has made real efforts to racially balance many other more informal roles in the school's social structure. It threatened, for example, to withdraw funding for a summer media program in order to persuade the program's faculty adviser to thoroughly integrate the group. However, the disparity in previous education and in socioeconomic status between whites and blacks creates considerable strain and leads to unequal status between the two groups. The differences in academic performance between blacks and whites illustrate the problem of maintaining equal formal status for black and white children.

There is no question that, for whatever reason, white children at Wexler academically outperform black children. Over 80% of the scholars' group in the eighth grade is white, whereas over 80% of the nonscholars' group is black, even though blacks are admitted to the program with slightly lower test scores than whites. On one fairly typical math test in a class we routinely observed, about 50% of the white students received As, compared with about 7% of the blacks. Similarly, year-end academic honors went disproportionately to whites. For example, 60 of the 68 sixth-grade children who received awards for maintaining an A average were white.

The effect of the disparity in academic performance on the status of blacks and whites in the school was felt when Wexler agreed to participate in a city-wide academic quiz program. Each school was to select a team to compete in publicly televised matches. Although Wexler's team was chosen from the seventh grade, the various homerooms in the other grades competed against one another in an in-school tournament. These competitions were shown on the school's closed-circuit TV. Observation notes show how academic differences separate white and black children.

> There were approximately 48 children in the TV studio, not counting the competitors. Of these, 19 were black. Six other black children who wanted to come in were not allowed to because they arrived after the program was on the air.
> The questions asked involved a wide range of general information, current events, mathematics, and recent history. Typical questions were, "Who is the lieutenant governor of our state?" "What country was host when Jesse Owens won several gold medals in the Olympics?"

"Who is president of the Watertown Teacher's Union?" and "What is the name of the actor who plays Fonzie on TV?" The game consisted of 20 questions. A child could signify willingness to answer by raising a hand. Two or three children generally thought they knew the answer to a given question. The black child raised her hand only once during the entire session. Two others on her team also wanted to answer. The team captain called on the black girl, who answered correctly.

The next round was played between Ms. Coal's team and Mr. Jackson's team. Both teams had five white members and one black member. Neither of the black males, Charles and Greg, raised his hand to answer a question until the eighth question, which was about a local sports announcer. The first boy, Charles, answered incorrectly, but the second's answer was right. Charles raised his hand and answered correctly two later questions. Greg didn't volunteer again. [March 1976]

Wexler's team for the publicly televised quiz competition was all white. It performed extremely well, losing a close match in the final round. An article in a Waterford Board of Education newspaper stated "any challenge to the Wexler 'Think Tank' [team] will have a difficult time if past performance means anything [1977:3]." Many of Wexler's students and faculty were very excited when their team reached the final round of the all-city competition. The fact that the team was all white, however, clearly affected the response of some of the black students. For example, one black girl refused to be quiet during a replay of the match on the school's closed-circuit TV. She muttered, "That's not Wexler School . . . might as well call it White School." At Wexler, then, in almost any situation in which formal or informal roles are assigned on the basis of academic performance, whites come out ahead.

The school does try to reduce the visibility of group differences in academic achievement. As noted previously, the principal discouraged academic honor rolls; similarly, to increase black participation in year-end honors ceremonies, awards were given for the greatest improvement as well as for the highest averages. All six improvement awards went to blacks. However, the unequal performance levels that students bring with them clearly affect the development of intergroup relations. In particular, they appear to have the strong potential for reinforcing stereotypes about racial differences in intelligence and creating resentment and hostility between black and white children. Black students often perceive the highest-achieving white students' performance as an arrogant display, a deliberate flaunting of knowledge that downgrades other class members.

Ms. Fowler tells the story of three black girls who frightened a smaller white girl in the bathroom by saying that she looked weak and giving her a light push. The black girl at first said that she had just been playing, but upon further questioning said of the white girl: "Well, I just don't like her attitude." Fowler asked, "Her attitude about what?" The black girl said, "Her attitude in class. She knows all the answers. She gets them right all the time." [October 1976]

Mr. James asks the class a question, and Howard (white) as usual has the answer. But Mr. James says, "Howard, you don't have to answer unless I have trouble getting an answer from other people. You don't have to keep putting your hand up." Steven, a black male, makes an apparently derogatory comment in a low voice. . . . Mr. James says to Steven, "Let him [Howard] be; he's done his work. You could be in the same position yourself." . . . Steven says, "I don't know everything." Mr. James responds, "Howard doesn't know everything either." Steven replies, "He thinks he does." [January 1977]

Whites observing the academic performance differentials often tend to conclude that blacks lack either intelligence or interest in scholastic achievement.

Occasionally students who are strong academically will offer to help others. This does not always have a positive effect on relations between the students involved. Ms. Short explains:

Ms. Short: A few [of the brightest white children] are exceptionally kind. . . . I mean that in the true sense of being kind. . . . They are understanding and oftentimes they will say, "I'm done with my work. Would you mind if I go over and help him?" That's never done with a sense of superiority or ridicule or anything. . . .

Interviewer: How do the kids who are offered help receive it?

Ms. Short: Sometimes they are receptive to it. Some children will not respond. . . . They are angry and very hostile and resentful. . . . They don't like people seeing the level of work they are doing. . . . [March 1976]

No matter what the motivation of the helper, it is easy to see why the child who is offered such help might feel anger or shame. Taking help from a peer is not like getting help from a teacher, whose formal role is that of helper and whose superiority in the field is widely acknowledged. However, offers of assistance from peers expose the level of one's present work to a peer and set up an imbalance that in a sense puts the person who has accepted that help under some obligation to

172

his mentor. Exchange theory suggests that such imbalanced relationships are often unstable as well as uncomfortable for the person who has received assistance, especially if there is little hope of his or her being able to pay for it (Blau, 1955; Homans, 1961).

It is clear, then, that personal characteristics that confirm traditional stereotypes and create unequal status relationships constitute a real barrier to positive intergroup relations. On the other hand, in spite of the differences between blacks and whites at Wexler in socioeconomic status and academic achievement, some improvement in intergroup relations occurred. Interviews with students and data on seating patterns in the school cafeteria indicate the improvement (Schofield and Sagar, 1977). However, intergroup attitudes and behavior are complex. It is possible that though certain types of interracial contact confirm some stereotypes, that very contact also leads to less avoidance behavior. A white child might conclude from experiences at Wexler that blacks are not as intelligent as whites but that his initial avoidance reaction on the playground was unwarranted, since the black students are as much fun to play with as white children.

In summary, at Wexler children do react strongly to the lack of equal formal status when it occurs. It is also clear that unequal personal characteristics make it hard for the school to maintain equal status between the children and cause considerable strain in relations between blacks and whites. Hence, regardless of whether equal personal status is actually a requirement for improved intergroup relations, it would seem to facilitate such relations. Where two groups bring unequal characteristics, it seems crucial not to transform these personal differences into differences that are reflected in formal status and to minimize the salience of such differences.

COOPERATION TO ATTAIN MUTUALLY DESIRED GOALS

Research on intergroup relations shows again and again the importance of cooperative dependence in reaching shared goals in improving intergroup relations (Amir, 1969; 1976; Ashmore, 1970; Johnson and Johnson, 1974; Sherif, Harvey, White, Hood, and Sherif, 1961; Slavin, 1978). Numerous experimental studies suggest that carefully structured cooperative work groups in interracial schools often improve intergroup relations even if they are used during only a small part of the school day (Aronson, Blaney, Sikes, Stephan, and Snapp,

1975; DeVries and Edwards, 1974; Weigel, Wiser, and Cook, 1975).
Also, there is evidence that competition between groups can lead to
stereotyping and hostility (Sherif *et al.*, 1961).

At Wexler students appear to enter with a strongly individualistic
and competitive orientation. Although the teachers generally agree that
the competitive orientation is strongest in the best students, the average and below-average students also seem very concerned with how
their performance stacks up against that of others. The academics-first
orientation that puts tremendous emphasis on conventional academic
goals helps to make academic achievement extremely salient in interpersonal evaluation even for students who are not at the top of their
class. The following interactions, illustrating attempts to clarify the
academic pecking order, all occurred in Mr. Cousin's seventh-grade
class, which he had divided into three homogeneous academic groups,
with Group C being the slowest:

> *Mr. Cousins stops by Harry's (black) chair and compliments him
> on his work: "Harry, that's very good. Very soon now I think I'll have
> to move you from Group C into Group B. Your work is coming along
> very well. I'm pleased." . . . Harry smiles and Mr. Cousins grins at the
> kids. Jimmy (black) and Denny (black), who are in Group B, hear this
> and are now looking in the direction of the boys and Mr. Cousins; they
> laugh. "Harry in our group!" says Jimmy, and he throws his head back
> and laughs again. His laughter indicates that he doesn't really seem to
> believe that Harry is capable of doing higher-level work. [February
> 1977]*

A couple of months later, Denny has to defend his own academic
status to a skeptical white male who has just been transferred into
this class:

> *Denny, a black male, and Bill, the white male who has been
> moved in front of him . . . are debating Denny's academic achieve-
> ments (Bill is a new addition to the class). Denny says, "I am, too."
> Scott, a white male, is walking back to his chair now and Denny says,
> "Hey, Scott, Scott; I'm on the honor roll, right?" Scott nods his head
> yes. Denny says, "See, you can look at any of my papers and see how
> well I do." [April 1977]*

The jostling and jockeying are apparent at the lower end of the academic distribution as well. Even Harry, still in Group C, finds someone
to downgrade:

*Richard (the only white in Group C), Harry, and Mr. Cousins
are talking about grades. Richard says, "Doesn't A mean you're
smart?" Harry says, "You'll never get an A; you're dumb." Richard
says, "Mr. Cousins, am I dumb?" Mr. Cousins says, "No, I don't
think so; but you could do better if you worked harder." Mr. Cousins
turns away from the boys, and Harry says to Richard, "You're a dumb
bum." [March, 1977]*

The students' emphasis on competition is evidenced in their responses to the question, "How often do students compare the grades
they get on tests or report cards?" On a 21-point continuum from -10
(never) to $+10$ (all of the time), the mean for the 20 randomly
selected students who were interviewed was 6.4 (between $+5$ [most of
the time] and $+10$ [all of the time]). No significant differences were
found between the responses of blacks and whites. Teachers, too, can
foster competition, even without realizing it.

Interviewer: How important is competition as a motivation for
students? When do you like to use it and when
wouldn't you?

Ms. Wire (white): Sometimes it gets obnoxious. Some of the better
students use it as a social popularity kind of thing.
. . . So, I don't like to play up the competition. I
feel that in too many cases, it is more detrimental
than it is beneficial. The students that are able
seem to have natural competition . . . or they have
gotten it from . . . their parents or one of the
schools they were in. They just seem to have a
drive to compete. But it works against the . . .
slower students.

Interviewer: Do you see more comparison of grades among girls
or boys? Is there any difference?

Ms. Wire: No. . . . Everybody does it. . . . Competition is all
over.

Interviewer: Would you say competition is the same for blacks
and whites or do you see more comparing in one
group or the other?

Ms. Wire: No. It is the same. . . . The happiest day is when I
publicly read the list of grades. They just love it.
They want to know what everybody did. . . .

Interviewer: Do you read them once a marking period, or . . .

Ms. Wire: No, like if I'm grading a test. . . . I read off the

> grades. . . . *They don't want to do something un-*
> *less there's going to be a grade.*
> Interviewer: *Is that the same for poor students as well as the*
> *good ones?*
> Ms. Wire: *Yes. . . . They are very conscious of success.*
> Interviewer: *Well now, the kids who got a D or an E on to-*
> *day's test . . .*
> Ms. Wire: *I wouldn't read that out. . . . I don't read out D's*
> *and E's. . . . I read out a list of grades and say,*
> *"People whose names I didn't call out know what*
> *they got." That way they aren't identified.* [March
> 1976]

It is unlikely that students oriented toward academic competition will cooperate with others whom they do not know unless the teachers structure the classroom situation so that such cooperation is essential. Even under these circumstances students are likely to object if they feel that they are learning less than they might otherwise, as evidenced earlier.

ACQUAINTANCE POTENTIAL OF THE SITUATION

Physical Proximity

Acquaintance potential, argues Cook (1969), is likely to have an important impact on the outcome of contact between two groups. He defines acquaintance potential as "the extent to which the situation provides opportunities for getting to know the other race as individuals [p. 211]." Several factors play a vital role in influencing the acquaintance potential of a particular situation. First is physical proximity. Unless students from two previously unacquainted and even hostile groups are physically close to one another, it seems unlikely that they will have much opportunity to get to know one another. Although proximity in and of itself does not ensure development of positive intergroup relations, it does seem to increase greatly the acquaintance potential of a situation.

Unfortunately, the types of behaviors that are most accessible to children who are physically quite distant in the classroom are the very behaviors that are most likely to cause problems in black–white relations. First, gross motor behaviors and loud talk (hitting, getting out of seat, showing off) are very noticeable, but more normative behavior is not so likely to gain attention. Also, these noticeable behaviors will be seen as discrete acts divorced from any context that could make them more intelligible. From a distance it is more difficult to differentiate out-group members as individuals. Hence, negative behaviors are likely to be associated with the group in general, if only because the particular individual cannot be identified or remembered. Second, disputes with the teacher or disciplinary activity by the teacher are also highly visible. Third, in most classrooms instruction is structured, at least part of the time, so that children are required to monitor the academic performance of other children, including those at considerable distance from themselves. For example, many teachers frequently pose a question and they call on a particular student, expecting that the rest of the class will listen to the response and learn from it. Since the teacher generally indicates clearly whether the student's response was correct, the children gain a clear impression of one another's academic capabilities without direct interaction.

Our observations suggest that at Wexler group differences in behavior occur in all three of the above areas. First, black children in Wexler's classrooms appear somewhat more likely than whites to engage in dramatic or very obvious sorts of motor behavior. For example, coding of field notes from a year's observation in six classes suggested a consistent pattern—black boys engaged in over twice as much physical play, such as boxing, in the classrooms as did white boys. Such play may lead to conclusions on the part of white children that blacks are aggressive, uninterested in academics, or both.

Similarly, the fact that over 80% of the children suspended are black suggests that black children are much more likely to experience serious disciplinary action in classrooms than are whites. A randomly selected sample of black and white students interviewed in their second year at Wexler showed clear awareness of the disparity in suspension rates for whites and blacks. Black students estimated that 72% of those suspended were blacks, whereas whites thought 62% were black. Although it is possible if not likely that some of the higher suspension rate for blacks is a reflection of teachers' racial attitudes, the important point for this analysis is that, for whatever reason, black children are much more likely to be disciplined for their behavior than white children. Hence, they are more frequently publicly cast in the role of deviant.

Close physical proximity can correct at least some of the problems inherent in remote observation of out-group members. The mundane behaviors which would hardly attract attention from across a room are continually apparent from close up and very likely will serve to humanize the impression gained of the person. Periods of quiet study, nonverbal indications of affect, and seemingly unremarkable comments can all be noticed. Thus, the more dramatic behaviors and statements can all be seen as part of a continuing, and perhaps therefore more intelligible, stream of behavior. Furthermore, the near observer is in a better position to note the stimuli to which the target person is responding. This does not, of course, guarantee that the outgroup person will be liked or the behavior approved of, but it does reduce the likelihood of misunderstanding and misinterpretation.

Sustained and Varied Contact

Two other factors that appear strongly to influence the acquaintance potential of a situation are the length and variety of the contact. Contact that is sustained and that persists in varied situations can provide the sort of information one needs in making judgments about what others are like. Kelley (1972) argues that individuals take three types of information into account when determining whether a behavior in question is due to a person's individual traits and tendencies or whether the behavior is primarily determined by the situation in which the person finds himself. Kelley labels these three factors as consensus, consistency, and distinctiveness. Consensus refers to the extent to which other persons act in the same way as the individual in question. Consistency refers to the extent to which the individual acts in the same manner on other occasions similar to the one observed, and distinctiveness refers to the extent to which the individual's behavior varies across different types of situations. As is apparent from the above definition, one can make judgments about consensus from a very fleeting interaction, since the behavior of the individual in that interaction is compared with the behaviors of others in similar circumstances. However, judgments about consistency and distinctiveness are quite different, since they depend on comparing the individuals' behavior at one time with their behavior in similar situations at other times or in a wide variety of situations. Thus, unless contact between blacks and whites in an interracial school is sustained, the children have little information on the consistency or distinctiveness of the behavior in question.

Interactions that are not sustained yield relatively little information for making judgments about the consistency and distinctiveness of the behavior; thus, the conclusions drawn from information about consensus become very important. Recall that Kelley says that information on consensus is gained by comparing the behavior of a particular individual with the behavior of others. He argues that if the behavior appears different from that of others, it is likely to be interpreted as due to internal causes, the individual's personality. However, if the behavior is seen as similar to that of others it is likely to be seen as a result of situational forces. Although Kelley's theory does not specify precisely with whom the individual being judged will be compared, it seems reasonable that children will compare the individuals with others in their own reference groups. Given the marked racial isolation in most interracial schools, reference groups are likely to be own-race groups. The out-group member's behavior is likely to be compared with that of in-group members. Hence, the use of consensus information to interpret behaviors in encounters that are not sustained can only exacerbate perceived group differences, because similarities in behavior are seen as caused by situational forces, whereas differences are seen as due to personality factors.

Opportunity for Actual Interaction

A third factor in the contact situation that seems crucial to the situation's acquaintance potential is the extent to which black and white students actually have the opportunity to interact with one another as opposed to just observing one another. Without interacting, people may remain what Milgram (1977) has labeled "familiar strangers"—people who recognize one another because of repeated occasions of physical proximity but who have little real idea of what the other persons are like.

Direct interaction is likely to lead to much fuller and more accurate learning about members of the other group than is mere observation. The children's behavior toward one another can be conceptualized as a sort of experiment, permitting them to test other students to see how they respond to particular events. Hence the children are able to explore questions that puzzle them and to fill in gaps that they recognize in their knowledge of one another. Furthermore, they are not limited to information that can be gained through visual and aural channels, as illustrated in the following example:

> *Tanya (black) runs her comb once through Karen's (white) short, straight hair. Then Tanya combs Lisa's (white) hair, which is longer and curly. She combs it with repeated strokes, pats it, feels it.*

179

Lisa doesn't seem to mind. Then Tanya pats Karen's hair and asks: "How do you get it like that?" Tanya's own hair is very long and fairly straight, tied into two slightly wavy pony tails, one at each side of her face. [February 1977]

Classroom Practices and Intergroup Learning

Decisions the teachers make about classroom practices also influence intergroup learning and affect the context in which interracial contact occurs. The analysis offered below is perhaps most appropriately interpreted as a set of hypotheses derived from intensive observation of a wide variety of classrooms.

SEATING POLICY

Students at Wexler are divided into classes of about 30 children. Because of the school's strong emphasis on providing an integrated experience, classes are generally roughly half black and half white. Students attend all academic classes with essentially the same group of children.

When asked to discuss why they used their particular seating policy, teachers almost without exception mentioned academic and/or classroom management considerations. Academic considerations were mentioned most frequently, as the academics-first orientation would suggest. Not surprisingly, given the colorblind perspective and the natural progression assumption, only one of the nearly 15 teachers interviewed mentioned racial mixing as a consideration. Ms. Wire's reasons for choosing her seating policy are fairly typical, although she, unlike many of her colleagues, eschews in-class ability groups.

> *Interviewer: How did you assign [students] to seats?*
> *Ms. Wire (white): Alphabetical. . . . So I could put a name to a face. . . . I had every name memorized.*
> *Interviewer: Have you ever used ability grouping?*
> *Ms. Wire: No . . . because if all the haves are on one side and the have nots are on the other, they aren't going to be able to share anything. So [when I group] I always group so that there are a variety of abilities in a group, so if one person doesn't have the ability . . . sharing information isn't cheating. Pure learning is very important. There were times when I couldn't*

> *get something across but a student could . . . explain it in one sentence.* [March 1976]

The seating policies used by Wexler teachers can be divided into two basic types—voluntary and assigned. Roughly one-third of the teachers observed at Wexler choose a voluntary policy and let students sit wherever they desire. Teachers adopting this course often feel that they have no seating policy, yet we suggest there are very significant and predictable social learning implications in such a choice. Teachers who assign seats do so according to a variety of criteria, as will be discussed later. Use of different criteria not surprisingly leads to very different seating patterns.

When students are completely free to pick their own seats, they generally choose to sit in quite clear-cut race and sex clusters. The strength of this tendency is shown in the following field notes.

> *There are nine tables in this science class. Most of the tables have three students around them. A few have two students, and there is one table occupied by a lone black girl, Thelma. Not a single table is racially mixed. Only two tables, both of white children, are sexually mixed. Three of the five black tables are right next to one another.* [September 1975]

> *Today, Terri, a black girl, is sitting with three white girls. All the other children at tables are sitting in racially segregated groups, although one white boy in an individual chair with its own writing arm is much nearer the black girls than the other white boys.* [November 1976]

Teachers who generally let students sit where they choose do frequently attempt to make temporary or permanent changes in voluntary patterns when they believe that it will improve behavior. However, since this involves breaking up friendship groups, such efforts are strongly resisted by the students.

> *Mr. Singer said that Mr. Count had changed the seating pattern in his class because there was too much noise and too much problem behavior. He had changed the seating pattern so that he separated friendship groups. Since the friendship groups are mainly within racial groups, the new seating pattern was much more integrated than the old. The students were unhappy with the new seating pattern and decided to boycott the class. They came to it, but wouldn't answer when Mr. Count would ask a question and call on someone. There was a lot of nudging, elbowing, and giggling. The child would stall and in most*

> *cases say that he didn't know the answer. . . . Mr. Count . . . asked the*
> *students what was going on and they told him that they wanted to sit*
> *in their old seats. He ended by coming to a behavior contract with the*
> *students—saying that they could sit back in their old seats, as long as*
> *they kept the noise and the problem behavior down. The students*
> *agreed to that and were allowed to go back to their old seats. [May*
> *1976]*

Similarly, students who normally get to choose their seating partners resist even temporary changes for academic purposes, as illustrated earlier in Mr. James's class. Hence teachers who initially allow voluntary seating often have difficulty gaining control over seating patterns later.

Given the clear tendency of children to sit in racially homogeneous groups, a voluntary seating policy results in heavily segregated classes that resist later change. The segregation ensures that black and white students are not physically very close to one another. Similarly, it makes prolonged and varied interracial contact most unlikely. Voluntary seating also renders cooperation between black and white children unlikely, since when cooperation does occur it is generally with students who are physically close together in the classroom. In summary, then, voluntary seating does not seem conducive to improvement in intergroup relations. It lets children avoid one another. Yet they are nonetheless in sufficient contact that group differences are apparent in academic performance as well as in unacceptable classroom behavior.

Teachers who assign seats, either in homogeneous or heterogeneous groupings, generally do so on the basis of academic achievement. A fairly large number of teachers believe that homogeneous grouping is conducive to academic achievement because it allows teachers to address one group at a time at precisely the right academic level. The small number of teachers who use heterogeneous groupings argue that more learning will occur because the brightest children will learn in any event and the progress of the slower children can be facilitated by assistance from their faster peers.

From the standpoint of intergroup learning, assignment to academically homogeneous groups is probably the least desirable seating policy. This policy was discouraged by Wexler's administration because it tended to result in racially identifiable groups, labeled either explicitly or implicitly as "fast" (white) and "slow" (black). One of the most extreme examples occurred in the class of a black teacher, Mr. Hue, who divided his classes into a fast group, Group 1, and a slow group, Group 2. In the class we observed, Group 1 was entirely white and Group 2 was entirely black, with the exception of one white boy.

> *Interviewer: You mentioned that when you group by ability level you*
> *get mainly whites in your upper group. I know that's the*
> *way it works out in the one class I have observed. . . .*
> *Do you have . . . blacks . . . in the upper groups in*
> *some of your other classes?*
> *Mr. Hue: Yes, I believe I have one. [March 1976]*

Mr. Hue's stated motive for grouping was to facilitate academic instruction, but the social result was enforced racial segregation that prevented black and white children from interacting in any extended way.

> *Class hasn't started yet and Steve, a black male who is in Group*
> *2, is standing near Sally, a white girl in Group 1. He has a sweatshirt*
> *draped over his shoulders and a pick in his hair. Mr. Hue says to Steve,*
> *"I'm going to tell you something. I don't want to see you over here*
> *again." Steve walks back into the Group 2 area. As soon as Mr. Hue*
> *turns his back, Steve returns to Sally. They struggle, slapping at each*
> *other. Kitty, a white friend of Sally's, calls out, "Mr. Hue." The black*
> *teacher says, "Steve, get back over here." Steve returns to the Group 2*
> *area, saying, "She's got my pencil." The aide says, "We'll get another*
> *one." [April 1976]*

In fact, about the only time that black and white children were allowed to mingle in this class was whenever Mr. Hue moved a child as a form of punishment. Not surprisingly, interracial contact under these circumstances is rarely either extensive or positive in nature.

In addition to preventing direct interaction and physical proximity, homogeneous grouping also emphasizes the status differences between white and black students in a number of ways. First, in Mr. Hue's class, as in other similar classes, the labels assigned to the different groups, Group 1 and Group 2, made the status order very clear. This was reinforced by frequent references to the differences in their work.

> *Steve and Brad, both black, occasionally do Group 1 work, al-*
> *though they are in Group 2. Today at the beginning of class Mr. Hue*
> *says to them, "I want you to work in Group 2 today. They are doing*
> *hard work in Group 1." Disappointed, Steve exclaims, "Oh." Mr. Hue*
> *explains the Group 2 problems to the class, saying, "This is very easy to*
> *do. I expect you to do it in about 5 minutes." Brad says, "Mr. Hue,*

183

can we do the other problems?" referring to the Group 1 problems. Mr. Hue replies, "You are going to find them very hard, I think. I think you'll find them frustrating." It's hard to pick up a clear yes or no in his answer. Brad and Steve watch as he explains the Group 1 problems. [Later] Mr. Hue says, "OK, how many people don't know how to do the problems?" Sonya says, "I don't," and Brad raises his hand. Mr. Hue says to Brad, "I'm going to have to put you in the other group. These are too hard for you." He goes over to Brad and Steve to get them to work on Group 2 problems. Steve protests, saying, "I'm on number three." [February 1974]

The clearly different work for children in the different groups also virtually prevents any sort of task-oriented interracial cooperation, since black and white students are performing different tasks.

More common than Mr. Hue's division of students into two groups is division into three groups. Mr. Cousins, a white teacher, had three academically homogeneous groups. In the class observed, Group A was all white, and Group C was all black except for one white male. The visual effect was muted somewhat by the presence of a racially balanced middle group, Group B. The social learning opportunities within Mr. Cousins's Group B, when considered in isolation from the rest of the class, seem ideal. Black and white students in close physical proximity, working on the same material at the same time and at the same general skill level, have an excellent opportunity not only to observe but also to interact over considerable periods of time on an equal-status, reciprocal basis. But, considering the class as a whole, the social cost of tracking seems high. The higher-achieving black students must surely notice that they have been paired with those in the lower half of the white distribution. And students in the racially homogeneous upper and lower groups scarcely have any more opportunity for interaction or close observation than those in the more completely segregated classes. Furthermore, the structural message of these racially unbalanced groups is still that the school considers white students better than black ones.

A relatively small number of teachers at Wexler assign students to seats in academically heterogeneous groups. Mr. Little assigned students in his class to one of five groups, breaking with the colorblind orientation and structuring the groups so that they would be racially and sexually mixed. The result was a class in which black and white students were in close and continual contact with one another. The heterogeneity of the groups ensured that no formal status differential developed among them.

The seating patterns in these groups initially appeared to be markedly influenced by race and sex. However, there was also a considerable amount of cross-race interaction:

> *As was the case last week when they were initially assigned to groups, the students sat around five tables of six chairs each. In four of these five tables there was a remarkably clear arrangement of students by both sex and race. For example, if one started with a white male at a table and looked to one side, skipping over other white males who might be at the table, one invariably came next to a black male. If you go around the chain of black males, one next finds the black females. The black females, however many there may be, abut against white females, which completes the circle. This circular arrangement was obvious in a pure fashion in all but one table. The last table was the same except one white male sat between two black males. The new seating arrangement seems to lead to a great deal of interaction across racial and sexual boundaries. Children seem to talk with considerable freedom to the others at their tables. For example, today I've noticed white girls and black boys talking several times. White boys and black girls seemed to speak with each other less frequently.* [September 1977]

The contrast between the almost total lack of cross-race interaction in Mr. Hue's class, where children are grouped homogeneously, and the very frequent interaction in classes where they are grouped heterogeneously is made clear from the following relatively typical excerpt from field notes taken in Mr. Little's class:

> *Mr. Little says, "I'll be right back. Finish your work alone." Daneen (black) and Susan (white) are working together. . . . Chuck (black) joins their conversation by making a comment about the assignment.* [November 1975]

> *A black girl with short braids has dropped an earring. She's now replacing it as a white female next to her helps. They work on it jointly for nearly 30 seconds. Mr. Little says to Bruce and Kenny, "Hey, you geniuses over there who are arm wrestling." Then Bruce and Jack (white) do the same. After they have finished, Kenny and Bruce start in again. Mr. Little announces in a bored voice, "It's time to clean up and get things put away."* [April 1976]

Even though Mr. Little rarely assigns group projects, the students frequently must cooperate to achieve desired goals. For example, students must learn to share the dictionary on days when there are writing assignments. Frequently, situations occur when the cooperation of all of the students at a table is necessary for each to achieve desired ends.

> *Mr. Little says, "Well, it's almost time to go. Which table is ready?" Students from all tables look up at him and about half of them are frantically waving their hands in the air. Mr. Little says, "OK, it's Table A first today. You all look cleaned up." [November 1975]*

Teachers also occasionally assign students to seats based on the alphabetical order of their last names. This achieves roughly the same amount of interracial mixing as does planned heterogeneity and hence produces much more interracial mixing than either voluntary seating or planned homogeneous seating.

The phrase *seating policy* is most frequently used at Wexler to refer to the teachers' rules for assigning students to particular seats, as discussed above. However, another more subtle aspect of a teacher's seating policy is the extent to which children are actually required to stay in assigned seats. Some teachers strictly enforce a seating arrangement and require students to remain in their seats during the entire class period. Others allow a great deal of movement around the class.

The effect on interracial contact of the teachers' attitudes to within-class movement varies, of course, depending on the particular seating pattern present in the classroom. Where seating is racially mixed, tolerance for a high degree of movement may actually serve to decrease integration by giving students an opportunity to gravitate back toward their same-race friends. But where seating tends to be segregated, interracial interaction and much positive social learning is dependent upon the teacher's tolerance for a certain degree of movement about the room. Students in relatively segregated classes seem to use a group of same-race students as a safe or comfortable base from which brief, low-risk forays can be made to explore cross-racial relationships. The teacher who permits students to select their own seats at the beginning of the class period but requires them to remain in those seats at all times throughout the class period has, perhaps inadvertently, selected a combination of strategies likely to keep interracial interaction to the barest minimum.

Although students tend to sit with others of their own racial group when they can, many students of both races seem motivated to explore, however tentatively, relationships with out-group members. Such forays sometimes but not always lead to positive interchanges.

186

*Karen (white) is standing by Sonya (black) with Nancy (white)
behind her, asking for something. Sonya reaches into her pocketbook.
Karen goes back, followed by Nancy, with a bottle of dark nail polish.
. . . Karen returns to Sonya and stands there a moment. The teacher
says, "Let's go; sit down." She does. . . . [February 1976]*

*Kelvin (black) heads toward the door, saying, "I'm going to get
my book. . . . [When he returns] he goes and stands for several moments between Sonya (black) and Kathy (white), who are seated at a
table with four other girls. Then he goes and sits across from Mark, a
white boy, at another table. However, he soon pops up and returns to
the girls' table. First, he taps Kathy's head with a pencil. He then
stands between Nancy (white) and Karen (white) and hits Karen
several times with the pencil as if fencing playfully. Karen tries to fend
off the pencil with her hands and finally looks very annoyed. Kelvin
then returns to his seat. [March 1976]*

*Nancy (white) and Karen (white) are standing at the table-cart
talking to Ms. Monroe. Darrin (black) is still there, too. He talks to
Karen; the two of them smile. Nancy's gone now; Richard (black) is
now at the table-cart also—he's clowning around, bouncing physically.
Karen laughs appreciatively. [March 1976]*

Note that this last example of friendly interaction took place around
the teacher; no other interracial interaction was noted in that class
that day, and the pattern was a recurring one. Centering the interaction on the teacher took the burden for sustaining and controlling it
off the individual children, making the encounter a very safe one. Interestingly, much of the social learning we observed had dubious
legitimacy in an academic classroom. Including the teacher in the
social interaction, as above, also has the effect of legitimizing it. A
much more common practice, however, is to try to keep the teacher
from discovering what is going on (not because the activity is interracial, but because it is nonacademic).

Finally, the type of furniture supplied to the teachers seems to
have a very real impact on the amount of interracial interaction that
occurs. Specifically, there appears to be more interaction among children who share a table than among the same children when they are
assigned to sit next to one another in individual chairs with writing
arms. Perhaps this is partially because the circular arrangement around
the tables is more conducive to eye contact and greater physical proximity than is the more traditional arrangement of widely spaced rows
of chairs. The tables may also lead to greater interaction because chil-

187

dren sharing them are often treated as a unit, thus sharing, in many ways, common experiences and a sense of belonging to the same entity.

INSTRUCTIONAL POLICY

Instruction at Wexler is generally organized in one of three basic ways. Most teachers spend most of their classroom hours using the method of teaching they like best. However, they also frequently use one or more of the other methods as these seem appropriate to the particular academic material to be covered. The three teaching methods—traditional, individualized, and group-oriented—have varying effects on interracial contact and learning.

The traditional method centers on the teacher and on one-to-one student–teacher interaction to which all students are supposed to attend. Teachers in traditional classes usually lecture, lead class discussions in which they call on students in turn, and pose specific questions that individual students are supposed to answer in front of the class.

In individualized work, each child is allowed to proceed at his or her own pace. Teachers frequently use work contracts in which the child agrees to perform a certain amount of work in a given period of time. The work is usually assigned according to the student's performance level. For example, Ms. Wire assigns 5 new spelling words a week to some students and 10 or 15 words to others. Since the students are working on different material, the teacher does not instruct the entire class. Rather, the teacher circulates from child to child, making comments and providing assistance. Although there is much teacher–student interaction, it is usually quite private.

Group projects, structured so that students must coordinate their efforts to produce a joint product, are by far the rarest teaching method. Thus, the group-projects method is very similar to the experimental methods employed by researchers seeking to study the effect of cooperative dependence in interracial work groups in schools (Aronson *et al.*, 1975; DeVries and Edwards, 1974; Slavin, 1978). The mere fact that students are seated in groups does not, of course, mean that they are engaged in group projects as defined above. In fact, during nearly 3 years of observations in academic classrooms at Wexler, we encountered fewer than 15 instances of true group projects involving more than two students.

The students form groups of three as they please for the science projects. (These students are assigned to racially and sexually mixed tables in class.) Interestingly, all four groups are racially mixed except for one group of two black girls. None of the groups are sexually mixed. In fact, when Mr. Little tries to get Carlos (black) to join this last group because he is in a big group with four boys, Carlos refuses and is sent back to the regular classroom. Mr. Little says, "OK, now each group appoint a secretary." The boys in one group are arguing over who should be the secretary. Bob, a black male in the group, says to the other two boys there in a disgusted voice, "Oh man. A boy can be a secretary." Mr. Little says, "But let's call it a recorder. . . ." In each group one child, the recorder, writes down what happens as the other holds sugar over the Bunsen burner. The third child watches but gets to participate in the next experiment. [October 1976]

The three basic types of instructional strategies have different implications for the development of relations between black and white students. Clearly, the traditional method makes the academic differences between blacks and whites as groups most obvious. Children's successes and failures are apparent to the entire class, as are their rates of participation. Black and white students generally agree that academic performance is a major route to peer status. Thus the very public nature of academic performance in traditional classrooms helps to create unequal status between blacks and whites and may well confirm traditional stereotypes.

The teacher says, "If you have 400 and 90 and 7½ how much would that be total?" He calls on Dan, a black male, whose hand is not raised. Dan doesn't know the answer. Three children, all white, are waving their hands in the air. Mr. Little persists with Dan and writes the three figures on the board. By this time there are six white kids and two black kids waving their hands in the air and you can hear little moans of excitement and pleas like, "Call on me." Finally, Dan gets the answer. (This class is roughly two-thirds black.) [October 1976]

Differences in academic performance are not so obvious in individualized classes for two reasons. First, students tend to interact privately with the teacher rather than publicly. Second, teachers using individualized strategies tend to grade somewhat differently than those using traditional instruction. In traditional classes, a student's performance is generally compared with the performance of the entire class. Students' grades depend not only on how well they do but also on how well others do, an inherently competitive situation. In an individualized class, grades are based more, although not exclusively, on how well the students do the particular task assigned to them. Children who do five spelling words correctly can get As if that was their task even if other students have done two or three times as many words.

In group project situations, each group member's performance is public to members of the group, but more or less unknown to others. However, the public performance on group projects differs from public performance in traditional classrooms. First, when groups are small, differences in academic performance between black and white group members may be attributed more to individual differences than to group differences. If the one black child in a group of three children performs less well than the others, all of the group members may be less likely to draw conclusions about whites and blacks in general than when two-thirds of the white children in a class frequently raise their hands and few black children do so. Hence, the small-group method of instruction may be less likely to reinforce or produce stereotypes than the traditional method.

On the other hand, poor performance will probably be much more salient in classrooms using the small-group situation than in those using individualized or traditional instruction because children are dependent on one another's performance to gain desired rewards. Hence, the failure of a particular child to contribute well to the group task may cause strong feelings of anger or resentment on the part of other group members. Experimental work with adults by Blanchard, Weigel, and Cook (1975) suggests that whites' liking for black group members is clearly influenced by the black's competence in performing tasks necessary to the group's success. It is interesting that competence plays no parallel role in attraction for other whites. However, other work by Blanchard and Cook (1976) suggests that if whites can actually be induced to help a less competent black, their liking and respect for that individual will increase. Little work has been directed toward assessing the less competent group members' reactions to those who help them. Our observations at Wexler suggest that help from a peer is often not welcomed. The research of Cohen and her colleagues suggests that even when blacks and whites have equal levels of competence, whites may dominate group interaction because of the prior expectation of both groups that whites are likely to be more competent than blacks (Cohen, 1976; Cohen and Roper 1972). Cohen argues that unless children actually experience a reversal of typical roles in which the generally subordinate group has superior, rather than just equal, competence, such expectations are likely to become a self-fulfilling prophecy. Thus, merely assigning students to work jointly on a project by no means ensures the emergence of equal status relationships. However, unlike traditional instruction, group project and individualized instruction at least do not emphasize group differences in performance.

The three instructional methods also differ greatly in the extent to which they foster academic cooperation. Academic cooperation is one of the few types of peer social interaction that is ever considered truly legitimate in a classroom. As will be discussed in more detail later, most other sorts of social interaction in the classroom are generally of very dubious legitimacy.

As pointed out previously, the traditional instruction method is inimical to cooperation because children are to a large extent graded in comparison with others. Hence, students generally hurt themselves by helping others unless they can develop mutually beneficial arrangements, and such cooperation is most easily worked out between children who are at similar achievement levels. Also, since such classes tend to be organized around teacher–student interaction, which the rest of the class is supposed to observe, student interchanges are likely to win the teachers' disapproval even if they are task-oriented.

Individualized instruction is not as likely to foster competition as traditional instruction, since the grades of one child do not affect the grades of another in as direct a way. However, it is not particularly conducive to cooperation either, since children are generally working on different projects than are those near them. Again, as with traditional classes, whatever cooperation occurs is most frequently between children at the same academic level who are working on the same material at a given time. The group-project method, of course, requires or at least legitimates cooperation. However, as discussed above, it does not ensure that each child is actually able to cooperate on an equal status basis with others.

One interesting feature in classes that are conducted traditionally or individually is the frequent ambiguity about whether cooperation is allowed at a particular moment or whether such cooperation is illegitimate and will be labeled as cheating. In fact, ambiguity concerning the legitimacy of copying seemed to be the most commonly prevailing climate in these types of classes. Occasionally teachers will indicate that students are free to work jointly or individually.

Mr. Little hands out the assignment indicating in his instructions that children can work either as a group or by themselves. [October 1975]

Other times teachers will take measures obviously designed to discourage collaboration and yet allow obvious collaboration to occur without even attempting to stop it. Copying and sharing of answers seem to be such common (and frequently tolerated) modes of working that they hardly ever disappear completely, even when the teachers suggest they are inappropriate.

The teacher says, "We're having a test today, three at a table." . . . (This spaces children out in the room so they cannot see one another's work as easily.) Stephenson, a black male who had been sitting with two other black males, goes and sits with Mark, Keith, and Steven, white males. Then he moves over with Dave and Lee, also white, saying, "I hear you guys got the answers (there is nothing at all surreptitious in his manner). . . . The class is fairly quiet. I can hear Stephenson consulting with Dave, who seems to be cooperating. . . . Collaboration among the kids sitting together is again visible, if quiet. Karen (white) looks at the work of Laura (white) and Sonya (black). Janice (black), Sara (white), and Nancy (white) all look at one another's papers. . . . Steven says to the others at his table, "What's number 20?" Mark says audibly, "I need the following: 1, 3, 18, 20. . . ." [June 1967]

The occasional failure of some students (often white) to give help when requested (often by blacks) seems to be perceived as honesty by the former and unfriendliness by the latter. Also, since collaborating when the rules are unclear imposes some risk on the participants, students tend to collaborate primarily when both parties feel sure they will gain something.

At Table A, Sylvia (black) is talking to Susan (white) from Table C. Susan has come over to swap answers. That is, Susan says, "If you give me 4, I'll give you 11. . . ." Later, another girl from Table A joins in the bartering, trading Susan another answer. [October 1975]

Most of the bartering for information appears to be within race, since friendships often follow racial lines and many black children are not in a good position to bargain for information with whites. Thus, race cooperation may occur between whites, whereas blacks are refused access to the cooperating group.

The group-projects method requires proximity, sustained contact,

192

and interaction in order for children to achieve their academic goals, but it also sets the stage for children to get to know quite a lot about one another's nonacademic attributes. This is extremely important, for, in general, the other teaching methods discourage and often prevent much interracial social contact. As previously discussed, in traditional and individualized classrooms academic consultation among students is frequently discouraged. Purely social contact is even more frowned upon because teachers perceive it as interfering with the attainment of academic goals.

Two types of social behavior that occur very frequently seem especially interesting from the standpoint of intergroup learning. In one type, the students try to gain information about the out-group:

> *As I entered the class today, I noticed Shirley (black) and Lisa (white) near the back of the room. Lisa was kneeling on the floor beside Shirley so Shirley could clip off a lock of her hair. [October 1976]*

> *Dick (black) is standing in front of three white boys who are seated in a row. He asks them each in turn, "Do you grease your hair?" Each responds negatively and Dick says in a surprised tone, "How come?" He is feeling Eric's brush cut when the teacher tells him to sit down. [November 1976]*

The school provides little opportunity for guided learning about group differences. The lack of such information not infrequently causes intergroup problems.

> *Mrs. Whitmore (white) told me that her daughter's worst experience at Wexler was the day when a black girl put some Vaseline on her hair. Mrs. Whitmore said her daughter and friends are now very concerned about having hair that is "squeaky clean." They can't stand the idea of having oily hair. The daughter got furious at the black girl who put the oil on her hair. She didn't know that blacks frequently grease their hair and thought the girl was somehow attacking her. [March 1978]*

The second type of social behavior of particular importance at Wexler is a kind of interpersonal testing to discover how others will react to various sorts of provocation. This testing seemed particularly widespread among the black children, who frequently seemed to be experimenting to see how other persons would respond to various actions on their part:

> *A white female walking toward the back of the room found her passage past a table blocked by a black male who had stood up just*

193

before she came. He didn't appear to stand up in order to block her, but once he stood up he was clearly aware of her progress and determined not to move in order to get out of her way. She walked around him, although she looked rather unhappy about it. [November 1975]

I noticed one of the social studies kids (black male) . . . with his belt taken off. He was holding the belt in one hand and using it like a small whip, slapping it down on his other hand so that the metal buckle was very obvious and made a lot of noise. He was about 2½ feet from Raymond, the only white child in a group of three. He said to Raymond, "If you're not careful, I'll beat you with this." However, his tone was not threatening, and there was a very small smile on his face that didn't look to me to be at all malicious. Raymond just walked away, and after a couple of minutes of playing with the belt, the other child just put it on. [October 1976]

Whites responded much less frequently to these provocations than blacks did when bothered either by whites or by other blacks. Furthermore, we observed few comparable incidents of whites' passively ignoring teasing or harassment from other whites.

It is easy to imagine middle-class white parents, anticipating their children's first experience with a desegregated situation, counseling them to "just ignore anybody who tries to give you a hard time." Interviews suggest that this did indeed happen.

Interviewer: Did your parents give you any advice about coming to Wexler?

Ann (white): Yes, they did. If someone comes and pushes you away and stuff and says they are going to fight, you just walk away or tell the teacher quick. [November 1975]

In a sense, many of the white children seem to have "flunked" the interpersonal tests that many of their black classmates have conducted. Once it becomes apparent that members of one group can generally be counted on to remain passive victims, it is almost inevitable that at least a few members of the other group will take advantage of that situation, either for some concrete gain or to enhance their own status or sense of power. Thus, by the second year of desegregation at Wexler, intimidation and extortion of food or money had become a concern of many students, with black as well as white students tending to report in interviews that the intimidators were often black and the victims more often white. The following incident, which did take place within a classroom, is not meant to illustrate a

194

typical incident, but rather is presented as an extreme example of the kind of negative behavior that depends upon a passive, ineffectual response from the victim:

> Matthew (white) sits with Eric (white) at the opposite end of the table. Then Richard (black) sits down between them at the table, simultaneously grabbing at Eric's math book. Eric resists at first, then lets go. Red-faced, he says in a strained, complaining voice, "I need my papers." Richard leafs through the book, and as he comes to papers he takes them out and slaps them down in front of Eric. Later on he comes upon another paper and throws it down in front of Eric, saying, "Get your shit out of my book." This provokes some amused laughter on the part of one or two other black males in the room. Matthew, sitting right there at the table, is impassive, not showing any kind of response one way or another to all this interaction. [March 1977]

Abusive behavior such as the above was rare in the classroom, but ignoring responses was not. Although ignoring may have been a self-protective tactic from the point of view of the white children who employed it, the ignored black child might reasonably have concluded that the white child was purposely being haughty and unfriendly. Such a conclusion could be plausible even when the black child's action had been ambiguous or playfully aggressive—the fact that even completely nonthreatening behavior by blacks was often studiously ignored by whites further contributed to the impression that the white children were unfriendly or considered themselves too good for the blacks involved.

> Taru (black) lightly hits John (white) on the arm to get his attention. He then asks, "How do you spell **grain?**" John makes no response whatever, not even acknowledging that Taru has touched him. [Later] Taru turns to John and says, "How do you spell **syllables?**" When John makes no immediate response, he hits the dictionary which is open in John's lap six times rather hard with the palm of his hand. Still John makes no response. . . . [February 1976]

In general, it seems that the ignoring tactic used by so many of the white children in response to a variety of black behaviors reflects an important social-skill deficiency, an inability to interpret accurately or respond openly and naturally to the actions of the out-group members. Much has been made of various social-skill deficiencies of lower-class blacks; we have taken pains to point out this parallel lack in the white children because so many of them cope with it in a way likely to go unnoticed in the academic classroom—the silent refusal to inter-act, or even to look up from one's work, will usually be seen as very compatible with the teacher's goal of silence and order in the classroom.

A Final Comment

It is apparent that simply putting black and white children in the same classrooms—even putting them at the same tables to encourage close observation and interaction—is not sufficient to ensure positive social learning. When the children are left to work out their own re-lationships without guidance in interpreting one another's behavior and viewpoint, their interactions are likely to be characterized by misun-derstandings, bravado and defensiveness, invidious comparisons, and unresolved conflicts. In fact, far from being colorblind, children fre-quently encounter situations that build or maintain their negative ideas about group-linked characteristics.

It is quite clear that the various policies that teachers adopt in matters such as seating or instructional strategies markedly affect the kind of experiences black and white students have with each other in interracial schools. In some classrooms children have little or virtually no direct contact with one another and have only the sort of distant contact that reinforces stereotypes without building humanizing ties. In other classes, children are in close contact under conditions that seem to build strong positive relationships in spite of the marked dif-ferences in individuals' backgrounds.

Unfortunately, even in a school like Wexler, which has explicitly stated integrationist goals, teachers are not adequately trained or strongly motivated to consider the impact of their attitudes and be-havior on relations between blacks and whites. Ironically, they are so busy meeting the demands placed on them by internal and external pressures to produce immediate gains in academic performance that they hardly have time to consider the ways in which the children's social experiences may promote or inhibit their academic development. As one teacher put it, "It just seems like there are so many things that we have to do during the school day that it's almost impossible to think about the social relations of children." Yet ignoring the social relations of children in interracial schools poses a real danger. As the following two excerpts show, some children are able to work out positive relations by themselves, but many others are not.

> *Shirley (black) is now sitting at the table with Lisa (white) and Karen. Ouida (black), nearby, says to Shirley, "I dreamed about you," and she describes an unpleasant dream that she had. Shirley says, "My dream wasn't nothing like that. It was a good dream. I dreamed about Lisa and you. We all went to the same college and we had an apartment together. I had a car . . . and we had an apartment together. I had a car. . . ." (Lisa interjects, "A Corvette.") The three girls continue in a social conversation. . . . [January 1977]*

> *Mr. Rider (white) has a son at Wexler. When he heard I was doing a research project there he said that something had happened recently that greatly upset him. His son had come home from school one day and said, "Dad, I know you won't like this but I think I'm becoming a racist." When Mr. Rider pursued the matter, it turned out that his son was angry about the way he felt black kids at Wexler acted. In particular, he felt the black kids were overly aggressive and were neither academically talented nor motivated. [March 1976]*

References

Allport, G. W.
> 1954   *The Nature of Prejudice.* Cambridge, Mass.: Addison-Wesley.

Amir, Y.
> 1969   "Contact hypothesis in ethnic relations." *Psychological Bulletin* 71: 319–342.
> 1976   "The role of intergroup contact in change of prejudice and ethnic relations." In P. Katz (ed.), *Toward the Elimination of Racism.* New York: Pergamon Press.

Armor, D. J.
> 1972   "The evidence on busing." *Public Interest* (Summer):90–124.

Aronson, E., N. Blaney, J. Sikes, C. Stephan, and M. Snapp.
> 1975   "Busing and racial tension: The jigsaw route to learning and liking." *Psychology Today* (February):43–120.

Ashmore, R.
> 1970   "Solving the problems of prejudice." In B. Collins, *Social Psychology.* Reading, Mass.: Addison-Wesley.

Blanchard, F., and S. Cook.
> 1976   *The effects of Helping a Less Competitive Group Member of a Cooperating Interracial Group on the Development of Interpersonal Attraction.* Unpublished manuscript, Smith College.

Blanchard, F. A., R. Weigel, and S. W. Cook
    1975   "The effect of relative competence of group members upon interpersonal attraction in cooperating interracial groups." *Journal of Personality and Social Psychology,* **32**:519–530.

Blau, T.
    1955   *The Dynamics of Bureaucracy.* Chicago: University of Chicago Press.

Clark, K. B.
    1973   "Just teach them to read." *New York Times Magazine* (March 18): 14ff.

Cohen, E.
    1976   "The effect of desegregation on race relations." *Law and Contemporary Problems* **39**(2):271–299.

Cohen E., M. Lockheed, and M. Lohman.
    1976   "The center for interracial cooperation: A field experiment." *Sociology of Education* **49**(1):47–58.

Cohen E., and S. Roper.
    1972   "Modification of interracial interaction disability: An application of status characteristics theory." *American Sociological Review* **36**(6): 643–657.

Coleman, J. S., E. Q. Campbell, C. J. Hobson, J. McPartland, A. M. Mood, F. D. Weinfeld, and R. L. York.
    1966   *Equality of Educational Opportunity.* Washington, D.C.: U.S. Government Printing Office.

Cook, S. W.
    1969   "Motives in a conceptual analysis of attitude-related behavior." In W. J. Arnold and D. Levine (eds.), *Nebraska Symposium on Motivation.* Lincoln, Nebraska: University of Nebraska.

DeVries, D., and K. Edwards.
    1974   "Student teams and learning games: Their effects on cross-race and cross-sex interaction." *Journal of Educational Psychology* 66:741–749.

Goldman, P.
    1970   *Report from Black America.* New York: Simon and Schuster.

Homans, G.
    1961   *Social Behavior: Its Elementary Forms.* New York: Harcourt, Brace & World.

Jencks, C. *et al.*
    1972   *Inequality.* New York: Basic Books.

Johnson, D. W., and R. T. Johnson.
    1974   "Instructional goal structure: Cooperative, competitive, or individualistic." *Review of Educational Research* **44**:213–240.

Katz, I.
    1964   "Review of evidence relating to effects of desegregation on the performance of Negroes." *American Psychologist* **19**:381–399.

Kelley, H. H.
    1972   "Attribution in social interaction." In E. Jones (ed.), *Attribution: Perceiving the Causes of Behavior.* Morristown, N.J.: General Learning Press.

Milgram, S.
    1977   *The Individual in a Social World.* New York: Addison-Wesley.

Pettigrew, T.
    1975   "The racial integration of the schools." In T. Pettigrew (ed.), *Racial Discrimination in the United States*. New York: Harper & Row.

Pettigrew, T., E. Useem, C. Normand, and M. Smith.
    1973   "Busing: A review of the evidence." *Public Interest* (Winter):88–118.

Read, F.
    1975   "Judicial evolution of the law of school integration since 'Brown vs. Board of Education.'" *Law and Contemporary Problems* 39(1):7–49.

Rist, R.
    1974   "Race, policy, and schooling." *Society* 12(1):59–63.

Schofield, J. W.
    1978   "School desegregation and intergroup relations." In D. Bar-Tal and L. Saxe (eds.), *Social Psychology of Education: Theory and Research*. Washington, D.C.: Hemisphere Press.

Schofield, J. W., and H. A. Sagar.
    1977   "Peer interaction patterns in an integrated middle school." *Sociometry* 40(2):130–138.

Sherif, M., O. J. Harvey, B. J. White, W. E. Hood, and C. W. Sherif.
    1961   *Intergroup Conflict and Cooperation: The Robber's Cave Experiment*. Norman: University of Oklahoma Book Exchange.

Slavin, R., and N. Madden.
    1978   *Race Relations in Desegregated Schools: An Activist Perspective*. Unpublished manuscript, Center for the Social Organization of Schools, Johns Hopkins University.

St. John, N.
    1975   *School Desegregation: Outcomes for Children*. New York: John Wiley.

Tomlinson, T. M., and D. TenHouten.
    1972   *System Awareness: Exploitive Potential and Ascribed Status of Elites*. Paper presented at the meeting of the American Psychological Association, Montreal.

U.S. Commission on Civil Rights.
    1967   *Racial isolation in the public schools*. Washington, D.C.: U.S. Government Printing Office.

Waterford Board of Education.
    1977   *Newsletter* 30(2):3.

Webster, S. W.
    1961   "The influence of interracial contact on social acceptance in a newly integrated school." *Journal of Educational Psychology* 52:292–296.

Weigel, R., P. Wiser, and S. Cook.
    1975   "The impact of cooperative learning on cross-ethnic relations and attitudes." *Journal of Social Issues* 31(1):219–243.

White, R.
    1968   "Sense of interpersonal competence: Two case studies and some reflections on origins." In R. White (ed.), *The Study of Lives*. New York: Atherton Press.

Wisdom, J.
    1975   "Random remarks on the role of social sciences in the judicial decision-making process in school desegregation cases." *Law and Contemporary Problems* 39(1):135–149.

Chapter 6

Contacts among Cultures: School Desegregation in a Polyethnic New York City High School

MERCER L. SULLIVAN*

The term *desegregation,* as well as the policy, is a controversial one in need of some solid ground. The tremendous body of legislation, litigation and administrative policy, public debate and case law that has shaped the meaning of desegregation attests to its ambiguity and to the fact that, ultimately, the term refers to an image of the future, of a state of affairs that is ardently desired by many but which no one can as yet describe empirically save in the broadest generalizations. What would a perfectly desegregated school look like? How would we know if we saw one? No one can answer these questions as yet, nor do we know all the right questions to ask. Perhaps the greatest service performed by qualitative studies of schools enmeshed in the desegregation process is to precisely define the concept of desegregation.

Desegregation is essentially the name both of a policy and of a continually unfolding and evolving process. But the problems of operationalizing the term *desegregation* are more complicated when one begins to ask questions about how a desegregated population is distributed throughout a school's complex curriculum and about such things

* This research was conducted by the Horace Mann-Lincoln Institute under Francis A. J. Ianni, principle investigator. Parts of this chapter are also based on reports by Margaret Terry Orr.

as access to various kinds of resources. Consequently, a systematic inquiry into the processes of social life in a desegregated high school must not itself be biased by the shifting and ambiguous meanings of the term.

Desegregation refers in the most general sense to "culture contact in school systems." Thus, a study of a desegregated school must take account of the school as a social system and also of the cultural diversity of the school and community population.

Sheridan High School: The Community Context [1]

HISTORY OF THE AREA

Sheridan High School is located in New York, a city that has seen many waves of immigration throughout its history. The spatial distribution of the population throughout the metropolitan area reflects the historical sequence of arrival of these groups. Sheridan High School itself is located in an inner-city neighborhood, which we shall call East Point, that has for more than 100 years housed new arrivals to the city. Only 20 years ago, most of the residents of this neighborhood were of eastern or southern European heritage. In the last 20 years, however, the population has turned over more than 50%. The newcomers are again immigrants, but this time they come from the American South, from the Caribbean and Latin America, and from the Pacific Orient.

History not only explains the contemporary distribution of the population, however, but also is a necessary ingredient for understanding the evolution of the bureaucratic form of the school system. Recent work by educational historians (Katz, 1971; Ravitch, 1975) has addressed this latter question.

Several conclusions emerge from this historical material that have powerful implications for understanding the interactions that we recorded from our observations in Sheridan High School:

1. For over 150 years, the "Great School Wars" have occurred during times of massive immigration into the city. This point is the theme and the original inspiration for Diane Ravitch's work. The major struggles over the purpose, organization, and control of public education have taken place during periods when the society was re-

---

[1] The names of the school, neighborhoods, and all individuals are pseudonyms.

ceiving large numbers of people with cultural differences from those who had preceded them.

2. These "school wars" have always involved an upsurge in ethnic identification and ideology, whether expressed in religious, racial, or cultural terms. These processes of ethnic identification on the ideological level are translated into social action by the formation of ethnically based pressure groups, voluntary associations, and political machines that have often been the driving force of politics in this area, especially during periods of massive population change. Conversely, the historical periods between waves of immigration have seen a decline in polarization of ethnic groups. During periods of immigration, however, the schools have often been the first social institutions affected as well as the focus of many political struggles.

3. The very organizational form of the educational system has resulted in part from these struggles. The first unified public system was created in response to Catholic demands for public funds for Catholic schools. The most sweeping organizational change in recent years, decentralization, came about during desegregation and civil rights struggles of the 1960s. The extreme political sensitivity of struggles over the schools has led to a pattern whereby solutions and decisions have been moved above the local level. In the past, municipal problems of this kind were often resolved at the state level. In the current era, federal intervention is assuming increasing importance.

4. A recurrent unanticipated consequence of the organizational development first of the school system itself and then of the professional unions within the system has been the emergence of school people as an interest group themselves, often divided internally but also able to assert their interests in opposition both to governmental agencies and to the community that the school serves.

5. Finally, we see that the absorption of new groups into society has now happened several times and must be described as a process of ethnic succession. Those who are now established were once themselves labeled as members of immigrant groups. Many stages of the immigration process, everything from recent arrival to generations of assimilation, are represented among the current population. Although every era faces new problems, certain paths of advancement and succession have been sanctioned by history. Newcomers both expect and are expected to establish themselves in ways similar to those that their predecessors employed. These ways include political organization, residential organization, entry into the labor market, and use of the public

schools for the advancement of their children. This tradition of ethnic succession sets the desegregation struggles of New York City off from the situation in the South in important ways. Whereas in the South only two groups have resided near each other in conditions of inequality over a much longer period of time in much greater isolation from the rest of the world, New York has often seen the arrival of new groups and their advancement over time.

NEIGHBORHOODS

Sheridan students are drawn primarily from two neighborhoods of the central city, East Point and Morganville. East Point, which surrounds the school, is a polyethnic neighborhood that over the years has housed successively arriving groups of immigrants. The white students in the school are mostly middle-class members of the Jewish and Italian and some Irish families that used to dominate the area. The largest single group in this neighborhood consists of Hispanic people, mostly Puerto Ricans but also including Dominicans and immigrants from all over the Caribbean and Latin America. This neighborhood also contains Chinatown, a closely circumscribed ghetto housing mostly poor and recently arrived immigrants coming directly from Hong Kong and indirectly from many points in the Pacific Orient. Chinatown's population has expanded 10 times since the revision of immigration laws in 1965.

Sheridan students are also drawn from another central-city neighborhood that lies on the other side of the main business district. This neighborhood is called the Morganville section and is one of the oldest and most famous black neighborhoods in the city. Students have been assigned to Sheridan from this neighborhood since the late 1950s as part of the school system's desegregation plan. When that plan was formulated, Sheridan was more than 50% white. At the time our fieldwork was completed, the population in East Point had changed to the point where the school was barely 10% white, but Morganville students have become accustomed to Sheridan and even report preferring it to some of the schools in their own neighborhood.

Morganville and East Point are similar neighborhoods with respect to many ecological and socioeconomic factors. Both areas are ecologically separated from the rest of the city and contain much low-quality housing. Many of the inhabitants of each neighborhood are either unemployed or members of the working poor, though each neighborhood does also contain some middle-income housing and population. Rates of social pathology, including crime indexes, drug addiction, health problems, and youth problems, are high in both areas.

Beyond these similarities, however, there are also important differences in the sociological profiles of these two neighborhoods. Though Morganville is a black ghetto, it has a fairly stable population and local institutions. A much higher proportion of Morganville residences have been continuously occupied by one family over the last 20 years. Furthermore, the area is politically well organized. The churches here are large and powerful and have often provided a political base for local politicians both in local desegregation struggles and later in community control struggles. The antipoverty agencies established in the late 1960s also contribute to the sociopolitical integration of this neighborhood with the rest of the city and the larger society. Morganville's cultural institutions, including music, dance, and theater groups, are nationally famous and give identity to the neighborhood and its inhabitants.

East Point, in contrast, is characterized by a much higher rate of population change and by the coexistence of several ethnic groups. The Chinese in Chinatown are perhaps more rigidly ghettoized than Morganville residents, but Chinatown is a small eight-block area mostly housing the poor Chinese. Chinatown has considerable local industry with tourism and garment manufacture, and these industries are controlled by a class of Chinese capitalists who live not in Chinatown but in better housing in East Point or farther away in the suburbs. Chinatown has its own internal government that is often respected by the municipal government. The voluntary associations in Chinatown have traditionally kept the Chinese separate from the larger society, although the recent expansion of the Chinese population has severely strained that traditional structure.

In general, the institutional structure of East Point is far more fragmented than that of Morganville, as a result of the diversity and rate of flux of the populations. The most characteristic institutions of the area are the settlement houses established to serve the immigrants of a previous generation. These houses still serve the elderly members of those populations (mostly Jewish) and now have programs for the newer arrivals as well. The settlement houses do not contribute to a political base in the same way that the churches of Morganville do. Indeed, many of the East Point residents, recent immigrants, are not U.S. citizens and thus are not able to vote. In general, one may ob-

205

serve that the Hispanic population's political organization in the city at large is just beginning to develop.

Within the East Point area, the degree of segregation of various groups in particular geographic concentrations varies a great deal from the relatively closed, though expanding, boundaries of Chinatown to the mixture of poor Hispanics and middle-class whites in the high-rise housing projects and the area around the school where the old housing is shared among blacks, elderly Jews, Hispanics, and Chinese. There is a major Hispanic concentration about Bridge Street, although the boundaries of the Hispanic area are not as rigid as those around other Hispanic areas in the city.

Thus, we see that patterns of interaction in the community within and across ethnic boundaries are pronounced and describable, although intricate. The neighborhoods that contribute the school's population exhibit varied but definite patterns of ecological, economic, political, and social organization. Much of the informal organization of turfs and networks and social control in Sheridan High School derives not only from the organization of the school itself but also from processes in the larger community of which the school is a part.

The Bureaucratic Context: Formal Organization, Administration, Curriculum, and Teaching

Sheridan High School served from 3500 to 4200 students during the period of our observations. It is one of over 100 high schools in the system and is rated as an "academic-comprehensive" high school. It is thus neither a vocational nor an alternative school, nor is it one of the prestigious specialty schools that admit only by examination.

This school system was decentralized in the late 1960s, and elementary and junior high schools were given over to the control of locally elected boards in various areas of the city. Sheridan and other high schools, however, were dropped from the decentralization plan at the last minute in the political controversy that led up to that plan. Thus, Sheridan is controlled directly by the central bureaucracy, a body that is dominated by members of earlier immigrant groups and that is often in conflict with the locally elected boards in districts that are predominantly populated by more recent immigrant groups. Another feature of social control of the school that deserves comment is the lack of parental influence. The governance of the school is largely

206

isolated from the families of the students it serves. This results both from the nondecentralization of the high schools and from the difficulty that poor and working-class people have in being able to attend meetings.

The size of Sheridan has an unavoidable impact on social relations. Students and staff alike cannot know everyone in the school individually. Few events are the common knowledge of everyone in the school. Everyone spends part of the day interacting with or at least passing in the hall hundreds of people whose names are not known. This fact of size, together with the ethnic diversity of the population, inevitably leads to a certain amount of stereotypical categorization on everyone's part.

Another characteristic of the formal organization of this school is the complexity of its curriculum, which, together with the diversity of the population, sets an enormous task of programming for the administration. Thousands of students must be fitted into dozens of course offerings. This programming process is the largest single influence on both sorting and territoriality within the school because it determines much of the time–space sequence of activities for both staff and students. Manipulation of the programming process is also one of the chief instruments of social control available to the administration.

The position of principal carries with it a great deal of formal authority, which the incumbent, Mr. Sontag, has operationalized into very real power. Although limited in many decision-making areas by state requirements, monetary allocations above the building level, and the very detailed union contract with the teachers, the principal still retains a great deal of discretionary power.

Legitimate recognitions of ethnicity and social class in the formal organization of the school include the desegregation that assigns students from the Morganville area to this school. Over half of all students receive free lunches by virtue of the level of family income. One special curricular program is also limited to low-income students. Recent mandates from the courts have prompted the initiation of bilingual classes for Chinese and Hispanic students, thus cutting against the desegregation mandate somewhat by separating these youths within the curriculum.

Other recognitions of a student's ethnicity or class, however, are forbidden. A rigid form of ability-grouping, a formal tracking system leading to differentially ranked diplomas, was outlawed several years ago as discriminatory. Similarly, the use of IQ tests was disallowed for programming purposes for the same reason. More recently, the Office of Civil Rights has imposed sanctions on the entire school system with respect to alleged discriminatory assignment of teachers.

The current administration of the school, headed by the principal (whom we call Irwin Sontag), has concentrated on three policy areas since Mr. Sontag's arrival in the school 7 years ago: establishment of security and control, standardization and evaluation of instruction, and programming and record keeping. The school's image as an orderly place has become firmly established throughout the system since Mr. Sontag's arrival.

Security has been greatly emphasized by the hiring of several full-time guards and the regulation of the student admittance to and circulation through the school. Manipulation and enforcement of these rules consume much of everyone's time. The principal also takes a great deal of personal responsibility for keeping order by walking through the school each day.

The principal's second policy imperative, the evaluation of instruction according to a strict lesson-plan format, resulted in an intense struggle for social control between principal and teachers. Several teachers sued him after his first year of evaluations, and those suits have now lasted for several years, even though most of the litigating teachers and those who openly supported them have since transferred to other schools within the system.

Finally, with regard to paperwork, the standards of the Sheridan administration are very high and the administration and office workers take pride in the superiority of their record keeping to that of other schools.

The curriculum of Sheridan High School has undergone a great deal of change in the past 2 decades. As mentioned above, the old system of tracking was a rigid ability-grouping system that stratified the population and provided students with differentially ranked credentials on leaving the school. The new curriculum also stratifies the population, but the mechanism is much different. Within the regular subject areas such as English, history, and mathematics, different classes are offered at different levels. This system differs in theory from the old tracking system in that students are assigned independently to levels of difficulty in each subject, rather than being put into a single stratified track. One of our observers recorded the ethnic percentages in these different-level classes and discovered that ethnic groups are to some extent stratified in these different levels, although the separation is not strict. Prestigious classes usually are mixed, although "slow-learner" classes are often almost entirely minority.

Special programs of two kinds have become increasingly prominent in the curriculum and further serve to stratify the population. Some classes—those for slow-learners, non-native speakers of English, and business and vocational students—serve primarily black and Hispanic youth, as well as poor, recently immigrated Chinese. Other special programs, including a school for international affairs, a communications school, and foreign language classes besides those in Spanish and Chinese, have percentages of white and middle-class Chinese students far out of proportion to their numbers in the school. Black students are also represented in these classes to some extent, but these are mostly middle-class blacks.

In extracurricular activities and student government, a curious mixture of activities follows ethnic boundaries, whereas others cut across those boundaries. Most of the clubs in the school are explicitly ethnically based, such as the Chinese Culture Club, the Latin American Club, and the Black Awareness Club. Other clubs, such as the Italian Club, are vestiges of population groups no longer predominant in the school and serve a mixed group of students. The chief activities that unite students across ethnic boundaries are the Theatre Club and the student government. The student council of the school, year after year, contains members of each major ethnic group in the school. In this case, the ethnic politics within the school mirror the "balanced ticket" that has been traditional in the politics of the wider community for years. Many of the athletic teams are dominated by one ethnic group. In general, however, only a very small percentage of Sheridan students participate in extracurricular activities.

The teaching staff at Sheridan is organized formally into a union that operates on a system-wide basis. Most of the teachers are white and Jewish and have been teaching for several years. A fiscal crisis for the whole system resulted in the layoffs of many younger and minority teachers throughout the system during our fieldwork, although the small proportion of minority teaching staff did actually increase somewhat during this period as a result of a new mandate for bilingual education.

The day-to-day operation of Sheridan High School, from the point of view of the staff, is handicapped by three kinds of organizational dysfunction: First, attendance rate is low and erratic; second, many of those students who do attend school cut classes, congregating and associating in spite of and in contravention of the bureaucratically ordained programming patterns; and finally, there is a low rate of graduation. Barely one-third of the students who come to Sheridan in the tenth grade will receive a high school diploma from Sheridan.

The latter two problems will be discussed later, but the issue of attendance deserves mention here. Attendance rate is directly tied to the formula for allocating money to the school. Beyond the direct financial impact, low and erratic attendance is a primary educational and organizational problem and contributes to both the difficulty in maintaining order within the school and the difficulty in maintaining continuity of instruction. Part of the attendance problem and the large rate of turnover can be attributed to movement of the population and to the insecurities and contingencies of life for the poor and working class. Another part of the attendance problem can be attributed to the structure of the school itself, especially its impersonality and size.

Social Relations of Students
Sheridan High School

Three kinds of data help to focus on the social relations of students in Sheridan High: profiles of eight Sheridan students, maps of territorial distribution, and utterances of linguistic labels. Sociological profiles yield information on three aspects of social process: *sorting, territoriality*, and *rule making* and *rule breaking*, with respect to both community-based and school-based constraints. The maps present more specialized information on territoriality, and the sociolinguistic section presents more specialized analysis of the labeling aspect of sorting.

The first body of data, the sociological profiles, has been constructed using the anthropological techniques of network analysis (Barnes, 1954, 1968; Ianni, 1972, 1974) and event analysis (Corsini and Howard, 1964). Originally, we analyzed narrative accounts of all actions and interactions of each of these students over the course of 1 or several days. We then combined information from both our observations of students' social contacts and these students' own statements about their friendship patterns.

SOCIOLOGICAL PROFILES OF EIGHT STUDENTS

The eight Sheridan students chosen for sociological profiles vary widely in sociological attributes such as social class, ethnicity, neighborhood of residence, length of time their families have lived in the region, language(s) spoken, and family structure. They also vary in their statuses within the school organization. These students are sorted into various areas of the curriculum by the programming process, and they also have different relations with the disciplinary and security system of the school.

In each profile, knowledge of each informant is summarized with respect to three characteristics: (a) the informant's place in the social structure of the larger community; (b) the characteristics of each informant's personal friendship network; and (c) the characteristics of the informant's relations with the school organization. After presenting all eight day-long observations, we will present a comparative analysis of the commonalities and the range of variation of these individuals' situations and attempt to assess the interrelationships among the three factors above. In this way, we hope to arrive at an understanding of the effects of both school-specific and community-generated constraints on individual students and their social and educational situations.

The first factor, the informant's place in the social structure of the community, must be placed in the context of the earlier community descriptions. Those descriptions emphasized processes of migration, ecological characteristics of neighborhoods and their spatial configurations, economic and political organization, and the historical development of ethnic succession in the neighborhoods.

The second factor, the characteristics of the informants' personal networks, focuses on two kinds of questions. The first is whether students associate in school with people they know from outside the school or with people they have met in the school. The second question concerns the amount of inter- versus intraethnic interactions that each informant engages in, both in formal classroom activities and in informal, personally chosen relationships. Sheridan is a particularly fascinating school in that it serves a diverse population. Its students come from many racial and cultural backgrounds. They also come from neighborhoods of the city that vary considerably in their degree of residential segregation. The school's official documents proudly proclaim that "Sheridan is one of the most uniquely integrated schools in one of the most culturally pluralistic communities in the country." The following analysis should serve to operationalize these concepts of "integration" and "cultural pluralism."

Finally, the individual's organizational status helps to clarify the relationships of community structure and individual networks to education and the design of educational organizations.

Daniel McKee, a white male, belongs to one of the middle-class, professional families that live in the subsidized moderate-income apartment buildings east of the school by the river. His personal friendship network of age peers seems to consist of two types of people. His closest friends, both in and out of school, are white, like himself, and probably also middle-class. Their bit of turf just outside the school is on the southeast corner, nearest the housing projects. He also has numerous casual acquaintances among Hispanic youths and Chinese youths inside the school, but he draws certain lines about these relationships. He does not report or exhibit any black acquaintances.

In his relations with the school, Daniel follows the rules, understands and manipulates the system well, and stays out of trouble. He does not, however, avail himself of an offered opportunity to participate in an elite program within the school's curriculum, the communications workshop, in which a large proportion of the students are white. The fact that the school and his family communicate directly and steadily through ties that are found in the community (e.g., his gym teacher's acquaintance with his family) is quite unusual for the majority of Sheridan students. Most students' parents are likely to have contact with the school only in case of extreme difficulties, in which case the parents must come to school to confer with the deans or counselors.

Follow-up note: When we last saw Daniel, he had graduated but he was still hanging out in his regular place in front of school, talking to girls coming out of school. He was not in college and was looking for a job.

Louise Marshall is a black female student who comes to high school from Morganville. Her socioeconomic status is probably low, although her appearance does not suggest extreme poverty. She is highly politically aware. That she knows the name of her Congressman is probably representative of Morganville's generally high level of politicization.

Her friendship pattern, by her own report, is dispersed and casual. Most of her acquaintances in the school are black, but she has met them in class and not outside in the community. This suggests that ethnicity has served as a powerful recruitment factor within the school.

Her relationship with the formal structure of the school is troubled by her propensity to absence and tardiness; she blames having to get up early to make the long trip downtown for part of these problems. When she does attend class, however, she is a lively participant in whatever is going on, whether in the formal lesson or in the informal interactions that often threaten to swamp the formal lesson in the classes to which she is assigned. Her English class (mythology) is a regular and not a modified (slow-learner) class, indicating that her reading scores are respectable. She has a lively verbal ability, and she reads the newspapers regularly. She is following the business curriculum, in which black and Hispanic students predominate.

Mike Edwards is a black male student of lower-income background who lives in the ethnically diverse neighborhood around Sheridan High School. His family migrated to the metropolis from the South within the past 20 years. He has always gone to school in this neighborhood and has always been in ethnically mixed classes.

His personal friendship network includes members of all the major groups in the school: blacks, whites, Chinese, and Hispanics. These friendships have grown out of school experiences as well as his activities in numerous community service organizations in the neighborhood. Even within his own family, Mike has a reputation for having many nonblack friends. His single closest friend, however, is a black male who lives not in the neighborhood but uptown. They met in school but associate in both neighborhoods outside school. This relationship suggests that in Mike's case, also, coethnicity has served as a recruitment factor in the composition of his friendship network. The overall ethnic diversity of his network probably also owes much to his having been labeled as "intellectually gifted" early in his school career and thus put into special classes that were more mixed than regular classes. In Sheridan, Mike is in a special program for low-income "under-achievers."

His feelings toward school are personal and intense, and his relations with the school are strong but often troubled. On the one hand, he expects a great deal from formal institutions and spends much of his time in them. He often takes constructive roles, such as doing extra work and supervising young children. On the other hand, he is cynical about rules and regulations, and he can become quite angry when he feels that he is being slighted. At the time of our interviews,

213

he reported that he had recently been having some difficulties and that his grades were falling. He conceives his relations to institutions in personal terms, as a set of mutual responsibilities between himself and specific adults.

Lucy Han is an American-born, non-Chinese-speaking Chinese female from a middle-class family. She lives in the East Point neighborhood but not in Chinatown. Like that of Mike Edwards, her personal friendship network includes members of various ethnic groups. She is one of the school's top academic achievers. The student government body to which she belongs in Sheridan is also polyethnic and contributes a large part of her close associates in school. Inasmuch as the student government is partially the result of ethnic voting patterns among students and partially the result of recruitment by faculty advisers trying to bring about an ethnically diverse group, we see here in microcosm some of the peculiarities of the ethnic politics of the larger metropolis. Voting and appointments along ethnic lines create a political structure with members of different groups who must then work together. Thus, the ethnic politician's interactions from day to day are with members of other groups as often as, or even more often than, with members of his or her own group.

Although Lucy Han spends more time with non-Chinese than with other Chinese students in Sheridan, she is intimately familiar with what the other Chinese students are doing. Her position in the school mirrors the position of a certain group of Chinese in the larger community. To understand this correspondence, it is useful to compare Lucy and Steven Wong, a Chinese-speaking Chinese student. Both Lucy's and Steven's fathers are professionals, but Steven's father was educated in China and Lucy's father in the United States. Steven is one of a number of Chinese students who do extremely well in math and science but who have language difficulties with subjects such as English and history, since they, too, received part of their education in Hong Kong.

Steven's group also controls the Chinese Culture Club, the most active student club in the school. Many of the members of the club are also primarily Chinese-speaking and recent immigrants from Hong Kong and elsewhere, but they are from a much lower class than either Steven or Lucy. Their parents are the waiters and factory workers whose lives are closely circumscribed by the Chinatown ghetto. We could also have included lower-class, English-speaking Chinese and Chinese youth gangs. Gang members are rarely found in school, however. In recent years, Chinatown has been troubled by rivalries between English-speaking and Chinese-speaking youth gangs.

Thus, the factors of class and date of immigration combine to include at least four groups of Chinese in Sheridan: middle-class and English-speaking, middle-class and Chinese-speaking, lower-class and English-speaking, and lower-class and Chinese-speaking. Middle-class English-speaking Chinese like Lucy are often among Sheridan's best students in most college preparatory segments of the curriculum. Middle-class Chinese-speaking students often do extremely well in advanced math and science classes and not so well in other subjects. Chinese-speaking students of all income levels, of course, fill much of the English as a Second Language and bilingual classes. Lower-class English-speaking students are particularly likely to become involved in trouble.

Cindy Ng is a recent immigrant to the United States from Hong Kong. She is bilingual, lower-class, and a resident of Chinatown. Both of her parents work long hours at low-paying factory jobs.

Her closest friend is Annie Moy, who is also bilingual, lower-class, and a Chinatown resident. Cindy has one other friend at Sheridan, Angela, a Hispanic female. This friendship, however, is largely confined to the several classes that the two of them share. They do not sit together in the cafeteria or associate after school or on weekends. Thus, Cindy's close personal friendship network is made up mostly of poor Chinese like herself. She has come into conflict with the youth gang structure that is currently causing turmoil in Chinatown. These gangs have arisen only since the post-1965 fivefold increase in the population of Chinatown. The swelling population has made it impossible for the traditional governance system of Chinatown, which is itself outside the formal structure of municipal government, to maintain its previous high degree of control and organization.

Despite her language difficulties, Cindy is making excellent progress in her education. She is assigned to reading and language classes and has already placed out of the English as a Second Language curriculum. Besides these reading and language classes, she is assigned to a science class. She has not been assigned to any of the business curriculum in the school. Cindy attends her classes regularly, with the exception of gym, and participates. Her degree of participation in the all-Chinese-language class, however, is much higher than her participation in the classes she shares with non-Chinese students. In these latter classes, she speaks out less frequently. Her Chinese class provides some continuity with the social organization of the Hong Kong schools. This class is also significantly different from the Hong Kong system, however, in that the Hong Kong system does not sanction much student recitation. Thus, the Chinese class at Sheridan provides continuity as well as a bridge to the social norms of the American classroom. Continuity with Chinese tradition is also provided by the activities of the school's Chinese Culture Club, whose meetings and activities she attends.

Carmen Nieves is a lower-class, bilingual Puerto Rican student who lives in the area just north of the school. Her personal friendship network is composed primarily of other students who were born in Puerto Rico or whose parents were. Carmen is English-language-dominant at this point, although her friends are both English- and Spanish-dominant. She associates with most of her female friends in the neighborhood as well as at school. Her father is quite strict about dating, however. Consequently, Carmen socializes a great deal in school.

She is a chronic class cutter. When she cuts classes, however, she does not hang out outside the way that male students do when they cut. She has established a set of relationships with the teachers and secretaries who work in the offices on the first floor. Since she often works there, no one questions where she should be. She manipulates this position to wander around the hallways while ostensibly doing errands. Her relations with her classroom teachers are as hostile as her relations with the office workers are warm. Carmen's program consists of courses in the business curriculum and modified classes designated for slow learners. Her experience with her program adviser is also rather typical at least in its brevity. The school must program several thousand students each term and must strain its personnel resources merely to accomplish this task.

Josie Fernandez is a lower-class, Dominican female student who lives in a small area of Dominican settlement north of the school. She is not an American citizen, but she and her family are legal immigrants. She is bilingual, but most of her friends speak with her in Spanish. Her friends are primarily Dominicans but include some Puerto Ricans. A Puerto Rican male student, Louis, is her close confidant, although she does not date non-Dominican males. In her lunch periods, she either sits with other Dominican females in the school cafeteria or goes outside to a sandwich shop that is frequented only by Hispanic students at this time of day.

She is assigned to academic classes in the school, including a re-

216

medial reading class. She is sometimes absent and sometimes cuts class, but she does so judiciously and hopes to pass her courses. In a marginal situation, her decision to attend a particular class is based on considerations of which of her friends are likely to be in the class.

Hutch is a first-generation resident of the city. His parents are from Puerto Rico. He speaks English but is Spanish-dominant. His closest friend, Starsky, who shares these characteristics, also lives in the same housing project as Hutch in the East Point area. The two are close friends and are also associated with a group of Hispanic youths who on occasion band together to fight with another group of black Sheridan students. Since Starsky and Hutch were unable to arrange their schedules for the same lunch period, one of them usually cuts class in order that they can eat lunch together. When they are outside the school, they have a habitual "turf."

Hutch does very poorly in school and does not expect to finish. By his own account, he normally attends class except for the following occasions: (a) if there is a fight scheduled; (b) if it is Starsky's lunch period; and (c) "if there is a teacher who doesn't try to help you in class." During the term of our observations, he consistently cut two classes, citing an unhelpful teacher as the reason for his behavior.

COMPARATIVE ANALYSIS OF
THE EIGHT PROFILES

From comparisons of the detailed school experiences of eight students from different backgrounds, a general pattern emerges. Generalizations drawn here will refer not only to the cases presented for illustration but also, of course, to many other cases recorded in our notes.

In comparing the personal network of the students, we will first examine the ways in which friendship networks in the school are recruited. It is important to know to what extent previous community-based ties account for ties within the school and to what extent school-specific factors account for linkages among persons. The question then shifts to how these processes work and how they are interrelated. Finally, we want to know how the social networks of the students relate to their statuses in the school organization and, again, what processes account for such patterns.

The personal networks of Sheridan students are recruited from five major sources, none of which is independent of the other four. These five sources are neighborhood of residence, ethnicity, social class, status in the school organization, and activities of special interest.

Neighborhood of Residence

All of the students we have observed have friends in the school whom they know from outside the school. In most cases, a student's best friend is likely to be someone known from the neighborhood. This is certainly true for Daniel McKee, Cindy Ng, Carmen Nieves, Hutch, and Josie Fernandez. The possible exceptions are Louise Marshall, Lucy Han, and Mike Edwards. Louise claims that she has met most of her school friends in school. They are predominantly black like herself. Mike Edwards's best friend is a black male from a different neighborhood, but he also has many friends of several ethnic groups from his own neighborhood. Lucy Han, who lives near but not in Chinatown, presents herself as separate from other Chinese in the school, but in fact she is intimately familiar with what they do. She also has friends from several ethnic groups from the neighborhood.

The implications of the importance of neighborhood ties with respect to the ethnicity of a student's friends are complex, since Sheridan students come both from highly segregated neighborhoods like Morganville and Chinatown and from neighborhoods with more fluid boundaries, such as many parts of the East Point area. Thus, Lucy Han and Mike Edwards have polyethnic associations outside as well as inside school. The others seem to have predominantly intraethnic relationships outside school.

Ethnicity

Common ethnic identity is a powerful source of friendship recruitment within the school. The meaning of ethnicity requires some disentangling, however. Ethnic identity itself is composed of many factors, including language, class, religion, phenotype, political orientation, and even, in our analysis, neighborhood of residence within the city. Morganville, for example, is both more highly politicized in terms of an ethnic ideology and more ethnically segregated than the East Point section. The examination of the politics of ethnicity requires, in turn, an analysis of social class. The ethnic politician is often either a higher-class or upwardly mobile individual who appeals to lower-class members of his or her group as a constituency. The student government in Sheridan replicates the patterns of citywide politics in this respect. This politicized process of ethnic identification must be distinguished from the more passive and unconsciously chosen identification that arises from common cultural patterns of speech, role expectations, beliefs and attitudes, and coresidence in an ethnically segregated ghetto. This second form of ethnic identification is likely to diminish with upward socioeconomic mobility. The politicized form of ethnicity, however, may assume increasing importance at the same time that the cultural content of ethnicity and the economic segregation that creates the ghetto are diminishing. In this community these two processes are strikingly evident.

With the foregoing qualifications, then, we may yet observe that students who make friends in Sheridan with youths previously unknown to them are most likely to choose others of similar ethnic background.

Social Class

Social class normally operates as a source of recruitment of friends within ethnic boundaries but, again, is also mediated by neighborhood of residence. The interrelations of class and ethnicity in American life are of great dialectical complexity. In New York newspapers, "Blacks and Hispanics" and "lower class" are used almost interchangeably. Thus, the position of the middle classes of these groups is obscured. In Sheridan, Irish, Italian, and Jewish youths are predominantly middle-class. Two groups of middle-class Chinese are distinguishable, the American-born Chinese whose parents or ancestors emigrated from China at an earlier time and the Chinese-speaking emigrants. The former group came from lower-class backgrounds in the Orient and has worked its way up through the American educational system. The latter group has been called the "stranded Chinese." These people come from higher-class backgrounds in China. Their parents came to this country for education or for political reasons and have remained. They speak Chinese and retain more of Chinese culture in their family lives. As we have seen in the comparison of Lucy Han and Steven Wong, there is both separation and contact between these two groups (Kuo, 1970). Many of the black students in Sheridan are poor, but the middle-class blacks still greatly outnumber middle-class Hispanics. Hispanics are the poorest as a group, yet the lower-class Chinese whose parents work in the factories and restaurants of Chinatown are also among the poorest students in Sheridan.

In general, individuals of higher class are less bound by the strictly cultural content of ethnicity, although they may or may not

219

still attach great importance to coethnicity. Their general institutional competence is much higher, and thus they find it not so difficult to relate to others who are similarly competent. The most prestigious classes in Sheridan are the most mixed. The striking exception to this generalization is the number of advanced math and science classes at Sheridan that are predominantly Chinese. These students are most likely to come from higher-class backgrounds in China. They bring with them educational and institutional competence, but they lack facility with the English language and concentrate their efforts on math and science. They are structurally assimilated but culturally segregated.

The phenomenon of the high rate of interethnic interactions of the ethnic politician, who is likely to be middle-class, is a special case of the effect of social class on ethnicity. Here the very process of activist ethnic identification leads the social actor into a wider arena of associations.

In general, ethnic boundaries are more rigid among lower-class members of the ethnic category and among more recent immigrants. The "stranded Chinese" are the exception to the general rule that the more recent arrivals are usually also poorer. Higher-class members of ethnic groups may still maintain their primary associations with coethnics, but they are thrown into more instrumental transactions with members of other groups, since the more prestigious classes at Sheridan are more mixed than the less prestigious classes, which tend to be predominantly lower-class and nonwhite.

Status in the School Organization

A student's individual path through a day at Sheridan is a primary determinant of his or her possibilities for informal friendship ties. The school's size and complexity and the stratification of its curriculum are the two factors that most influence a student's informal associations. The size and complexity of the school most often serve to fragment the associations that are brought into the school from the neighborhood. Students are often not able to see their best friends because their programs diverge. Much of the high rate of class-cutting that constitutes one of the school's major organizational problems is attributable to this fact. The profiles of Mike Edwards, Hutch, and Carmen Nieves all illustrate that students cut class in order to be with their friends, who are separated by their schedules. This pattern is repeated throughout our field notes. One of the great curiosities of

Sheridan is that students will come to school day after day and yet miss their classes. Instead, they congregate on the immediate periphery of the school, in stairs, hallways, the cafeteria, and even the administrative offices under the very noses of the adult staff. They do not like classes, but they love school for the opportunity it gives them to congregate with their age peers. Only a small percentage of them manage to structure their informal associations within the extracurricular activities that the school provides and legitimates, such as the student clubs, teams, and activities. Other students make clandestine appropriations of whatever unsupervised space and time they can find.

The stratification of the curriculum to some extent cuts against the fragmentation that results from size and complexity. The complexly divided curriculum with its many special programs tends to reinforce class and ethnicity. Recent immigrants are funneled into the ESL, bilingual, and other language classes. White and Chinese students are disproportionately concentrated in college preparatory classes and programs. Black and Hispanic students are disproportionately concentrated in slow-learner and business classes. Even when two students who are of similar background and who are already friends are placed in the same segments of the curriculum, however, they are still likely to be separated by their programs, since there are several sections of each class. Thus, the curriculum tends to fragment neighborhood ties even though it also reinforces class and ethnic divisions. This fact is partly responsible for the phenomenon of ethnicity as a recruitment factor inside the school. A student finds himself in a classroom with other students he does not already know. Some of these other students are of similar background and some are not. Those with common elements of identity are likely to strike up new relationships. Mike Edwards and Louise Marshall both report such situations. We have also seen examples of this situation for white, Hispanic, and Chinese students.

SPECIAL INTERESTS AND INSTRUMENTAL TRANSACTIONS

Sheridan students often associate with others on the basis of common interest. Although some interests may be culturally specialized, this source of recruitment of associates is the most likely to cut across ethnic boundaries. The Chinese, for example, predominate on the math team and, in some years, in art and photography work for student publications. Several of the sports teams appeal to particular

221

groups. Blacks predominate in basketball and track, Hispanics in soccer and baseball, whites on the girls' swimming team. The girls' modern dance classes appeal equally to blacks and Hispanics. The culture clubs appeal overtly to ethnicity and reify ethnic identity within the school.

Other extracurricular activities, however, represent the most noticeable loci of recurrent interethnic interactions among Sheridan students. The student council, the drama group, and the peer group organization all usually have polyethnic membership. The informal associations in these activities operate with clearly defined rules of how to deal with ethnic boundaries. To some extent, the students who participate in these three organizations overlap. They constitute a minority among Sheridan students both in the fact that they look to the extracurricular activities of the school for their friendships and in the polyethnic makeup of their networks. Since the same group, more or less, provides the basic membership of all three of these organizations, their relationships are often those of diffuse friendship.

In contrast to these relationships of diffuse solidarity across ethnic boundaries, the other domains of interethnic association that we have observed represent limited instrumental transactions that occur in specific situations and not in others.

The first of these situations of instrumental transaction is labeled by our observer Samuel Henry as the "learning underground." This phrase refers to a recurrent pattern of classroom behavior in which students share help with their lessons, either licitly or illicitly in the form of cheating, but in either case without direction from or apparent awareness on the part of the teacher. In cases where students have diffuse friendships and are in the same classroom, their sharing of their work is predictably more regular. However, we have observed that students are quite willing to share their schoolwork across ethnic boundaries. This sharing may include cheating, as when Daniel McKee gives his answers to a Hispanic male student in the accounting class, or it may include permissible sharing of textbooks and classroom exercises, as in the case of Cindy Ng and Angela. This pattern of cooperation in schoolwork across ethnic boundaries that would separate the same individuals in social encounters outside the classroom is very common.

The second common pattern of interethnic instrumental transactions is the buying, selling, and, to a lesser extent, consumption of marijuana both inside the school in clandestinely occupied areas and outside on the immediate periphery of the school. Shared consumption implies a more diffuse friendship, whereas buying and selling are more strictly instrumental transactions.

To assess the significance of all this for the process of education and the design of educational organizations, it is necessary to address the question of whether associations across ethnic boundaries are related with success in school. The Chinese-speaking honors students immediately seem to refute such a supposition. Among our eight students, however, the two with the best academic records, Lucy Han and Mike Edwards, are also the two with the mixed sets of friendships.

Social class does seem to correlate highly with academic success. Middle-class members are the best students, regardless of ethnicity. Again, however, we are confounded in any simple correlation of class and success by the differential school success of lower-class Chinese and lower-class blacks and Hispanics. Among our eight students, we may observe that Cindy Ng maintains a much more mutually productive relationship with the school than does Louise Marshall, Carmen Nieves, Hutch, or Josie. Thus neither class nor ethnicity, difficult to separate even conceptually, is sufficient to explain differences in school performance.

To resolve this dilemma, we must differentiate between structural and cultural assimilation. The Chinese students in Sheridan are more structurally than culturally assimilated with regard to the predominantly white and Jewish faculty and administration. Blacks have far less cultural distance from the adult staff than the Chinese. They share native English speech, citizenship, and political socialization. The two groups are, however, structurally opposed, especially in the aftermath of the 1968 teachers' strike and the dispute over community control. Hispanics have been structurally allied with blacks since that strike, although the interests of these two groups are also now diverging as Hispanic political organization begins to emerge. Hispanics are also separated culturally from the adult staff by speech and by their circular migration to and from the Caribbean. Dominicans are noncitizens, more politicized than Puerto Ricans, and consequently even farther in social distance from the staff.

Structural assimilation appears to be the most important criterion for academic success. Close personal friendship across ethnic boundaries does not seem to be necessary for academic success. The ability to deal with members of other groups in instrumental transactions, however, is necessary for success. The Chinese students and the teaching staff of Sheridan have different cultural backgrounds. Their assump-

223

tions about schooling, however, are similar enough to permit a workable structural alliance even across a great gulf of social distance.

Middle-class students of any ethnicity are also more likely to share with the staff certain assumptions about schooling. Lower-class black and Hispanic students, however, do not share such assumptions. They expect little from the school and the school expects little from them. They have the poorest academic records, encounter more disciplinary sanctions, and participate the least in extracurricular activities.

SOCIOLINGUISTIC ANALYSIS OF ETHNIC LABELING BEHAVIOR

In an earlier comparative study of three high schools, we identified a basic social process that we called *sorting*, which took different forms in each of the three schools. Simply put, high school students in each site did not associate randomly but formed cliques and personal friendship networks. In each site, this process of social differentiation was accompanied by a set of categorical linguistic terms that students assigned one another, although the correspondence of these terms to actual patterns of association was by no means perfect. In the rural school, students sorted one another in terms of their places of residence—the names of each of eight local towns and villages from which the school drew its population—thus providing names for various cliques. In the urban school, Sheridan, the most common sorting practice involved the assignment of labels referring to racial phenotype, language, religion, culture, or place of origin. In the suburban school, which served a highly undifferentiated population living in a circumscribed local area, the sorting labels most commonly used were "jock" and "freak" and did not correspond to any identifiable structural attributes of those so labeled such as class, ethnicity, residence.

As mentioned, the correspondence between these systems of labeling categories and actual patterns of association is not perfect. Therefore, no statements about the relevance of these labeling systems to the processes of social action can be made before examining the use of these labels in actual situations. Language categories are instruments of social action, but they are also the results of social action.

The complexity and pervasiveness of ethnic labeling in Sheridan clearly indicated to us the need for understanding and recording the different ways in which ethnicity is invoked in various situations.

Ethnic groups and internal divisions of these groups in Sheridan High School are many and diverse enough that the uses of ethnic labels for the identification of self and others are quite varied, and the meaning of such labels, the choice of which label to use, or indeed the choice to employ such a label at all can change from one situation to another.

The focus here, then, is the relationship of the language behavior of ethnic labeling to the reality of social action in the school.

Collecting the Corpus of Utterances

Having noticed the prevalence of ethnic labeling and wishing to investigate this phenomenon more systematically, we assembled a set of data for analysis and comparison. From a selected portion of our

Utterances

ETHNIC LABEL	NUMBER OF OCCUR-RENCES	ETHNIC LABEL	NUMBER OF OCCUR-RENCES
black	32	Chinese	26
nigger	1	Hong Kong	3
Negro	6	Taiwan	2
black kid from uptown	1	white	16
colored	1	American (referring to white Americans)	3
black American	1	Italian	4
Afro-American	1	Wop	1
dudes (referring exclusively to black, non-Hispanic males)	1	Jewish	5
		Irish	2
African	3	honky	1
half-Negro, half-Puerto Rican	1	German	1
Hispanic	4	Polish	1
Latino	3	West Indian	2
Spanish	5	Bajan	1
spick	1	Indian	1
Puerto Rican	28	Pakistani	1
Puerto Rican hick	1	Brazilian	1
Negro Puertoriquena	1	non-Chinese	1
P.R.	16	non-English speaker	1
Dominican	1	alien	2
Domingo	1	Christian (specifically meaning non-Jewish)	1
R.D.	1		
Cuban	1		

notes, we extracted all utterances that seemed to constitute ascriptions of ethnic identity by the speaker, either with reference to others or reflexively to the speaker himself. The preceding list is a compilation of all utterances possible ascribing ethnicity that are contained in the field notes of three observers (Sullivan, Henry, Mavros) for the field-work period September 1975 through March 1976.

Because we were looking for labels that were significant categories to our informants, we could not judge questionable instances by our own categories. Therefore, our rule of thumb was to include all questionable cases at the beginning.

A data sheet for each utterance was constructed containing a situational description of the circumstances in which the utterance occurred. The format of the data sheets was as follows:

Data Sheet

Referential meaning	color (phenotype)
	religion
	place of origin
	language
	pejorative/not
	residual
	combinatory
Social meaning	speaker: name
	color (phenotype)
	place of origin
	language
	religion
	class
	neighborhood
	organizational status
About whom	name
	color (phenotype)
	place of origin
	language
	religion
	class
	neighborhood
	organizational status
Situation	where
	who present

Data Sheet (cont.)

Circumstances	equality–inequality
	formality–informality
	affect
	results
	given meaning if any

These sheets allowed space enough for narrative qualitative descriptions by observers.

Analysis

Comparative analysis of the data was based on the distinction in sociolinguistics between referential and social meaning (Blom and Gumperz, 1972; Ervin-Tripp, 1964). *Referential meaning* of a word is the denotative, dictionary meaning. *Social meaning* refers to the control that a speaker has over several words with the same referential meaning: One of these words is chosen according to situation, in response to social factors that are separate from the bare denotation of the word. Similarly, a given term may have different meanings according to different social contexts in which it occurs.

In order to analyze and compare the referential and social meanings of the utterances, we constructed a matrix to correlate the referential semantic content of each term with the situational context of each utterance of the term. Each utterance was matched against a set of exhaustive categories of referential meanings. These categories were inductively generated from the corpus of terms. The categories included the following semantic domains: color–phenotype, religion, place of origin, language. In addition, the terms could be differentiated from one another along with the following dimensions: Some are pejorative in manifest content and some are not; some are residual categories (non-Chinese) and most are not; some are combinatory categories (half-Negro, half-Puerto Rican).

Also added to the matrix was a set of categories that differentiate the situation and social context of the utterance. These social categories referring to the situation included the following: where, who present, equality–inequality of speaker and person labeled, formality–informality of the situation, affect, results, given meaning.

Having constructed a matrix, we first asked this question: In what sense are all of these terms ethnic labels? Do these terms stand for one system of mutually exclusive identities, or are they merely isolated descriptors? Admittedly, our hypothesis was that an ethnosemantic domain of ethnic labels exists, and we designed our matrix in an attempt to examine just this question.

The difference between the terms *Puerto Rican* and *black* is a specific example. In a strictly referential sense, the two terms do not seem to be mutually exclusive. One refers to a place and the other to a color. In our field notes, however, Louise Marshall says, "She's not black, she's Puerto Rican," in referring to a female student with dark skin. No formal linguistic elicitation procedure was used to obtain this statement. It is an everyday utterance that clearly indicates that, in this speaker's understanding, the two terms are mutually exclusive. This mutual exclusivity indicates that these terms are part of a single semantic domain. According to the results of our matrix, the term *black* is consistently used to refer to people with a wide range of skin colors but never to a person of Hispanic heritage. Similarly, the terms *Puerto Rican, Dominican, Latin, Latino,* and *Hispanic* are often used to refer to people with dark skin.

The data indicate that terms that seem referentially to refer to language, like *Chinese* and *Spanish*, are in fact used to refer to people who both do and do not speak these languages. The terms that seem to have place referents, like *Puerto Rican, Dominican,* and *Chinese,* are sometimes used to refer to people who have never set foot in these places.

Our conclusion is that there exists an ethnosemantic domain of social classification in which all of these terms are of a similar order of reality. This order of reality, in turn, cannot be reduced to any of the separate referential domains of phenotype, language, color, religion, or place of origin.

This ethnosemantic domain of classification, which we shall call *ethnic labels*, does indeed exist, but this process is a dynamic one in which people identify other people in real situations and not a closed, absolute, static system. This caution is important in that several of our informants may ask such questions as "What race is he?," thereby embedding this social process in a spurious biological ideology.

These considerations lead next to the question of how this system of classification is used in practice. How consistently are these terms used to apply to the same individuals from one situation to the next? This inquiry refers to the process that Blom and Gumperz call *code-switching*. They emphasize that social meaning can often be found in the systematic switching of referentially equivalent terms among different situational contexts.

For example, the two referentially equivalent terms *Latino* and *Hispanic* have referential meaning that imply a language—Spanish—and/or a place of origin where that language is spoken. However, the matrix indicates that these terms are used almost exclusively by different kinds of people. All recorded utterances of the term *Hispanic* were by adult teachers and administrators in the school. All uses of the term *Latino* were by students. The term *Spanish*, again with the same referential meaning, is used by both adult staff and students. Thus, the use of one or another of these referentially equivalent terms may convey a social identification of the speaker who has chosen the term.

The data suggest that two kinds of code-switching occur that have broad significance for understanding how ethnic identification operates. The first systematic form of code-switching is the process of *segmentary identification*. It will be noted that, in a strictly referential sense, some of the terms in our list are subsets of other terms. For example, all Puerto Ricans are Hispanics, but not vice versa. According to the matrix, speakers tend to identify someone more specifically when they share more elements of common identity with that person. Thus, a student born in New York City of parents born in Puerto Rico calls another student recently migrated from the rural areas of Puerto Rico by the term *Puerto Rican hick*. A third student, however, of non-Hispanic background altogether, calls both of the first two *Puerto Ricans* indiscriminately.

Similarly, students who are phenotypically Chinese make many linguistic distinctions among themselves according to the part of China they or their families originated from and, especially, according to whether or not they speak the Chinese language. Non-Chinese students, however, lump all these subcategories as *Chinese*.

The second type of systematic code-switching was more difficult to discover, since it involved the question of the null set—that is, the question of whether the ethnic labels are sometimes not used at all, in a manner that indicates social meaning. Obviously, it would not be valid to attempt to confirm the null hypothesis by presenting every recorded utterance that has no reference to the domain of ethnic identity. If we had found no such references at all, that fact would certainly be significant, but, in fact, we found many such references. How then do we show whether or not these terms are sometimes deliberately not used? One manner of achieving this is to look for cases in which one person performs a verbal classification of this sort and another person disagrees with that entire practice. Indeed, the list of utterances contains several such examples.

In this analysis, two utterances of two speakers, one student and one administrator, help to explicate the null hypothesis. In the case of each speaker, one utterance applies an ethnic label to someone and another utterance denies the validity of ethnic labeling altogether. We will call the student Nancy Travis and the administrator Bill Morgan.

Nancy Travis is a middle-class Morganville resident with dark skin. She is a senior, an honor student, and the president of both the Student Organization Executive Council and of the Black Awareness Club, of which she is also a founder. In the following passage from our field notes, Nancy and a few other students of different ethnic groups are in the student organization office, along with a teacher–adviser, Mr. Gormley:

> The students were trying to plan an upcoming trip, but, as usual, there was a lot of horsing around. Mr. Gormley was sitting at the desk by the wall grading papers and sometimes putting in a remark. Nancy was joking a lot and digressing from the subject of the trip, but whenever a decision came up, she seemed to make it and tell the others what they would all do. At one point, they were talking about another student government group, the Senior Council. Nancy remarked, "There is not a single black, white, or Chinese person on the Senior Council."
>
> A few minutes later, everyone had left the office except Nancy, her friend Linda—the other founder of the Black Awareness Club—and Mr. Gormley, who had finished grading his papers. As Nancy was about to leave the office, she and Mr. Gormley were joking around and kidding each other about the way Nancy was running the SO [Student Organization] Council. He kept accusing her of not letting anyone else make decisions. She kept smiling and saying, "Somebody has to decide." Just as she was about to leave for her class, Mr. Gormley delivered his parting shot: "Nancy, is it true that you used all the SO funds to order Afro-American T-shirts?" Nancy replied, "I'm not an Afro-American, I'm just a person," and walked off to her class. Mr. Gormley looked at me, shook his head, and chuckled.

When talking about the Senior Council, Nancy is not reluctant to use ethnic labels. In the cross fire of her verbal jousting with the teacher, however, she does not hesitate to switch from using ethnic labeling to denying the validity of being so labeled herself. Thus, the null set, the denial of the validity of such labeling, is just as much a part of Nancy's cognitive system as are the various labels themselves. The fact that she uses the labels for others but protests being so labeled herself in a situation of verbal competition suggests that perhaps these labels are sometimes associated with situations of unequal power and that, although these labels are often used, they are also regarded as threatening in some situations.

Adults make similar code switches. Bill Morgan is a white, non-Hispanic department chairman. The following utterances occurred in two separate situations:

(1) *I was talking to a new student teacher, Ellen Stearns, in the cafeteria. She was complaining about Mr. Morgan, her supervisor. She said, "The first day I came here, I went in to talk to him and he kept telling about the problems of teaching black and Puerto Rican students. I finally got mad at him and said 'I grew up around blacks and Puerto Ricans all my life, thank you, and I don't find any particular problem in dealing with them.'* [Note: *Ellen Stearns herself is white and non-Hispanic.*]

(2) *Today, I sat down with Mr. Morgan in the cafeteria. He showed me a questionnaire he had just received in the mail from Washington and asked me if I had heard about it. I told him no. He showed me the inside of the questionnaire, which asked for information on the ethnic mixture in each of his classes. Mr. Morgan said, "These forms don't mean a thing. They can't tell you anything. What about Spanish kids who aren't at all Spanish?"*

In each example, an individual speaker attributes ethnic labels to others in one situation and disputes the entire practice of ethnic labeling in another situation. Again, the denial occurs in a relationship of unequal power, in which the speaker feels threatened. Not only Mr. Morgan, but, indeed, many of the teachers in the school were upset by the questionnaire mentioned above. Practically speaking, they had good reason to be concerned. The information collected in this manner by the Office of Civil Rights of the Department of Health, Education and Welfare was later used to impose sanctions on the personnel policies of the school system.

Conclusion

The analysis of social meaning of ethnic labeling behavior reveals that these labels are often used and accepted in a variety of social situations. Such behavior, however, has not achieved complete legitimacy. Although many people label one another in this way, the option to

231

challenge the meaningfulness of these classifications remains a lively possibility, an important part of the cognitive domain we are describing. The examples of Nancy Travis and Bill Morgan reveal this aspect of quasi-legitimacy in everyday conversation. Above the level of everyday interaction at the level of policy formation, interest-group politics, and formal litigation, however, many disputes go on over the legitimacy of ethnic labeling. After the Office of Civil Rights sanctions against the school system's personnel policies, for example, the system began assigning minority teachers separately from nonminority teachers. That practice precipitated lawsuits from several community groups. The legitimacy of using ethnic classification in public policy is once more tied up in the courts.

Many of the utterances culled from field notes were spoken in a neutral tone of voice, implying no positive or negative evaluation of the person being categorized. In a dense population where everyone does not know everyone else by name, these descriptors seem quite useful to everyone. In situations of conflict and inequality, however, these terms can easily become charged and threatening, and many people will deny the meaningfulness of these terms.

General Conclusions

A number of problems are associated with the presentation of research results from field studies. In large measure, the problems result from the nature of ethnographic inquiry itself, which is holistic, situational, descriptive, and generally designed to provide a statement of system characteristics rather than the inevitable association of elements or variables within the system. Eventually we do produce a typology of systems, and any generalizations that can inform social action programs, professional practice, or policy and decision-making processes are dependent on the analyst's or the practitioner's ability to identify his operational system with one of the model system types. Much of educational research has been narrowly deductive and has purported to present interrelationships among elements or variables that are conceptually independent of any given situation. As a result, educational policymakers have come to expect statements of lawlike regularities from research. Such statements do not emerge from ethnographic field research, and techniques and standards of application and operational utility for qualitative data are just beginning to develop.

Thus, generalizing from our study of desegregation in one urban high school requires some caution. The problem is further complicated by the setting of our study. New York City has a number of unique characteristics, and the overwhelming importance of ethnicity as an organizer in political, social, economic, and educational systems may be idiosyncratic. Despite these caveats, however, we have attempted to present both our conclusions and the recommendations that we have derived from them in terms that can be generalized to high schools in general and to urban, inner-city, polyethnic high schools in particular.

The conclusions emerge from two levels of analysis: the political and historical context within which desegregation and culture contact have taken place in the community surrounding Sheridan High School and the school context itself. Because recommendations should grow out of a clear research base, we have included most of our recommendations within the body of the report where they emerged and we recapitulate them here in association with the conclusions that lead to them.

CONCLUSIONS ABOUT THE CULTURAL– HISTORICAL CONTEXT IN WHICH SHERIDAN HIGH SCHOOL OPERATES

Much of what is school-specific about the educational program and the structure of order at Sheridan High School grows out of the history of ethnic succession in New York. In the Americanization period of the twenties and thirties, eastern European and Mediterranean (primarily Italian) immigrants who lived in Sheridan's attendance area were willing and indeed eager to become assimilated into American society even at the price of their own ethnic identity. The schools, as the agents of Americanization, could be patently paternalistic and offer access to American society and eventual social and economic mobility in exchange for becoming American. The new migrants in the area—black, Hispanic, and Chinese—not only are less willing to give up their ethnic identity and heritage, but also generally find less access to social mobility than seems to have been true of the earlier migrants. To a major extent, this change reflects the illusion of the melting pot and the ethnicizing of political and economic power in New York City.

The ethnic factor in power politics is most dramatically seen in the

233

composition and leadership of municipal unions in the city. The police department in New York has been traditionally an Irish stronghold, although other ethnic groups are beginning to make inroads, so that the Emerald Society (Irish) within the department now competes with the Shalom Society (Jewish), the Columbian Society (Italian), the Steuben Society (German), and the Guardian Society (blacks). Yet the Patrolmen's Benevolent Association, the major police union, is controlled largely by Irish members and, throughout the period of this study, was always headed by an Irish-American. The same ethnic concentration is true in the sanitation department (Italian) and the United Federation of Teachers (Jewish), as well as in the supervisory associations in education.

Today, black, Hispanic, and Chinese in the attendance area of Sheridan are asking for access to power through education as did previous migrants, but they do not propose to surrender their ethnic identity. One of the interesting results of this refusal is that it has led to a reassertion of ethnicity among previous immigrant groups and their children, once again intensifying the importance of ethnicity. Minority students and teachers often see these earlier immigrant groups as holding on to the power inherent in administrative positions in education, thereby blocking them from legitimate access to power.

The question of why Sheridan seems to be particularly bureaucratic is demonstrated and affirmed by the Gerry Report. In effect, this report maintains that the administrators of New York Ciy's schools are defending their control against the incursions of more recently arrived groups. The principal of Sheridan, as is true of all New York City High Schools, is given his job by the central board and not by a locally elected decentralized board, such as the one that is responsible for the elementary and junior high schools that surround Sheridan.

Diane Ravitch's work (Ravitch, 1975), although it often fastidiously avoids political interpretation of events in an attempt to "present both sides of the conflict," amply demonstrates that urban education has been highly politicized since its inception. In fact, the schools have been the field of conflict where immigrants have first made their political power felt for a century and a half. Education, as a public enterprise, is more directly approachable through politics than through private employment or privately owned housing. In this context, the politics of ethnicity may be more prominent in the school arena than in others. Studies of ethnicity in construction unions, for example, could shed needed light on this question. Certainly, the rest of the New York City municipal unions (police, firemen, sanitation workers) are organized within the context of ethnic politics.

How an educational system controls the jobs within it is, of course, a different question from how that system functions in ranking students who pass through it and funneling them into different sections of the labor market, including unemployment. Clearly, Sheridan is an institution highly concerned with ranking. A small elite, mostly white and Chinese, is channeled into special "prestige" curricula. Others, mostly lower-class black and Hispanic, are channeled into "remedial" and "alternative" programs, some of which may in fact be desirable alternatives for these students from a strictly educational standpoint (one of the alternative programs at least has been highly successful) but which also confer certain labels on them that limit their future possibilities. The teaching of basic English to very recent immigrants is a task that the school performs remarkably effectively, reflecting an established heritage of Americanizing newcomers and conferring minimal skills for entering the labor market. A sizable portion of the curriculum, the business segment, seems unlikely to produce executives and more likely to provide a pool of clerical labor for the Manhattan office industry.

Michael Katz's (1971) statement that bureaucracy in education came into being to promote the illusion of social mobility (while strictly regulating it) gains some support from this study. All high schools are rule-oriented institutions. Large high schools, in which social control cannot be accomplished by everyone's knowing everyone else by sight, are even more rule-oriented. Among large high schools in New York City, Sheridan itself is particularly rule-oriented. The security system and the control over teachers and students exerted by the following of the Developmental Lesson Plan format are rule systems in point.

Formal rules are the essence of bureaucracy, and, in Weber's conception, they provide democracy, fairness, and efficiency in comparison with traditional or charismatic types of authority. Yet rules can be enforced for some and overlooked for others, thus perpetuating relations of power that exist outside those rules. The proliferation of and emphasis on rules works to the advantage of those in the position to formulate and enforce them. In this sense, Sheridan demonstrates Katz's contention that bureaucracies do not come into being neutrally, merely as a necessary concomitant of urbanization and the increasing density of population. They come into being as agencies of social

235

control, and they represent an alternative rather than a complement to electoral local control.

Yet, as Ravitch demonstrates, the creation of bureaucracies also has unintended consequences. She stresses that huge bureaucracies may be created to keep power at a distance from one group only to evolve into powerful interest groups themselves, separate from either of the original contending groups. The potency of the United Federation of Teachers' political machinery under decentralization was not anticipated by those who constructed that legislation. In addition, the very insistence on rules and the inculcation of legalism can also backfire on groups using this strategy. Members of groups that are out of power learn to manipulate the rules, and those in power are caught in the middle. For those out of power and kept out of power by the manipulation of rules from above, two possible strategies exist. One is to break and ignore the rules. This is what many Sheridan students do when they cut class and appropriate for themselves the school's facilities in a clandestine manner. That was also an important component of the strategy of both pro- and antiintegration groups in the 1960s during strikes, boycotts, and demonstrations. The other strategy is to accept legalism and to try to manipulate it to one's own advantage. This strategy seems more characteristic of the 1970s, a period when the conflicts of the 1960s have become institutionalized. Ethnic politics in the city seem certain to continue to dominate both the management of the schools and the processes of affiliation among students. Desegregation in this context may well mean the manipulation of political power in the community as much as, if not more than, any school-specific changes.

CONCLUSIONS ABOUT CULTURE CONTACT AND DESEGREGATION IN SHERIDAN HIGH SCHOOL

To describe, define, explain, and correct the wide range of problems seen as disrupting schools, it is necessary, but difficult, to separate analytically what is "school" and what is "society." This is, of course, not a new problem, nor is it restricted to questions of how to deal with segregation and desegregation. Distinguishing between what is school-specific about culture contact and what is simply reflective of what is happening in the streets is central to explaining and remedying the problems. Failing to distinguish the two, we are likely to view culture contact through the same personal ideologies and institutional perspectives that have failed to do away with inequality in the general society.

The School Context

Sorting. The process of sorting at Sheridan is clearly based on ethnicity. In our earlier studies where community of origin in the rural high school was critical, the characteristics of sorting were established outside the school and carried into it. For example, school personnel might label a student from "Apple Valley" as "a student with good learning potential." Over time, the sorting might be adjusted, but the initial labeling set a tone for the student's entry into the school. In the suburban school, on the other hand, where ethnicity and social class were homogeneous among both students and school staff, sorting ("jocks" and "freaks") was clearly established within the school itself. In Sheridan, surrounded by ethnic enclave neighborhoods, ethnicity is not only established outside the school and brought into the building as the basis for sorting, but it becomes internalized on the part of the students even before they enter the school. Because of the ethnic characteristics of the feeder schools, students entering Sheridan usually will have accepted a degree of self-sorting along ethnic lines by the time they reach Sheridan. This self-sorting, born in neighborhoods and nurtured in elementary and intermediate schools, establishes in the student a self-image that serves as the basis for affiliation among students in Sheridan High School. Students use linguistic labels to reinforce the image and establish social boundaries among students. Although the school further reinforces these boundaries through its curricular programming of students, the essential point for the desegregation process is that it is the student and not the school that establishes the primary level of group affiliation and the social boundaries among students. Certainly this is true at Sheridan and in other New York City schools we have seen. Its saliency elsewhere is dependent upon the strength of ethnicity in communities and the relationship between that ethnicity and school assignment of students.

Territoriality. There are a number of territorial aspects to desegregation and to the process of contact among cultures in schools. The division of the school from the outside world is, in itself, a primary territorial demarcation. The ethnic turfs immediately outside the school are determined by neighborhood of origin. Within the school itself, sorting is reinforced by territorial division over time and space. As a result, obvious ethnically controlled spaces exist, as particular stairwells and even floors within the school. Once again, whereas the primary sorting is done by students themselves, who determine ethnic self-labels and social boundaries, the school reinforces the social boundary setting by programs that further isolate students into ethnically determined life spaces in the school. Although most of the teachers and administrators at Sheridan would maintain with conviction that academic streaming or tracking does not consciously take place there, the net effect of programming students into sequences of courses and events on the basis of perceived ability is to reinforce the ethnic pattern of sorting.

These affiliations and movements in time and space maintain the effects of segregation despite the mixture of students from a wide variety of ethnic identities. Students at Sheridan do cross ethnic boundaries in forming friendships and do violate territorial integrity established along ethnic lines, but not as a result of conscious efforts by the school or any other special institution. What leads to cross-ethnic affiliation is some event, cause, activity, or "equalizer." School disruptions or student activities may result in cross-ethnic affiliation characterized by either conflict or cooperation. Causes and activities seem to operate in the same fashion. Equalizers are those common interests—drugs and drug use are the most salient examples—which cut across ethnic boundaries and bind individuals into networks that supersede ethnicity. Movement over time and space is, we believe, a more "naturalistic" area for observation than sorting because it can be charted from direct observation. Yet both provide evidence of how the school refracts the ethnic boundaries established in communities.

Rule Making and Rule Breaking. Finally, systems of rules and conventions regulate and regularize behavior and social relationships within the school. Sorting and territoriality are interrelated with rules. Violations of formal rules may result when individuals compete for power within the system, as when students of different ethnic groups compete for territorial control. Or they may challenge the order of the system itself, as when students violate a teacher's control over the territory of the classroom. The imposition of the formal rules of the school is dependent on sorting and on territoriality as well. Rules are differentially enforced according to ethnicity. Black students, for example, who are considered potentially violent, are sometimes ignored when they violate rules. Student restrooms are considered student territory and are relatively free from adult supervision. These variations in rule enforcement are negotiated on a day-by-day basis. The social organization of Sheridan High School seems to be set up around the demarcation of identity and power.

Because power and autonomy in the school are limited, much of the boundary maintenance is symbolic. That is, since it is not possible to enforce rules successfully in a large school like Sheridan, emphasis falls on occasional enforcement and broad parameters for most rules. From this perspective, sorting, territoriality, and the making and breaking of rules are identifying procedures that mediate between the formal structures and informal systems. Whereas the formal structure of the school can be adjusted through desegregation, the informal social systems of the school wherein culture contact occurs are not responsive to such adjustment and continue to reflect ethnic identities and affiliations in the community. Thus, racial balance among students and staff and coethnicity between them tell us little about the sociocultural context within which education takes place. The formal organization, the rationally planned and directed programming of students for careful scheduling and movement—the *gesellschaft* of the school, to use Tonnie's term—fails to do much more than identify and enumerate the individuals involved and the sequence of events. It is the *gemeinschaft* character of social relations in the school that provides the true measure of desegregation of attitudes and behaviors among the participants in the school.

The School and the Social System

Viewing desegregation or culture contact within the context of the social action of schooling is not, however, an easy task. Boundaries separate the school and the family, the school and the community, and the school and an increasing number of educating systems, such as the media, which make it difficult to say where formal schooling begins and ends. Even if this problem is dealt with, there is an additional one inherent in how researchers have traditionally looked at schools. Most studies of schools have focused on individuals as learners without examining the social organization of learning. Research that has been done on schools as organizations has focused primarily on administration and management. Consequently, although we know something about how children behave as learners and are beginning to get some ideas about how adults organize and manage schools as places to work, we know very little about how schools are organized as social systems. We know even less about the social controls that govern relationships among the school's children and its adults or about its socialization structures and how they function to promote or hinder learning. We must examine the role that schools themselves play in producing, aggravating, or reducing racial and ethnic tensions and we must determine how the schools mediate between students and poverty, employment, family, the media, and other extraschool areas of culture contact. And, finally, we must answer the ultimate question of whether and how changes in the way schools are organized and the way they relate to students can remedy the problems we identify with segregation and desegregation.

References

Barnes, J. A.
  1954   "Class and committees in a Norwegian island parish." *Human Relations* 7(1):39–58.
  1968   "Networks and political process." In M. Swartz (ed.), *Local Level Politics*. Chicago: Aldine.
Blom, J., and J. J. Gumperz.
  1972   "Social meaning in linguistic structure: Code-switching in Norway." In John J. Gumperz and Dell Hymes (eds.), *The Ethnography of Communication*. New York: Holt, Rinehart and Winston.
Corsini, R. S., and D. D. Howard.
  1964   *Critical Incidents in Teaching*. Englewood Cliffs, N.J.: Prentice-Hall.
Ervin-Tripp, S.
  1964   "An analysis of the interaction of language, topic, and listener." *American Anthropologist* 66(3): Part 2.
Ianni, F. A. J.
  1972   *A Family Business*. New York: Basic Books.
  1974   "Social organization study program: An interim report." *Council on Anthropology and Education Quarterly* 5(2):1–8.
Katz, M. B.
  1971   *Class, Bureaucracy and the Schools: Illusion of Educational Change in America*. New York: Praeger.
Kuo, C.
  1970   "The Chinese on Long Island—A pilot study." *The Atlanta University Review of Race and Culture*, Third Quarter.
Ravitch, D.
  1975   *The Great School Wars: A History of Public Schools, A Battleground for Social Change*. New York: Basic Books.

241